SAVAGE TRAVEL

Memoir of a Beach Warrior

By

G. Jurij Zebot

DORRANCE
PUBLISHING CO
EST. 1920
PITTSBURGH, PENNSYLVANIA 15238

Cover art photo composite background black and white photo credit:
Twisted Vine, Killing Fields, Cambodia: G Jurij Zebot
Dragon sculpture photo credit: Imperial Palace, Hue, Vietnam - G Jurij Zebot
Concept, design and graphics: G Jurij Zebot
Design and graphics: Larry Safady

Dorrance Publishing Co
585 Alpha Drive
Suite 103
Pittsburgh, PA 15238
Visit our website at *www.dorrancebookstore.com*

ISBN: 979-8-88729-997-6
eISBN: 979-8-88729-560-2

"You go away for a long time
and return a different person.
You never come all the way back."

–Paul Theroux

ACKNOWLEDGEMENT

The journeys and stories alluded to here are all part of a collection of personal events that were experienced sometimes by choice and sometimes not. A reoccurring pattern of finding myself in areas of conflict was not always in the best interest of self-preservation. The urgency seemed always to seek out the remote.

My thanks to my parents Francek and Lija who endured everything and gave me all the necessities to allow my life to unfold the way it has. To Ava my loving and giving wife and my ultimate travel partner who never needed to change me and makes me a better individual than I would be on my own probably because of my desire to return the favor. I recognize I would not be the person I am today if it had not been for my mentor Dick Oden, a man who opened my eyes to light. I concede to my good fortune to have had these people and others in my life. And I want to acknowledge all of my students over the course of the years for having taught me as much as I taught them.

I owe my brother, Frank and Lou Pumphrey a debt of gratitude for their literary support and William Finnegan after our brief encounter for showing me what was possible even though in all likelihood, he was probably not aware of his influence.

It is crucial to say I never wanted, nor was satisfied, to limit my travel to an annual two weeks of regimented vacation. I hoped to be all in wherever I went. Thanks to those who joined me on my journeys with apologies to those who might have wanted to be mentioned and to those who were included but didn't want to be.

CONTENTS

The Balkans
CHAPTER 1

His life started off with a bang but the funny thing was he didn't remember much. His mother said the British were dropping bombs the day he was born in the southern part of what was formerly the Hapsburg Empire. It only got more confusing after that. War had a sick way of twisting the natural course of events. His grandfather, a true patriarch, was a senator in parliament, mayor of Maribor and well established. But the fallout from the second war punctuated an upheaval that wasted his family history leaving it an aftermath of an earthquake cast in stone like some artist's torturous vision. A future that never allowed for the eminence and station he worked so hard to secure and deserve. The war reached its critical juncture over the last two winters. The Third Reich had already taken big pushes from allied forces. Juri's father, Francek went to Gestapo headquarters in search of Franjo, his father, not only to discover under massive doses of adrenaline that his father had been railed off to Dachau but that he himself was also on the list. He found this out by chance. Revealed by a logbook thrown at him and his persistent questions by a thoroughly pissed off, disgruntled desk sergeant.

Juri's grandfather was absent at the head of the family for the first time anyone could remember. It left the household in the throes of abject grief and uncertainty. Faced with his probable fate, they were paralyzed with the unacceptable and the unknown. Demons dictated the unholy. They were at the end of their days.

Against all odds Franjo reappeared. He just walked into the house and sat down, somewhat broken but alive. His unexpected return proliferated a spectrum of emotions that were short-lived. The rollercoaster of war toyed with their sanity. The perverse minds that spawned the internment camps intentionally released him only to recapture and incarcerate him again. It was the last time anyone in the family saw him alive. A Dachau survivor reported Franjo died two weeks prior to the camp's liberation by the US Seventh Army.

The war turned tribal. The partisans under Tito, and the Chetniks under Mihailovic, were fighting the Germans. And the partisans and Chetniks were battling each other. After horrendous reprisals by the Nazis, the British in their infinite wisdom, countering a previous strategy, handed control of Yugoslavia to Marshal Tito. His distrust of the Slovenes, especially the political arm backed by the young boy's family, put everyone in immediate jeopardy. Tito announced the closing of the borders. That meant sure death to those who couldn't get out.

Escape, cigarettes, a bicycle and an illicit ride into Austria through the Julian Alps would leave the young boy without knowing he was drawing lines on a map, scribbling what might be a composition tracing random patterns of movement on that part of the world. So began the irony that would seal the genesis of travel in his life from those very first days.

The bicycle would be for Francek who would not accompany the three of them in the car. Educated as a lawyer, the eldest son was groomed to step into his father's political shoes. He was too recognizable at the checkpoints assuming liability for their secure passage. After taking some light scattered small arms fire the bicycle instinctively forged forward. It was his only ticket out over the high mountain passes to the safety of the allied encampments in the valleys on the other side. By chance they had safely crossed the border. As arranged a family friend transported the mother and children after the crossing and on the ensuing drive, they miraculously came across their father who had fallen asleep on the side of the road after his ordeal. The depth of joy his mother felt was hard for the boy to totally grasp. The family commiserated for much longer than the children could tolerate. After his sister meandered off for a while she found live ordnance, including a grenade. A frantic father asked her for the "toy" so she would willingly hand it over. It might well be pointed out here that particular rest stop had its share of overload. The sheer idea of the thoroughly impossible happened on that mountain road on a spring day in 1945.

The cigarettes were a bribe to a train guard acquiring passage for his mother Lija, his sister Minka and himself for the second great escape out of Spitall in the British zone to Asten in the American zone. Fleeing was necessary. The British Army in Spitall was sending back hundreds of Slovene refugees to Yugoslavia, and certain death at the hands of Tito. On the train at an unscheduled stop Juri's cries had to suddenly be muffled by his mother's hand. The guards had noticed. Again, the cigarettes came into play. Nicotine was currency. The Americans were heroes to his parents. America represented a safe haven from fear.

In the middle of conflagration one can still breathe easy depending on circumstances. What makes war common is looking back on it. At the heat of the moment in the baptism of fire any fork in the road can be your undoing. Choices are debilitating. With the benefit of history, you already know which road to choose. They are all uncharted until you take them. He would learn this lesson twenty some years later in the jungles and rice paddies of Southeast Asia and come to understand why his mother, because of earlier experience, would always be conditioned for "worst case scenario".

While living conditions in Austria were Spartan, it was a paradise absent of most horrific unspoken fears. His father, fluent in nine languages, landed a job as a translator with the Americans whom he favored over the British. Among other reasons, he had transcribed radio broadcasts of the X Olympiad from Los Angeles in the summer of 1932 prior to the Berlin games when he was in college. Larger choices that shepherd the path of one's life are sometimes made for seemingly insignificant reasons. His two brothers were born in different outposts of allied territory, swelling the family to four young children. The creativity of play trumped the bleakness of all the displaced persons camps where they resided. What he remembered was the cold and hunger. What lay ahead was passage to his new world. Out of the chaos of the adult world came a journey to a new country. What he left behind was playing in the snow with his brothers and conversations with people who spoke an assortment of different languages. The trek to America would go on from Linz situated in the U.S. sector of Austria through Nuremberg a town yet to be known for its war crimes tribunal and a defeated Germany and finally to the port of Bremerhaven on the North Sea.

Transatlantic

CHAPTER 2

The USS Hershey, a 522-foot battleship, powered by a Westinghouse turbine engine with two Babcock/Wilcox boilers, was part of the Asian-Pacific Theater in the Leyte Island Amphibious Operation under the command of General Douglas MacArthur. Possibly the largest naval battle in history, it certainly was the largest naval conflict of WWII. The ship, after seeing action, was converted to function as part of the Military Sea Transport Service (MSTS) in Europe. Capable of carrying over 1,200 passengers, it was assigned to the International Refugee Organization. On its previous sailing the USS Hershey responded to distress calls issued from the SS Tecumseh Park 840 miles off Nova Scotia. All concerned survived. The family "ride" was now docked in Bremerhaven and scheduled to take 10 days to Ellis Island. On a subsequent voyage the USS Hershey, in a thick fog, would collide with the Argentine cruise ship MS Maipo in the North Sea. The Maipo would sink three hours later off of Wangerooge Island. All concerned would survive. With this frenetic narrative in the background the family boarded, all smiles and trust, ready for the home of the brave and the land of the free.

As the sun broke through a lifting mist, Juri spotted a glimpse of the white chalk cliffs of Dover. There had been nothing but water as far as the eye could see for some time. The immense size of the ocean caught him off guard. He wasn't expecting it. He had never seen big water. This was really readjusting his perception. The sighting not only changed the scenery, it was in his mind "land ho" and they weren't even out of the channel into the Atlantic yet. Somewhere out in the open ocean he was exploring the many decks of the ship. He leaned his arms on the railing of an upper deck, secluded aft of the few people venturing out into the brisk air. He noticed orange peels one after the other floating by in the deep teal water scalloped by white foam pushed by the forward motion of the ship. He concluded that someone in front of the bridge that he could not see was enjoying an orange. For a boy his age, that was a *Holmesian* conclusion. The memory had been so lucid that to this day he could still smell the pebbled grain of that particular orange in the water. He was one of the fortunate few who along with his father avoided the ravages of the waves. He was blessed not to endure the aftereffects of the pitching and yawing of the ship on heavy seas. Lots of passengers spent an inordinate amount of time at the rails of the decks. Somehow, he got along with the ocean. It seemed to pass him over. This affinity would bond him to many subsequent ventures into the water, seemingly, as a natural rite of passage. The transatlantic crossing took a small lifetime and the power of the ocean was washed onto his soul.

Transcontinental

On a grey foggy dawn in New York's upper bay past the Verrazano-Narrows bridge the passengers could not make out where the sky and the water met. There was no horizon, just a blanket of grey serving as a seamless backdrop to the lady of the harbor. And she did command an audience. Every single immigrant paid her respect. All 1,283 passengers had their epiphanies on the deck that morning. In the terminal at Ellis Island, it was a cattle call of humanity. He enjoyed leaning against the shiny subway tiles that sparkled glossy white and left him feeling cleaner than he could remember. The induction process faded to nothing in his head and all he could think about were bits and pieces of his new country. The family boarded the train and headed west with a front row seat to take in this new land. This land was their land, from California to the New York Island.

The first whistle stop was Pittsburgh. The family stayed with Cyril and Itcha, Francek's younger brother and sister-in-law. They had preceded the family to the states and Cyril had already procured a position on the faculty at Duquesne University. Juri had no way of knowing how accomplished the family was. Cyril later became a doctorate professor and head of the Georgetown Graduate School of Economics and authored numerous books on the subject, some even controversial. As a young boy, Juri didn't really engage in the late adult conversations that kept his parents and guests up all night but he intuited that they must have been about things that mattered. Somewhere in Ohio his father telegraphed ahead to Esther, the woman who opened up her home and her heart to the family through one of the many service organizations established to handle the refugee crisis. She was a single woman, rare at the time, and a teacher by trade. She happened to be a person who cared. Juri's family would forever be indebted to her.

The train tracks ambled through the plains states then labored up through the Rockies, coasted down the windward side through the deserts of the southwest. In New Mexico Juri had to be swept up by his father from the fascination of Native Americans in full-feathered dress just as the train was pulling out on the final leg to the Pacific Ocean. He had received a geography lesson before he had even enrolled in school. Union Station, the terminal end of the Union Pacific, was everything it always had been in the old classic movies. That was before the coming of jet airliners and freeways.

Esther lived in Long Beach, which was really the port of Los Angeles. Peacetime Long Beach was still a navy town. There were subtle vestiges that reminded civilians what the country, and beyond that, the world, had recently endured. On the streets, sailors in uniform were more common than car salesmen. Big grey battleships double-parked just beyond the busy ocean front skyline and remnants of Uncle Sam posters dotted buildings on the side streets. America and the family were turning the corner.

Orange County in 1949 was a bygone era. Brisk mornings, the smell of orange blossoms and snow on Mt. Baldy was real life imitating an old fashion travel sticker. Their first house had a cavernous front porch and was plopped down right in the middle of 40 acres of oranges. His lawyered-up father took on work as caretaker of Mr. Kellogg's citrus grove.

This would turn out to play a contributing role in his father's preferred passion in the coming years regardless of his job title. Horticulture was at the root of who he was. In Juri's college years his father turned out to be an acknowledged fuchsia grower and botanical photographer.

In the new America, Francek's name evolved into Frank and the dinner conversations turned into a hybrid of Slovene and English. In the mornings Minka took a school bus whose interior didn't have an aisle running down the center. Instead, the bench seats went from window to window across the bus and it had outward opening doors exiting both sides of *every* row. With all the doors open the large squared up transport looked more like a huge yellow accordion than a school bus. Transit was definitely not rapid in those days. He would wait for viscously slow periods of time at the side of the road under large shade trees in anticipation of the Long Beach to Riverside bus. Going into Santa Ana could be counted on as an all-day affair. The eucalyptus trees were used as windbreaks for the citrus groves. They were everywhere. They were the signature of the times walling in large tracts of agricultural land that would later become suburbia. Listening for the frost warnings on the radio in the winter with his dad was not an option. 32 to 34 degrees meant putting on thick jackets and loading the tractor with smudge pots to protect the crop. In a few years modernization would assault them with mechanized turbine driven windmills.

Black Habits
CHAPTER 3

Columban nuns in archaic black habits, who were mostly well meaning, overly strict and absolutely pious, schooled Juri. His parents imported their Catholicism from the old world. It gave the young boy a safe and accessible place for his individual sanctuary until he came of age. Sister Thadeus was a quiet gentle rebel not cut from the same cloth as the other nuns. She imprinted on him an artistic independence that expanded and shaped his creativity. Her encouragement opened a Pandora's box to the world of art. She saw something in the boy and believed in him. When he showed his drawings to the adults he knew, he was showered with praise that generated more art. He found a conduit that gave him a voice and in a subtle way made him proud.

He sensed he was different, maybe even foreign. His two older cousins came to the states a couple of years after he did. They both spoke with a marked accent. Juri flew under the radar. His English was indistinguishable from his classmates. He was just young enough that his first language didn't affect his speech. Outwardly he seemed typical. Inwardly he knew better. There were entirely distinct "ways" at home. The customs were not the same when he visited his friends. Other parents had a personal ease he didn't recognize. But he had some essence of the old country that they didn't. He had one foot in the American dream and the other in Eastern Europe and didn't quite fit in either one.

His father passed on the finer points of table tennis to Juri and his brothers with his old school "pen" grip. His dad also encouraged them at new games by putting up a backboard and rim on the pump house in the back yard. During the school year of his 6th grade, the basketball coach came into the classroom and spoke privately with the teacher. Juri was summoned to the front of the class and followed the coach out of the room. He became officially part of the school team comprised mostly of 8th graders that traveled to play Holy Family in the city of Orange.

Bill Russell, before he was an NBA hall of famer, visited Blessed Sacrament Elementary School as a USF Don and an Olympian prior to the first Melbourne Games. He was a big deal. He towered over people in the school's cracker box gym. Juri was in awe of this articulate black giant. The impact of rubbing elbows with his hero made an indelible mark on an impressionable young boy. Basketball became his first love. He would run home after school and shoot hoops late into the evening's dim light. The game was on. His love of sports had awakened.

Because of construction on the new Interstate 405, a main north-south artery in southern California, his family was forced to relocate yet again. They purchased a modest home with ample acreage two miles on the other side of town. He moved one block up and one over into the adjoining city's southwest Little League district. While he didn't live in Garden Grove, he was required to play ball with strangers. Having new roots tied him down. He wanted to move again. He was devastated not to play with the friends he had grown to know. Another of life's lessons stared him in the face. Devastation turned into opportunity. Because he was a latecomer and the team rosters were already selected, a special tryout was arranged for the young transplant. Juri would go through the paces and display his skills for coaches of opposing teams. People were paying attention to him. He was drafted to play for Mr. Barr, skipper of the Evans Sporting Goods Red Sox. The coach, an ex-Marine, hit ground balls to Juri from the perch of his wheelchair in the dirt around home plate. The opportunity became an unseen chance to play with winners, not because they scored more runs than anyone else but for the deep bonding and camaraderie.

Sonja had come along later. She was first generation and the only one in the family born in the states. In her early years, she was one to always tag along. The kid sister got left behind at a Little League game after some late inning heroics captured everyone's attention. It wasn't until they all got home the entourage realized they left the five-year old. During all the excitement she wandered off to play on some far-off swings and luckily the good Samaritans who were responsible for closing the snack bar rescued her.

As an eighth grader he went across the street from school to Sigler Park where Mater Dei, the high school he would soon attend, was having spring football practice. A young freshman a year his senior showed early to the workout and asked Juri to run some patterns. The tight symmetric spirals were things of beauty. The future quarterback was going to become a Heisman Trophy recipient at Notre Dame and Juri was going to be his battery mate on a Monarch Baseball team that would go deep into the state playoffs 2 years in their future.

Along with his brothers, the three of them became gym rats. They frequented gymnasiums from Huntington Beach to Anaheim to Newport Harbor. They honed their skills in pick-up games across the county. He seemingly couldn't get enough basketball. At night lying in bed his legs would jerk and sputter from the over-activity. He was a diehard basketball junkie.

High School was different in unexpected ways. He attended a parochial school, which were mostly gender segregated. As a student attending Catholic school you either went to an all-boys school or an all-girls school. Juri enrolled in one of the few in the entire archdiocese that integrated boys and girls. The curriculum was a severe college track. Privately he actually appreciated the discipline. It gave him a path forward instead of being at the mercy of fate. What was more difficult was the willingness and bravado to break the rules. He later told his younger siblings that he alone took the heat for resisting the strictness and discipline at home by pushing the envelope to circumvent their parents' regimen, control and curfews. He would say, half in jest, that he sacrificed taking the punishment in order to make their adolescence easier.

Detention at Mater Dei amounted to slave labor at the Brothers' of Saint Patrick monastery on weekends. It truly was a sanction to be avoided. After being busted for hoisting the student body president's pants up the flagpole at school on a particularly mischievous day, Juri, the designated perpetrator was sentenced to hard time in Midway City.

In hindsight one of the smartest decisions, but unknowing at the time, was to drop football after his freshman year to concentrate on playing basketball and baseball. Winning the basketball league championship and going to the CIF playoffs his senior year and in his sophomore-year making the varsity squad in baseball that went to the semi-finals of the state playoffs. Then in his senior year he was selected captain of the baseball team. The positive outcome of his decision had nothing to do with the other sports. It just felt to him if he had stayed out for football his testosterone levels would not have suited him well as an artist. This was an odd thing to feel. Maybe it was somewhat irrational but his senses told him different.

Another oddity was the fact that even though he knew of his long ambition to study art in college he resisted taking art courses in high school. Again, this aversion was very hard to explain. It seemed unreasonable. In the future he would tell himself that his evolution as an artist began with an unconditioned and moldable beginning. The innocence didn't require a period of un-training to begin.

Juri actually liked high school. He seemed to break with the consensus of most adolescents. His street smarts might have been in question. Peer pressure played on his shyness but his convictions drove him to introspection. For him that was something very different from "herd mentality."

After graduation Jay a teammate of Juri's on the Mater Dei basketball team contacted a disc jockey at radio station KRLA in Pasadena and offered himself and his friends to save face for all the radio personalities who didn't finish their publicized 50-mile hike. It was the era of President Kennedy's push for public health and awareness. Jay said that he and each of his friends would adopt one of the disc jockeys and complete the hike in their name. The entire week each radio personality mentioned the upcoming hike for a few moments on their broadcast. The plan was the group of young hikers would call in on their progress each hour of the Saturday marathon. During the walk listeners would honk as they drove by and young ladies offered prepared lunches for the marchers. At a point near the destined radio station at a railroad crossing a long freight train halted their progress. Juri remembered walking in circles around a traffic signal because his legs couldn't stop in jeopardy of cramping. The father of one of the participants drove a giant RV to the station and after all the ceremonial regalia transported all eight hikers, home in a reclining position.

The Grassy Knoll
CHAPTER 4

The world was going to change that crystal clear brisk Friday morning. No one knew it yet but the body politic was going to be brutally and permanently different from that day forward. It was to be one of those monumental events that calendared time before and time after, as does the birth of Christ. A midweek storm had just passed through Orange County transitioning into a high-pressure system and light Santa Ana Winds with Mt Baldy's archetypal snow-capped peak commandeering the landscape and the fragrance of orange blossoms maybe a premonition of incense for the upcoming horror that was going to become a litany of tragic ritual assassinations that forever would change Juri's America.

He just finished his morning class as a college freshman conflicted but eagerly taking in a surf check at 18th Street just south of the Newport Pier. Turning his back on the San Gabriel Mountains standing outside his Volkswagen van Juri focused his gaze on the ocean swells wrapping across the shallow point when a young acquaintance, clad only in a bikini, wiping away tears ran up to him crying… "the president has been shot". He could vaguely hear the breakers in the background. The breaking news on the car door speaker drowned out the rustling bouquet of the orange groves. A strange numbing was in the air. Juri felt as if his solar plexus had been gutted. Little did he realize that moment was portending events beyond his pay grade that would somehow find him later in the decade in Southeast Asia in a war that was not of his choosing.

At the onset of his college studies Juri had been completely and duly impressed by the artwork of one particular art faculty member and enrolled in one of his classes. He had not yet met Dick Oden but was absolutely fascinated and drawn to the imagery in his work. He had never seen such intellectual and graphic grace consistently married together in the work of an individual artist. Legendary status preceded the man. Professor Oden's drawings and paintings took your breath away. The buzz around the art department was that the teacher was a magic man.

Eager to catch a glimpse of the fabled professor, he showed up at that first 9:00am class session early with heightened expectations. Juri struck up conversations with a group of students he did not know. Strange was beginning to be part of the norm. 60's fashion seems so innocuous now but then it was the experimental badge of the Avant Guard. People expressed their politics through what they wore. This small assembly of art students was obviously from divergent circles and for the moment circumscribed only by Juri's intuition of who they were. They ringed into a semicircle between the front row of drawing tables and the instructor's desk. David was tall and lanky and had a regional intelligent drawl for a west coaster. Jennifer easily stood out as the most attractive female in the room with pulled back red hair. She obviously had that magnetism of drawing people into conversation evident by the number of individuals she engaged. Ken was clearly a surfer like Juri confirmed by his sun-stained skin and his conversation. Then there was Richard, a bit quirky and the shortest of all of them. He was harder to get a fix on. Witty and quick and wore pointy shoes. His dress code was undecipherable. Unlike the others that were definitely going somewhere specific with their manner, his attire suggested vague places that you could almost remember.

As the clock on the wall made that final vertical click to its zenith it was time to start the class and the semester. Everyone seemed to be anticipating the arrival of the instructor. Quietly without anyone really taking notice Richard morphed into Dick Oden and negotiated his way around the desk and faced the entire room. This was Juri's first encounter with the master that would emphatically change how Juri would measure time before the influence of his new mentor and time after studying with him. Lessons learned were exhilarating and always full of surprise and risk. His offerings were nothing short of visual ambushes. In the months

16

and years to come he would learn and listen from the man that made these exquisite marks with the ease and mastery of a sage. Baryshnikov was a maestro on his feet. Dick Oden dispensed magic through his fingers, hands and arms, with his entire body. He danced on paper. While he was a consummate artist, he seemed not to need recognition, something very rare in an artist. Art and teaching were of consequence to him. Most his accolades and awards were gained because other professionals were astute enough to submit his work when Dick didn't or wouldn't. He was exceptionally well read and had a voracious literary appetite. Juri would nod to himself to signal he understood Dick's words and watch his mark-making in awe but it was not until years later when Juri was working on his own art that he fully grasped the depth and nuance of what Dick had said. It would come full circle in the reckoning of a true aha moment, a lesson in slow time.

Rugged individualism encouraged us to credit only ourselves for our achievement and station in life. Recognition belonged to those who went before and crossed our paths because they were instrumental in shaping not only our character and our humanity but also in what we attained. It countered those who believed they did it alone. That act of acknowledgement is balance by passing it forward. It paid respect to those that helped with the art of learning. The universe got its due. Gratitude could be cyclical through generations making a significant difference.

Because they lived in proximity to each other, first in Newport and then Laguna Juri would ride his bike to Dick's home on Balboa Peninsula and later to the house perched on an outcrop at Pirates Cove. Those conversations were the bedrock of their life building relationship. They would talk art and the possibilities of esthetics. They would philosophize, analyze, compromise, improvise and surmise well into the hours and then throw in a game or two of chess. It was because the honored teacher was becoming a friend that Juri was coming to see some of the human imperfections in the mentor he lionized. That allowed for the seeding of a lifelong friendship as peers rather than one that had always been student / teacher. Years later when they both did individual artwork commissioned by the NFL, *Psychology Today* and *Westways* Magazine Juri could see the respect he had not only for Dick, but for himself, was earned.

Maple Syrup
CHAPTER 5

Mike was from Vermont but had the attitude of someone from Brooklyn. Dogs sometimes take on the personality of their owners. Mike had the composure of a bulldog. He once ate a ceramic plate at a coffee shop solely on a bet. Bit into it like it was an Abba-Zaba. Swallowed it whole. Juri saw him do it. Mike came out for the California dream, wintering in the OC. He just showed up on the beach one day. He played football for UV and you could tell. His short stature belied his toughness but his compact, stocky build and tree trunk legs spoke to the linebacker's fierceness. While he wasn't a water-man he fit into the group seamlessly both with the surfers and the ladies. His behavior was performance. He occupied attention.

Their turf was between 18th street, for the waves and 15th street for the social life. Sixteen and seventeen-year-olds need to fit in somewhere. It was right on the doorstep of the Beatles and the Stones who weren't quite there yet. Bal Week on Balboa Peninsula and Balboa Island was still the Coachella and Lollapalooza of the day before municipal restraints forced the informal gatherings out to the desert or across the country to Lauderdale.

Cruising Bal Week was a rite of passage for anyone under 30. Easter Week, Mardi Gras and Carnival all rolled into one. It summoned youth by the thousands. Bal Week was the Pied Piper of any red-blooded adolescent who wanted to party. Traffic would back up on the peninsula over the Arches and onto Newport Blvd all the way to Costa Mesa.

In fact, the driving force to stagger and spread-out spring breaks across different high school and college districts nationally was precipitated by Bal Week. The bottleneck it would create for 10 days every Easter on the tiny stretch of beachfront real estate in south Orange County turned unmanageable. It was a classic case of youthful revelry pushing the envelope against the restraints of civil authority. There was blatant disregard for all the rules. Drinking in public normally never tolerated in conservative Newport Beach was simply too rampant to deal with for the cops. Young kids walking down the boulevard with gallon jugs of Red Mountain slung across their shoulder dragging a sixer of Schlitz or Olympia were a common sight. Chronologically it was still a bit early for sinsemilla. It all seems lame by today's measuring stick. Mike was in his element. This was his canvas. Somehow, they felt safer with him having their back. And back it up he did on several occasions.

It was a pleasant spring before the June gloom. The closer Mike got to the date of his return flight the more he coveted his tan, a badge of honor in his native New England. Normally he was always agitated and restless as if he had Attention-Deficit Disorder, a non-stop windup toy. But during those last two weeks on the beach, they couldn't get him to move. He lowered himself to tanning with reflective tin foil. As a poser they started calling him David in honor of Michelangelo.

It was mid-summer and Terrance, Pete and Juri reminisced over a couple of beers in Mike's honor when someone said, *"let's go visit Mike… yeah…let's go visit Mike"*. After the third refrain they took out the passenger seat of a brand-new VW Beatle and replaced it with a piece of plywood and a really small mattress. Within an hour of that fateful toast the three amigos were on the road, a road trip with little or no beginning.

They were on a mission. Three bad asses were bookin' it cross country with only one stop logged in on the itinerary and that was only because they had to launder the clothes on their back. In the enthusiasm of bon voyage they didn't think to pack a change of wardrobe. Cleaned up and fully fed they missed seeing the sign that read leaving Amarillo. Years later he would recall making an impromptu rest stop on the lawn of the same hospital mentioned in the novel *Surely, You're Joking, Mr. Feynman!* Somewhere outside Erie, Juri had his arm resting on the driver's side door and his bent elbow pointing out through the window. He had just come up over the rise and in his side view mirror spotted a highway patrolman momentarily looking down at his radar gun. Instinctively he switched over to the slower lane on his right. As their luck caught up with them the patrolman sped past and pulled over the driver in front of them who was traveling at the same rate of speed they were.

One hour less than three days from Anaheim where Terrance's parents lived to Bellows Falls. Expediency made possible by alternating positions with one person driving, one sleeping on the passenger side while the third was sheathed into the tight space behind the driver. You had to believe that was the shift no one wanted.

Vermont hospitality like throughout most of New England was tradition. For the road trippers it was welcomed because of their neglect of travel details. They planned on surprising Mike but were clueless on what they were going to do next. Every evening it was dinner at someone else's home and a comfortable bed for the night. Many of the households were eager to see Mike's friends that they had heard so much about. When the myth superseded reality there was somewhat of an obligation to live up to the hype. They all took their turn in the spotlight. Then it was Mike's moment to showcase his neck of the woods. Not the chamber of commerce's view but a particular spin on what the boys from California would like to see. It was the 75 feet of guardrail taken out one night a couple of weeks prior by Tom while racing someone home from Walpole. Mike needed the ladies to be up to par. Sami was Mike's version of a California girl. She was sweet on the eyes and a bit of a rebel. There was an edge to her that made her very interesting. She was strong and tactful enough to make a conversation go where she wanted it to go. Mike not so much. He would just cut to the chase. Somehow, they ended up driving to a quiet spot on a wooded country road. Juri sensed something was being orchestrated. It turned out to be a short make out session. Sami had her tongue down his throat with so much force it muffled his speech. It was like an oral arm-wrestling competition and she had gotten the jump on him. She took her turn with Terrance and Pete. Then as fast as it began it turned to playful conversation. It was understood that was all that there was going to be. They laughed and told jokes and learned a little about each other. It was an awkward but spirited adolescent afternoon.

Aloha

CHAPTER 6

During the second semester of his freshman year Juri would car pool to Cal State Long Beach on Tuesdays. Larry drove a cherried-out vintage 1949 Ford. That morning on the way to school they inched out to the middle divider separating the four lanes of Highway 39. The traffic on Beach Blvd was backed up in both southbound lanes from the red light at the signal a block away. The idled cars immediately to their right waved them through the two gridlocked lines of traffic. The vehicle in the far-right lane signaled him to cross. Larry slowly pulled out into the opening. Juri sitting in the passenger seat had his mind on the unfolding events at school that upcoming day. How long was the blink of an eye? What happened in that fateful moment when time seemed to stop, when that jolt of adrenaline addressed you unexpectedly and with the suddenness of a bolt of lightning? A millisecond before impact Juri's kneejerk reaction was to lean away from the gunmetal grey Simca bearing down on him at 50mph. The runaway vehicle was trying to pass halted traffic by using the shoulder of the road. It was another case of needless urgency to get somewhere in Southern California traffic. The Simca driver took the pace of traffic into her own hands. Juri ended up in a full fetal position. They were in the crosshairs of that runaway missile on tires. The antiquated Ford rocked onto its two left wheels teetering a precarious balance. As all the crushed metal and broken glass settled their vehicle luckily righted itself with all four tires in contact with the pavement Juri turned to see if his friend was ok. Larry had been smoking a pipe prior to the collision. As he gathered himself upright in the driver's seat and turned toward Juri there were dozens of small shards of glass embedded in the side of his face with lines of blood everywhere. Ironically the pipe was still clenched in his mouth but without a shred of tobacco in the bowl. It can be deduced that the crash coming from the passenger side, the window was blown out and the glass fragments embedded in Larry's face. The collision thrust Juri forward toward the dashboard luckily out of the line of fire of the glass shrapnel. He had two tiny transparent slivers in the back of his lower neck just above the collar of his t-shirt. The tank like construction of the old Ford and its sheer weight probably saved their lives.

At the hospital the doctors diligently extracted each and every glass fragment from Larry's head. The injuries were dramatic because of the blood but not life threatening.

Juri accompanied the ambulance to the hospital out of concern for Larry. The following day Juri went to his life drawing class but felt nauseous. In the restroom he vomited blood. He managed his way home and called the doctor later that evening. It was suggested he come in immediately. He convinced the medical staff that he would come in first thing in the morning. Still living with his parents whom he felt were overly concerned he didn't have the strength to negotiate his options. Minnie, a long-time friend in the neighborhood, came over to visit Lija. Juri not feeling cordial or in any condition to be conversational walked slowly down the 2 flagstone steps into the patio.

The next thing he remembered was opening his eyes 2 days later in a hospital bed. Juri had blacked out and was unconscious for 48 hours. He had vague recollections of blurred vision and garbled apprehension about his blood pressure. The nurse's voice projected a serious and unsettled tenor. *"Oh shit… his blood pressure is 80 over 55"*. To Juri it was a viscous dream. He had suffered a serious concussion and some internal bleeding. His concern the day of the accident was focused on Larry while he initially felt fine. The danger for Juri was that his symptoms didn't raise a red flag until sometime after the crash. Juri didn't remember it but a lawyer representing the other party visited him in the hospital and he would find out later that to protect his client's legal interests a private investigator was assigned to shadow Juri all summer after he was released from the hospital.

The accident left Juri with some short-term medical issues for the next couple of years. He would get up in the middle of the night to relieve himself and on occasion would find himself lying in the bathtub. Standing at the toilet he would black out and fall precariously into the tub. Anytime he would stare directly at a bright light he would become dizzy. Getting up suddenly from lying down would make him light headed. These symptoms lasted more or less for another 2 or 3 years. The time in between these episodes got further and further apart until they eventually dissipated. The accident was to become one event in a string of other similar unforeseen circumstances that would play a significant part in a life changing drama that would affect Juri for years in the future.

The car accident happened just before finals week of his second semester. While he was in the hospital, he asked his sister Minka to explain to all his teachers what had happened. All, but one teacher, were very considerate of the situation and allowed him *incompletes* in his courses which made it possible to submit the work at a later date and get credit for the course due to medical reasons.

John Lincoln was a notorious curmudgeon and an absolutely gifted teacher with an attitude. Juri took life drawing from him that semester. There were stories going around that Mr Lincoln had, during a critique, ripped a student's drawing off the wall, crumpled it up and threw it out the 3rd story window of the classroom just to make a point. John would turn out to be a future personal friend and colleague in later years when Juri joined the faculty but that first encounter with him was harsh. It was the only non-passing grade Juri ever got in a studio course.

That summer was a blur. Juri's palate was sweetened again. The fog was slowly lifting. Healing from a head injury and a concussion were indistinct and indefinite. When it came time to register for classes, he had second thoughts. He needed to clear his head and an opportunity to do just that appeared on the horizon in the form of a trip to Hawaii. John, a surf buddy suggested they go for a few months and catch some fabled waves. What John didn't tell him was the incentive for going was a female he had his eye on had recently moved to Oahu for work. The heightened sense of travel enticed Juri's palate again. Gauguin sailed to the South Seas when it was nearly impossible to cross the Pacific. They arrived in Honolulu via Pan Am. It had been Juri's first time on an airplane. That sensation of stepping out on the gangway in the tropics was a wonderful assault on the senses and something he was sure he was going to repeat over and over again. That day it was more familiar than it should have been. The summer months sport waves on the south side of the island so they set up shop in Waikiki. They rode the mushy waves in front of the high-rise hotels and braved more of a challenge at Ala Moana. They even did a little body surfing at Makapuu and Sandy Beach. John became despondent when he found out "his lady" had quit her job and moved back to the mainland. Like a puppy dog, he put his tail between his legs and followed her back to California.

Juri by chance ran into a lady he knew from the mainland. They decided to back pack into the Waipio Valley on the big island for 4 days. One day hiking in, two days of natural perfection camping on the beach next to a stream and a waterfall, then the one-day hike back out. When they got hungry, they would put their clothes on, roll over and pick mangoes, guavas and bananas growing wild just off the beach. He dove with a hand-held spear gun for protein. During the short jaunt to the waterfall, they saw wild boar in the bush. It was Edenesque. It rained the night before the return leg with a rare dramatic display of lightning lighting up the inside of the tent. In the morning they had to build a raft from driftwood to ford the swollen creek and reach the path for the way out of the valley.

It was when the Beatles were first touring the states. John, Paul, George and Ringo came across the pond about when Juri met a gang of Aussies that lived on the North Shore. They were all a few years older and definitely had more miles on their tread. He learned the fine art of grifting for meals at sunset luaus from his new mates. They would drive down to Waikiki from Sunset Beach and cruise the buffets on the sand and evening gatherings scrounging for free food. They were a gang of nine, eight Aussies and one Yank. He cut his teeth on the North Shore surrounded by the entourage from down under. Having a wave to oneself was nearly impossible. Juri tried to sneak off by himself quite a bit. One time he caught it un-crowded at Haleiwa. As he paddled out, he spotted two of his all-time surf heroes, Ricky Grigg and Paul Strauch. Strauch was riding his favorite surfboard that was so well known that it had its own name, *The Black Knight*. It was solid black with a yellow diagonal racing stripe across the deck. It would capture so much heat in the tropical sun it probably melted the wax on the deck of the board. One day when Wiamea Bay was breaking big the two of them in tandem on the aforementioned board stroked to catch a 30 ft wave and as the nose of the surfboard started to plane down the face Ricky Grigg sporting Voit UDT swim fins slid off the front of the board and body surfed the gigantic breaker across the bay. It might have been the first prototype for tow-in surfing. That was what myths were born of.

Juri honed his wave riding skills that season on the North Shore. He learned to handle his apprehension of big waves with some grace. Confident in the fact that what needed to be purged from the vestiges of the automobile accident was now whole and his mind and body were healed. In total, he spent a year in Hawaii before he tossed his lei in the water and said aloha. It was time to pursue the art of art and go back to school.

Prodigal Son

CHAPTER 7

Back on the mainland in the middle of a semester, not enrolled in school and living with his parents again was not ideal. It was a household where education was non-negotiable and definitely an expectation. A father with a doctorate and a mother who taught German were not going to be happy with a son who turned his back on schooling. Dropping out, especially to go surf for a year stretched the boundaries of what was acceptable. To do his part for family harmony before the next school term started Juri took a job at Voters Registration in Santa Ana. The work was absolutely menial and numbing for an artist surfer who at the moment was really only a surfer artist. There was no challenge, no freedom, and absolutely no risk to the job. He would find himself staring through the window that faced the direction of the ocean even though he couldn't see the beach. The situation didn't last. He pondered taking an evening job on the night shift, anywhere. He found one at an electronics factory testing diodes in Costa Mesa and now his days were free to beach it and surf again. The labor consisted of testing electronic parts mostly tedious repetition but the work force was more interesting, more diverse and definitely spirited. They suited his liking, ranging from a broad number of minorities from countries he had traveled. The one oddball other than Juri was a very light skinned middle-aged man who seemed way over qualified for the job. He was obviously intelligent and he was in a wheel chair. One evening when the workload was slow Juri asked him without much tact how he came to be paralyzed. His answer was remarkably candid. It turned out an enraged husband had found him in bed with his wife and unfortunately the husband had a gun.

Labor Day was right around the corner and Juri was enrolled in 15 units that included 3 studio art classes, Astronomy and African Geography. The long hard climb to a bachelor's degree was re-engaged. Shifting gears was surprisingly a smoother transition than expected. The curiosity and love of learning instilled by caring parents apparently was paying dividends. And then there was Dick Oden. A return to the mentor fate had intended for him seemed only natural. Creativity, inspiration, surprise and risk were again part of the job description. It was all fitting into place.

It was energizing to have the creative juices flowing again. To play with inspiration and birth an idea into a physical thing was akin to spiritual alchemy. It was play in its purest form, for adults. Juri thought the reason he gravitated to art as a child was because it brought so much pleasure, so much pride. He would have to remember to take a thing of joy and put it under the microscope of formal education and made it seem like work. He would take a newly minted work of art and put his *"pleasure meter"* over it. When the needle kicked all the way into the green he was fulfilled.

As an undergraduate he had confidence in his drawing abilities but constantly had doubts and dissatisfaction about his understanding of color. When he drew both he and the image were robust. His painting was another story, at the time mostly an unhappy one. Color was more than theory. In a random sample group one or two out of 30 in a classroom have the innate ability to see color for what it is, not a cosmetic, decorative component but a sculptural element that toys with space in a painting. Color was something that could put things in their place. For most, this was a long-term process that needed to be learned. For the first three years of his studies, it was mostly disappointment with the outcomes. But then somewhere in the middle of his junior year there were small parts of his compositions that he liked. He spent time transfixed on a portion of a painting he was working on and wondered why it made him respond the way he did. It made him feel good and he could stare at it for hours. Then sometime at the beginning of his senior year he did a painting of his mother's family from a picture taken when the century was in its infancy, when she was very young. It wasn't that the painting had a fidelity to the photograph but that the color did remarkably unexpected and risky things. It was brash, brave and unpredictable. From that point on it was like riding a bike. Even if he fell off it was easy to get back on and progress. Soon his color was an ally and he could count himself as a colorist.

Society was changing. The war in Vietnam was consuming the country. Nightly broadcasts brought the savagery to the dinner table. The campuses were enraged. Young people questioned the generation in charge. The times they were a changing. The rules were altered. He got a letter from the draft board. Prior to the notice Juri had a student deferment in addition to a 1-Y classification for the dizzy spells and the acute concussion from the accident. It seemed draft policies had suitably been reversed during the peak years of the war. August of 1966 saw the highest induction rate of the entire Vietnam era. The notice in the mail informed him that the draft board was reviewing his case and deferment status. The ground rules were changed probably based on their need for numbers. Student deferments were now allowed only eight consecutive semesters or four years from the date one initiated their studies. Anyone who interrupted his schooling to go surf in Hawaii was eligible for the draft. He was obligated to report to the induction center in Los Angeles. It was customary practice when reviewing draft status for all potential draftees to have two reviews. The first, a pre-induction physical, decided through a medical review the draft status of the person. Based on that first review a notice would be sent out whether that individual was required to report at a later date for a second induction physical and transported to a military assignment which was usually in the US Army.

He had just taken on a job, as a waiter at the Newport Chart House owned by Hawaiian surfers Joey Cabell, Buzzy Bent and Bobby Daniels. It was where his childhood friend Lee was employed and with his endorsement Juri's job was secured. Most everybody from the owners to the busboys, were all avid beach people. They surfed, played beach volleyball and partied together. It was an extraordinary camaraderie in a hierarchy of bosses and employees. Shortly after his hiring at the Chart House part of the ownership split away from the original group and formed a new restaurant called the Ancient Mariner. It gave everyone an opportunity, a choice to stay with the Chart House or throw in with the Mariner. Juri chose to go with the new guys at the Ancient Mariner and his friend Lee stayed with the old guard at the Chart House. The choice was based more on pecking order and seniority, which translated to money more than anything else.

The two restaurants became the social hub of younger Newport Beach. The Mariner crew, mostly twenty-something, was going to take full advantage of their vigor and active enthusiasm. Any excuse for a gathering would do. Sometimes they initiated friendly competition among the local restaurants and bars. Kite contests, raft races, surf offs, flag football games, all were excuses to come together. They had all the beach time they could hope for, money in their pockets from tips and social connection after work. It was righteous and it was happening.

The mailman produced a manila envelope addressed from the draft board that required Juri's presence at the Induction Center. With his student status invalidated, his medical history of the accident was his only hope to remain a civilian. He drove into the heart of Los Angeles planning to be back in time to cover his shift at the restaurant that evening. Lined up and herded in skivvies, young men of all races and beliefs were being berated by uniformed cadre. One particularly unpleasant sergeant told him…*"maybe your mama has them"* in response to Juri's question as to why his medical records weren't in his folder. Seems the draft board overlooked forwarding his records. No small oversight. In his naiveté he didn't insure to bring copies of his medical records along just in case. Why shouldn't he trust the draft board? Surely, they would have his best interests at heart. He soon realized through conversations with the other candidates they were all there for their second induction physical. Red flags went up. He could feel the white heat in his gut and both temples on the sides of his head were pulsing. There was a sense of urgency here. To compound things a cadre of three marines showed up and was plucking every third person from the cue for induction into the US Marine Corps. Their uniforms were subtly different but there was nothing nuanced about this. It was absolute horror. Draftees into the Marines were a rare contradiction to the enlisted infantrymen who signed up for a four-year stint. And you could be sure a draftee in the Corps would be low man on the totem pole, always with the most vulnerable assignments on their sure-fire patrol duty in Vietnam. From where he stood, he did a quick head count with some urgency. Gravity abruptly had more influence on him. His number fell directly on a multiple of three. It was like hoping for red and hitting black on the roulette wheel. For one time in his life having a name starting with the last letter of the alphabet literally saved his life. When they got to "Taylor" the marine contingent stopped for the day because they reached their quota. He tried to tell another of the staff that there were missing medical files. The retort was…*"ask when you get to the end of the line"*. The next sergeant told anyone that needed to see a doctor to follow the yellow line. Juri made sure to pay attention to stay on course when that line braided with other colors on the hallway floor. The mousy little man in the lab coat asked him what his problem was. After a flustered explanation about dizzy spells and a concussion there was a long silent pause. Finally, the doctor asked if Juri had a driver's license. That was it …*"follow the red line downstairs"*.

He had to call his father and ask him to come pick up his Volkswagen van and to phone the Ancient Mariner for him and tell them he wouldn't be in for two years.

FTA

CHAPTER 8

Fort Bliss

The historical definition of Shanghaied is…*"someone forced to join a ship lacking a full crew by drugging them or using other underhanded means"*.

A more adept and experienced person would have told them to go screw themselves and challenge being abducted into the military under those circumstances. Not yet having come of age politically at that point in his life he was basically a beach bum with the only politicking he had been exposed to was from a distance on campus and from further away in his father's legitimate anti-communist views. Juri's strategy was to see the doctors at Fort Bliss where he was being shipped off for basic training. The nightmare of boarding buses in the night parked next to dimly lit rows of austere barracks was freshly burned onto his visual cortex.

The plan from day one was to find a rational human being who could see the injustice in all of this. Home was "C" company on an asphalt quad in a barren barracks building in the west Texas heat. The drill sergeant was a combat veteran of the Korean conflict. You could look into his eyes and see the steel. For an NCO he was uncannily quiet. You could feel he had been through some shit. You just sensed that he could back up anything he said simply by the blue Combat Infantry Badge pinned over his breast pocket that confirmed he had been under fire in harm's way.

Somehow Juri felt invisible. No one knew who he was. It was at least a week into training until he was able to match the shaved head version of each PFC with the longhaired hippie edition he rode in with on the bus. Dark memories haunted him of sitting in the barber's chair wearing olive drab and watching pounds of hair pile up on the rubber mats. They were marched into a movie theater to watch *Dr Zhivago* immediately after their domes were buzzed. Because of being immersed in movie storytelling and the films length when the lights came back on the cold reality was that they didn't know where they were. The long slow trailing of the film's credits really made that fact sink in. The movie was an odd choice for the military. Were they playing with the minds of the recruits or were they simply ignorant of the revolutionary overtones of the film? Had it been later in time, knowing military mentality, he was sure it would have been *Rambo* on the marquee.

Reveille was at 5am and their bunks had to be made taunt before they fell out on the quad. Physical Training better known as PT was a grind. On the shooting range Juri who had never fired a weapon in his life was surprised by the exhilaration of discharging an M-16. He was good at it but it unnerved his psyche. It was an uncanny surprise at how tight his shot group was. He qualified Expert for his marksmanship, something he never expected of himself.

The drill sergeant took more of a liking to him after the company's forced march. They would be rated according to how the entire group finished. There was always one person who lagged behind, who didn't have the stamina to keep up. The 50 miles with helmet, full pack and rifle was strenuous and challenging. The weak link was a Kentucky boy mercilessly overweight. Half way into the hike he was lagging hundreds of yards behind. Juri dropped back until he had the straggler in sight. He took the soldier's backpack and strapped it to his own chest. He then instructed him to lean back against the pack on Juri's front side as they mimicked two stock cars playing bumper tag down the road. Juri pushed with his legs for 2 people the last 20 miles.

The entire basic training facility at Fort Bliss was scheduled for an IG inspection. The company commander noted that Juri was an art major in college usually a point of derision but on this occasion, it was deemed a useful skill. He was asked to paint military coats of arms and insignias on buildings and floors. This assignment was so significant that he was given *special duty* classification. It gave him a get out of jail free card when it came time to fall out for PT. When they called out the whole troop for haircuts, he would simply grab his brushes and avoid the un-pleasantries. A month into the project he had hair on his head. He did not look like the new recruit he actually was.

The last week of boot camp everyone's orders came in. Each and every individual's Army future depended on those assignments. The majority were to be shipped straight off to Vietnam with an infantry MOS or military occupation specialty and without any leave after basic training. Less than 20% received non-infantry assignments and drew a two-week furlough before relocating to their new assignment. Juri was one of those fortunate in the minority. He was not headed for Vietnam, at least not yet.

JFK Special Warfare Center

81E20...was a particular designation that was probably a life-saving proposition. At Fort Bliss no one at company headquarters knew what that particular MOS was. Prior to the general use of desktop computers no one could Google it. A short hike to the brigade quartermaster unit led to an enormous faded blue binder that was dusted off of an upper shelf and answered the question. What they did know when the original orders came down was that Juri was assigned to the 13th Psyops Battalion at the JFK Special Warfare Center at Fort Bragg, North Carolina. Christ...this was home base to the Green Berets. Psyops was Psychological Operations and was in part an element of the intelligence wing of the military. What was a California surfer dressed in olive drab doing in a place like this? The old blue binder answered that question, ILLUSTRATOR...what the *friggin'* hell. He was going to be an artist in this man's Army. Now if that wasn't an ironic slice of surrealism. People were marching in the street against the war and he was going to confront Charlie with his paintbrushes. The Viet Cong were probably preparing their palettes and easels to counter this new offensive.

In a less-than-sobering moment he was coping with what had just transpired. On the back burner he still planned on pursuing his health records issue and a medical discharge with a faint flicker of hope.

13th Psyops was a ragtag band of brothers who were mostly malcontents. They were not quite the caricatures of the MASH unit of TV fame but only because it was real life. Creative types across all organizational lines tend to be more anarchic, progressive troublemakers. They were after all, journalists, artists, photographers, writers, radiobroadcasters and offset printers. Only a stone's throw from the antithetical unit in the adjacent Quonset hut but kilometers away philosophically from the analysts, auditors, accountants, statisticians and data scientists.

Lou was from Painesville, Ohio and a brilliant writer. He had the gift. In Vietnam he wrote articles for Stars and Stripes and ended up being a journalist and editor for the First Infantry Division newspaper. He would be one of the few after their time in the service that kept in regular contact. Rafa called Miami home. He was of Cuban descent and someone Juri counted as a friend. "Rat" from Chicago was a funny man with plenty of street credit who was also a competent writer. Don was a paradox to say the least. He was an artist, a surfer and drove a VW van. Very few enlisted men had cars. He was from Newport Beach, Juri's hometown. Don rattled off names of dozens of people Juri knew back home yet he had never met or heard of Don until he arrived at Ft Bragg. After a group of them in the barracks listened to the newly purchased Beatles version of Sgt. Pepper, they took a walk to the PX that was very much the prototypical precursor of the big warehouse Costco and Walmarts of today. "Fig" took a hit of acid and Juri served as his night nurse to assure he wouldn't get in trouble with the MP's or other ranking individuals. Juri's comrades were always pushing against the Army Code of Conduct. FTA was their battle cry.

Stapled to a kiosk in a neighboring quad Juri noticed a neon orange flyer announcing tryouts for the post basketball team. Having some interest in round ball he showed up at the suggested time. The gymnasium was impressive but then most any permanent structure would be compared to standing tents and Quonset huts. There were some players who could ball.

Juri held his own enough to make the squad. He always felt the east coast coach was preferential, a closet UCLA fan and Juri was from SoCal. Close enough. During an early season game while running wing on a fast break an errant pass high and behind him put him in a precarious landing and tore a lateral meniscus.

The base hospital was adjacent to the 82nd Airborne Division's landing field. At first, he declined surgery remembering that a few recruits at Fort Bliss while chasing medical records were discharged for refusing operations. But the Army played hardball with him. He was tactfully put into traction. They were simply playing a waiting game. The cartilage wasn't going to heal itself. Confined to the medical levers, lines and pulleys of the girders above his bed he lost his patience. His incarceration to a bedpan was intolerable. He quietly undid the binding to the traction and hopped on one leg down the hallway to the latrine during the evening shift. Then one morning when urgency didn't allow for stealth the hardcore head nurse on the day shift busted him in the middle of the hallway. His patient gown was confiscated and his only covering was the top sheet on the bed. The straps attaching the traction lines were upgraded to shackles. It was a pissing contest that Juri couldn't win. Despondent he stared out the window to witness what from all points of view was a horrific accident. Two parachutists entwined in each other's rigging free fell to their death. Being worn down over time at that moment he realized he wasn't so bad off and consented to the surgery. Big mistake. When the anesthesia wore off the pain was unbearable. The surgery was at a time when arthroscopic procedures had not yet been perfected. When Juri awoke he experienced intolerable throbbing pain in the right knee and uncontrollable racking pressure on the heal bone from the full cast that was applied too tightly. He was plastered from mid-thigh to the bottom of his foot. It was Sunday morning and there was no doctor available. They must have all been out skydiving. Juri was moaning in agony. The nurse couldn't reach his doctor to prescribe stronger pain relief. He resorted to grinding his teeth after taking a couple of aspirin.

Post-surgical recuperation was a bitch. The pain was hollow. It reverberated through his whole body. And he knew this was going to be a long process. Convalescence and recovery were strained, because in his opinion the Army Captain from Missouri was not a competent physician.

Belief is probably everything and maybe for that reason his recuperation was painfully slow and disappointing. In the adjacent bed a green beret from St Louis who had been shot in Vietnam arrived at Fort Bragg via medivac. Bryan and Juri were good for each other and talked around the clock. He told Juri that he had been on point during a patrol and a sniper's round hit him dead on between the nose and the upper lip. He cartwheeled in mid-air and landed on his feet. The sniper got in a clean headshot. The bullet missed the spinal cord by the slimmest of margins and exited through the back of the lower neck. Damage assessment was the loss of three teeth and a few stitches. When it's not your time it's not your time.

Juri's knee joint remained swollen for a worrisome amount of time. It was now months not weeks since the surgery and he still couldn't put his full weight on the leg. His quadriceps had atrophied significantly. He planned to play his medical discharge card again. In a long string of office visits he slow played his strategy to focus with his doctor that the urgency was the knee and not necessarily getting a medical discharge. After repeated visits and tests on the health of the joint the doctor was starting to ask questions about what kinds of physical things Juri did in civilian life. Juri sensed that negotiating a medical discharge was on the table. He estimated it was going to take one or two more follow up visits.

He cautiously approached the next appointment monitoring his anticipation with his practitioner. Walking into the waiting room something was amiss. There were a lot of new faces. The entire medical staff along with the undistinguished good doctor had shipped off to Southeast Asia. In his stead Colonel Stern stood there in front of Juri more a paratrooper than a physician. A green beret tilted at just the right angle and a heavily starched khaki uniform with enough ribbons and medals to make a Christmas tree light up. His pant trousers were tucked into spit shined jump boots topped off by the jump wings of the parachutist badge. This full bird was *strac*.

What Juri remembered hearing next was…*"run it off"*. The hardliner had no time for any version other than the Army version. The game was over. It was time to relent. Time to cut losses. He was in, up to his knee.

Suddenly it felt like jail time. The summer of love was still a year and a half away as was his remaining time to serve.

Juri wasn't keen on returning to his company after being on limited duty for the last 4 or 5 months so he went to his former basketball coach and asked if there was any special duty assignment he could help with. Timing is everything. There was an opening for a lifeguard at the base swimming pool that suited the PFC from the Golden State. He became the 12th and final guard on the crew. Ten of the guards were from California, one from Tennessee and one from New Jersey. The chain of command had a single NCO, Staff Sergeant Fredricks, who oversaw the lifeguards and his immediate superior, a lieutenant colonel who was never present. That said, they didn't see much of Sergeant Fredricks either. They rarely were in uniform being on Special Duty status. Red Cross regulations stated one hour on, one hour off. One day on, one day off. The crew extended that to two weeks on and two weeks off. They would cover for each other and be able to take unofficial leave to assorted destinations up and down the eastern seaboard. Besides a trip to Florida and one to New York City he frequented the outer banks at both Cape Hatteras and Nags Head as an undocumented defender of peace, freedom and the American way. The waves on the Outer Banks were a step up from anything happening at the pool at Ft Bragg.

Juri developed a rapport with Jonathan a surfer from Virginia he met in the lineup at Hatteras. He was reserved but still conversational in a clever way. On multiple trips to the Outer Banks, Juri would seek him out to share waves and stories. Then late in the summer Jonathan's parents came down and invited him over for a dose of southern hospitality and a home cooked meal.

Conversation was pleasant enough ranging from business endeavors and the drive down from Virginia Beach. Something dark started to pervade the discussions. An antebellum attitude of ascendancy was making Juri uncomfortable. As if in time with a drum beat the discussions got unpleasant. When the "N" word became punctuation, it was time to end the sentence. He excused himself and never saw Jonathan again.

41

The pool deck was a great place to check people out. Usually frequented by military wives and family it would occasionally cater to unwinding soldiers out of uniform. Small and subtle intricate customs would divulge regional idiosyncrasies but the gangly exuberance of adolescence was always universal.

The California guards were not a homogenous group. In some ways they couldn't have been as different from each other had they arrived from varied locations in different states from around the country. There were two that were from the San Gabriel Valley who were strident and grating. The adolescent daughter of a senior officer who was a regular at the pool and tended not to have much in the way of filters became playful and flirtatious with the Valley boys.

The season was coming to an end when a surprise roll call was ordered. They scrambled to find the uniforms they stowed away a long time ago. As the lifeguards fell out on the pool deck, a contingent of brass with the young girl in tow accompanied her father the colonel.

What happened next transfixed everyone's attention. The colonel demanded his daughter proceed forward and point out each individual she slept with in military parade fashion. The fact that she was pregnant didn't please the old man. Shortly after, the unit was disbanded Sgt. Fredrick and all but two of them moved on to more routine assignments.

Good Morning Vietnam
CHAPTER 9

The fateful news a soldier of that era never really was prepared for no matter how much they trained. Orders came down for Vietnam. It would be a Flying Tiger charter out of Pope Air Force Base in Fayetteville, N.C. where the takeoff had to be aborted due to a tire blowout on the runway. The cabin was evacuated when it filled up with smoke. Not particularly the way you want to start out a vacation to a combat zone. After trying again, it was on to Travis Air Force Base in Oakland, CA. Then by troop transport shipping out with a stop off in Subic Bay in the Philippines and on to Vung Tau, the first port in Vietnam. The entire travel itinerary consumed a month. Sailing under the Golden Gate leaving San Francisco Bay in the rearview mirror and cruising by the Farallon Islands, the breeding grounds of the Great White Shark seemed somewhat appropriate for a boat full of killers.

You can see strange and remarkable things on the open ocean. On a pristinely calm and sunny day a huge inverted V shaped fin was spotted seemingly half way to the horizon following the ship's wake. Distance plays tricks on size but how big that pelagic monster was any PFC's guess. One of the cooks procured a slab of meat the size of a basketball. They secured it to a grappling hook whose mass took two people to toss overboard. The leader line was rope that begged large hands to grasp. They tied a 50lb weight to the line so that it would submerge trailing the boat. Within seconds the fin that was now easily 300 to 400 yards behind the stern darted forward in a series of slaloming S curves and then submerged. By the time you could hum the tune to Jaws the entire line snapped up above the water line with the weight dangling like a ping-pong ball. It turned into a team effort as sailors from the mess staff were joined by dozens of curious soldiers. It became a tug-of-war on the open ocean. At that point an army manned the lines. After pulling on the rope for what seemed like an endless amount of time the hook came up bare. It didn't matter that they didn't hook a Megalodon. Anyway, they say fishing is not about what you catch.

On an especially clear and warm evening Juri ventured topside to see if he could possibly catch a glimpse of the Southern Cross. He did spot his sign of Scorpio low on the horizon. Just then he was distracted by a slow clockwise rotating circle of bright yellowish lights submerged not far under the surface of the water. Whatever it was, he estimated was half the size of a football field. He knew enough about meteorology to know that the rotation of the lights should have been counterclockwise in the northern hemisphere and they were still above the equator.

When they cruised into Vung Tau the first landfall in Vietnam he felt like a little kid playing with toy soldiers hiding behind any structure on deck that could protect him from a stray bullet. Soldiers to be stationed in the Saigon area were deposited and the remainder sailed on to Cam Ranh Bay and then his final stop in Nha Trang and the 1st Psyops Battalion.

Nha Trang was an idyllic coastal resort town where General Nguyen Coa Ky a very public figure and chief of the South Vietnamese Air Force had a summer home. Mun and Bich Dam were but two of the islands that dotted the waters offshore. If Juri could have erased the war it might have been a place he chose to visit. The American encampment as you would expect was stark and out of place by any measure. It looked and felt like an enigma especially compared to the culture of the coastal town that had it not been for the war would have been on the map. America had that effect on a lot of places.

Greeted to a fireworks show that first nightfall in the temporary tented city, he was yet to be billeted in his nothing-is-permanent quarters closer to his worksite. Blue detonations from incoming rockets brought the color and the munitions expedited the pyrotechnics. Besides the visual onslaught, the air-sucking clap of explosions shook the base and cratered the tarmac. Mutilated bodies of the unprepared were peppered across what looked like a movie set to the citizens back home.

It was the first time he experienced an amount of fear that left him little control of his body. He was on total override and on automatic pilot. It was the white heat of an adrenaline let down, the baptism of fire. He was stunned by the indifference of experienced bunkmates who had time under their belts in this wasted paradise. After the first rockets and mortar shells hit most of them remained on their cots knowing full well the barrage would last a very short time. If you made it past the first volley you were good to go. The Viet Cong would head for their tunnels while the good guys turned on the sirens, scrambled the Phantoms and broke out the flak jackets. The Americans would be up all night behind sand bags, bunkers and retaining walls. Those with street credit and in the know knew the game. Hit and run. What you learned quickly was that you couldn't afford to be scared except when you first got there and when your time in country was short, only at the beginning and just before you went home. The other choice would be to fry your nerves. Drugs were balm. Total burnout was disastrous when your life was on the line.

The company commander, a second lieutenant straight out of Officer Candidate School was even greener and less suited for the job than Juri. He was shipped to Nam and thrown into battle after only 12 weeks in the service. He was so unpolished, so unadulterated that his belt buckle shined in the middle of jungle. Juri proposed a second shift of artists would double the output of the shop. There were already three shifts of printers producing leaflets, handbills and propaganda along with data sheets and military accounting. Juri said he would be more than willing to man the swing shift for the good of the company. In Juri's mind having days off for the beach was sacrosanct even in the middle of a war. He sold the idea to the lieutenant, privately thinking the leaflets were an ineffective form of marketing.

Being able to enjoy the beach felt like a crime. A secret he didn't want to advertise. It felt like R & R and he didn't have to get on a plane. Walking south along the strand he couldn't believe his eyes. Sure, the palm-dressed shoreline with the emerald islands a stone's throw from where he was barefooting it were an unwarranted privilege but what seemed to be an apparition were two small silhouetted figures in the water sitting on surfboards close to the airstrip. His pace picked up considerably.

Larry and "Midget" respectively from San Diego and Santa Ana were assigned the late shift at the control tower on the airbase. Both were in the Air Force so their stint in the service was for an extra year. They informed him surfboards were available to check out from special services. Juri could not believe what had just transpired. Was it fate or some bizarre form of reality in an alternate universe? The three of them became inseparable. They carved up the waves. They shared time and surf wax. They toasted their good fortune over a few beers.

One eventful day out at the lineup directly perpendicular to the airstrip they had a foreshortened telescopic view of the F-4's gunning their engines lining up for takeoff. Their exhaust created a mirage of heat waves distorting the shape of the jets capable of a top speed of 1,473 mph. The aircraft shook, rocking violently side to side in a threatening way. The three of them were in the crosshairs of the squadron pointed right at them. The runway wasn't flat. From the head-on view of the dips and swales it exaggerated the undulating approach of the Phantoms. It reminded him of the stalking of a great cat just before it pounced on its prey. It became a repeated ritual for the pilots to buzz them paddling out in the water by tipping their wings in a simple gesture of greeting merely a few feet above their heads. The aircraft would hiss a long howling whine kicking in their afterburners and circle out towards the mountains and valleys to complete their missions.

On that particular day after the familiar wing tipped salute three F-4 Phantoms circled the basin that reminded him of a smaller version of Southern California. The ring of mountains surrounded a sprawl of dwellings all the way to the sea. The jets screamed to their targets in the hills. Juri's sanity was being challenged to a literal nightmare of surrealistic and horrific proportion. As the Phantoms approximately 5 miles in the distance dove relentlessly at ground zero dropping their payload huge fireballs of orange Napalm and clouds of black billowing smoke were burned onto his brain. Armageddon was right in front of him and all he was wearing were his board shorts.

Authority has a habit of oppression. Many of the soldiers were ordered to do things that just felt like bullshit. Not necessarily crimes against humanity although there were those but things that felt like they were against one's own private self. It was very difficult to feel like an individual in the army. You always started off as a grunt. From the very first day of basic training, you had your face in the mud. To break away from the suppression there were many forms of distraction. And most of them got perverted. Some 19 years later Juri would remember seeing Stanley Kubrick's *Full Metal Jacket* and even though it was an intentional hyperbolic parody and nothing to do with reality the texture of the film was the only time he was transported back to that place by a movie. He felt that all the Hollywood attempts at Vietnam all fell short. He would for the rest of his life stridently question authority. So much so that his anti-war rhetoric sometimes offended certain people and alienated him. He felt his fellow soldiers didn't know if they were qualified to call themselves men. They were crossing the line from adolescence to becoming full-fledged adults. The way they conducted themselves would shape the world. Drafted into the Army to be a soldier was the definition of slavery to the idea of waging war. America's voracious appetite for the cult of war drove a dagger into its own heart. It had divided the country and lingers to this day. It seeps into our psyche and has become the genesis of dysfunction to the point where we can't even listen to each other.

As he got closer to separating and returning home, he became more anxious. He promised himself he wouldn't go off base and into town those last weeks, where he would be more vulnerable. Stories of returning troops being shot through the head on the gangway by a sniper's bullet as they boarded the plane at Tan Son Nhut Air Base for home played to many short-timers' worst fears. Larry and Midget wanted to party his separation. They lifted their Bai Hoi for going to town and toasting the end. The end wasn't the end for Juri until the charter flight was out of harm's way. He rejected the idea as if a couple of serial killers had offered him a drink. Their nothing-to-lose persistence won over the invitation. He relented that last night in Nha Trang to say his goodbyes in the town's active beachfront bars.

Dressed for the heat in the usual shorts, t-shirts and flip-flops, they eventually gravitated to the club that was in a fortified compound where they often gathered over drinks a couple of blocks off the oceanfront. The bar girls were overtly friendly. It was before karaoke so tight mini skirted ladies lip-synced into a microphone and the beer flowed freely.

YELLOW ALERT... a uniformed MP jumped to the stage, interrupted the performer, took the mic and repeated with urgency...YELLOW ALERT. You could now hear automatic weapons fire off in the distance. It was time for hard choices, stay at the club and possibly get over run or try to make it back the five miles to the base with the possibility of taking fire. That same adrenaline rush he felt his first day in country could now be his last. Why the frigging hell did he backpedal and go to town against his instincts. They were decked out for margaritas but the sentries wore helmets and flak jackets behind the sandbag bunker guarding the 30 ft. high chain link gate topped off with razor wire. They were dressed for something a little different. They were in the middle of it. The Tet Offensive initiated on the day Vietnamese celebrated their New Year. The surge in 1968 started in late January and came in 3 phases. It would endure beyond his scheduled flight home if he made it. Juri would never forget the sound of that chain link turnstile clanging shut leaving them naked in the street. The small arms fire seemed realistically closer. They flagged down an Air Force pickup that was running dark in the moonless night. The road back was now the road home and it bottlenecked on a narrow stretch along the beach at a place with no chance of turning around. Neon colored tracers from machine gun fire zippered all around them. The bullets drew rapid red-orange lines crossing their path and occasionally sounding off with a resonant heavy metallic THWACK when they struck the truck. Larry, Midget and Juri made like abalone on the bed of the pickup. It was an escalated plan for a low profile. The actual encounter lasted only about two or three minutes as their driver fishtailed and sped through the gauntlet. Every subsequent recount of the incident became more heroic. The psychological release within the safety of the barracks produced seven degrees of separation and a lightness of being. Needless to say, in the aftermath and relative safety inside the green zone they were emotionally spent. When Juri came to his senses he was angry. Absolutely enraged for putting his safety on the line like that. He was now of an age to understand the depth of fear his parents endured when he was an infant. The jungle boot was on the other foot. The next day he could not get comfortable. He was separating on the way to Saigon on a C-7 Caribou an especially slow, low flying twin engine aircraft. He spent his final night in country with the Psyops unit in Saigon and boarded a United Airlines Charter at Tan Son Nhut in the morning. He held his breath a lot on those last two flights.

He lost his faith in Vietnam, in his religion and in his government. At a critical time when he needed them, they both failed him. He had been in harm's way, literally in the line of fire. For months he contemplated kissing the ground when he would arrive stateside. It was a dramatic and patriotic thing to say but it was a meaningless gesture except in novels. *"Thank you for your service"* wasn't something he subscribed to. In fact, he didn't much care when he arrived at Travis Air Base. He was alone in Northern California among hundreds of family reunions. He was just fine by himself and he would let the journalists and the politicians sort things out, at least for now.

Orange Coast

CHAPTER 10

Looking back to those early days going to the beach with his parents, the ocean was something that easily filled his day. The memories of when he first learned to swim were cloudy. It was an overcast day in Seal Beach with Lee, his childhood friend. They put inner tubes into an oversized gunnysack. At low tide, in front of the power plant they launched their way to an exposed sandbar that had about the same footprint as the tree house they built together. As sometimes happens he lost track of time. He was hungry and hadn't yet had lunch. He overlooked that Lee had slipped away with the raft leaving him marooned. The tide came in and he was up to his neck. He scanned the shoreline some 30 yards away and couldn't spot a familiar face. Time to jump in headfirst. He flailed and floundered thrashing his arms like they did in the movies. He watched grownups around him and tried to do his best adult imitation. Because his breathing was erratic, he started to sink a stone's throw from shore. Time altered. He was not in the expected state of panic but was extraordinarily calm on the bottom of the channel. As he looked around underwater, he wasn't sure if his slow measured movements were dream-like or if it was the resistance of the water that slowed his pace. Starting to enjoy the weightless feeling, he was abruptly wrenched to the surface by his hair. A hand that belonged to the foot of someone he drifted into yanked him to his senses. He gasped a big gulp of air and time snapped back to its normal state.

The first couple of years of high school he hung out at the pier in Huntington Beach. Blackie August, father of *The Endless Summer* star Robert August was a mate of Lee's. That film would have a profound effect on beach culture. An entire generation of young surfers was going to be subconsciously prepared to chase waves across the whole planet. Also in the circle of friends were Jericho Poplar, a celebrated women's international champion and her brother Pepe. Some of the untouchables included Hawaiian legend David Nuuhiwa, Chuck Dent, Dick Pendergraft and shaper extraordinaire John Grey. Some of them later migrated south with Juri to employment at the Chart House and Ancient Mariner in Newport Beach. It was a time when John Grey crafted a few of Juri's favorite surfboards.

Newport Beach

Surfers tend to take time off to travel in search of waves. Juri was no exception. The number of places he lived was proportional to how many trips lasted more than a couple of months. Rent money could go a long way in Hawaii, Tahiti, Fiji, Indo, the Caribbean, France and Peru. During the time he spent in Newport he lived at 4 different places. He was going to surf, travel and play volleyball, his new love, and forget Vietnam. Surfing at 56th Street jetty he would watch the players on the sand court while he was in the water. He said to himself he could do that. Basketball in high school and in the service required the same skill sets as volleyball... jumping, passing and spatial court awareness. Some of the athletes were top-flight volleyball players and it was an opportunity to hone his aptitude for the game. He won an unsanctioned tournament in Bear Valley that instilled confidence. As his volleyball improved, he moved his game south again to the other side of the harbor entrance at Corona Del Mar State Beach. It was one of two beaches that were home to the elite tournament players in Orange County.

At first, he shared a two-story four bedroom on 35th street, in the first block off the water with three Newport Beach lifeguards. Tony and Randy waited on tables at the Mariner with Juri. The rental became a catchall with the addition of a girlfriend and a dog, then another girlfriend and a child. The last straw was when a flock of snowbirds from Sun Valley and Ketchum settled in. One day Juri went into the kitchen to get a bite to eat when a mountain of each and every dish, cup and piece of silverware in the house piled up in the sink and assaulted his sense of community.

They shared stories about Rocky who when he was a rookie lifeguard at Huntington Beach was low man on the totem pole and assigned to go into the water under the pilings of the pier to winch up a floater who apparently drowned while scuba diving. Rocky secured the strap around the body as the pulleys started to lift the lifeless form up on to the pier. Suddenly all the contents of the wetsuit exploded under the weight and emptied all over Rocky who lost his lunch in the water.

Peter and Juri spent the bulk of one summer at the Wedge, which was in those days exclusively a body surfing beach. It had a rebounding wave that bounced off the granite rock jetty on the north side of the entrance to Newport Bay. The wave would redirect toward the next oncoming swell and amplify its size significantly. The wave had a reputation and only bodysurfers who were accomplished in the giant gnarly conditions braved going out. Long before the era of boogie boards Ron Romanowsky was shredding the Wedge on a kneeboard. Peter had a cast on his wrist and forearm that summer from a swimming pool accident. He had a custom neoprene glove made that Juri would help duct tape securely just below the elbow allowing Peter entry into the water without risk to the cast. That was unless he hit rock bottom, which was a distinct possibility with a wave that had a 20-foot face and broke onto near-bare sand.

After a surf session at the pier, they noticed a couple of young outstanding ladies getting up from their spot on the beach to make a run to the market across the parking lot for refreshments. The boys hung up their neoprene wetsuits and were in their shorts drying off. Juri convinced Peter to pick up one of the vacated towels, dig a small trench under it and lay down in the depression. Juri placed a t-shirt over Peter's face and then covered the rest of him with a thin layer of sand then placed the beach towel exactly where it had been before. Peter was more patient than Juri waiting for the pair to return. The girls sat sipping their drinks as the mischievous played a waiting game. Unsuspectingly one of the girls lay down to get comfortable and bag some sun. After a pre-choreographed number of minutes, the earth moved for her. The ladies were gracious sports about the prank and accepted an invitation to Blackies, the infamous local hangout.

While in a good mid-day mood a group of six from the 18th street crew sat in the sand approximately 25-30 yards from the busy pedestrian-bike path. There were a few sunbathers between them and the pavement. They chose one spotter who faced the bicycles and foot traffic and had the best line of sight on potential targets. An industrial sized fire extinguisher with a ridiculously long extension hose attached to the nozzle had been buried in the sand aimed directly at the sidewalk. What made this a devious plan was that the spotter would whisper for the triggerman to release a blast of carbon dioxide gas at unsuspecting passers-by. The rubbernecking to figure out where the burst of cold gas came from was hysterical.

And for the trifecta, Graham who had a coatimundi as a pet would walk down the beach a good sprinting distance from an unaware candidate, preferably young and good looking, semi-comfortable and ideally lying down taking in some sun. A small piece of sweet bread was stealthily dropped on the corner of her towel and at the quiet chirp of an imperceptible signal the primal anteater looking creature was bearing down on its victim. The speed the coatimundi could realize in pursuit of the morsel was impressive. The after-the-fact histrionics didn't always turn out well.

They ended up renting a beachfront unit with Daniel on West Oceanfront east of the River Jetty. Jose Feliciano was their next-door neighbor and because he wasn't sighted would show up all sorts of hours of the night. His wife didn't much appreciate the encouragement he received from the trio.

On New Year's morning before the sunrise Juri went to the playground of the elementary school on Balboa Peninsula that was on the beach just south of 15th Street. In the dark he propped himself against the backboard of a handball court to take in the New Year's dawning. Just at the break of the day he saw the headlights of a patrol car pull out onto the sidewalk and head his direction across a large blacktop area of the schoolyard. He was miffed by the cop's approach. Had someone phoned in a complaint about his presence on the school grounds? But moments later his perspective changed dramatically. He realized the policeman was unaware of his presence and was simply drinking in the sunrise for himself. He was on the same page as Juri reflecting on what the New Year had in store. He was practicing consciousness on duty.

Juri was enjoying time with his friends at the restaurant. Stephanie could distill the abstract and the good in just about anything. She introduced him to pot and a wholesome attitude towards play. The unwritten rule particularly when the wait-list was long and a waiter was out on the floor taking an order the others would prepare his salad and heated bread in a small compact oven. This allowed him to turn in the order and immediately take the first course out to the table. Ron, one of the newer waiters fancied himself a ladies' man. His high beams went on when the hostess sat two lovely ingénues at his table. He turned on the charm with casual conversation leaning with one hand on the table for closer comment. What he didn't suspect was that Juri and Jack had written devious little notes, put them in the breadbasket and covered them with a cloth napkin. After Ron took out the salad and bread to the table he had to attend to his other diners. When he returned, he was sure he had positioned himself to pounce. He just couldn't figure out why his ladies had turned cold on him.

On a really busy Saturday night after a long and extended surf session during the day he put on the blue pants, white shirt and short apron and waited on a four top. Two couples engaged in expanded conversation ordered three New York steaks and a lobster dinner. Weekend evenings were considered *"turn 'em and burn 'em"* nights. It was especially hectic with as much as a two-hour wait for a table. In the meantime, the customers on the wait list were known to have a drink or two. Phil was the guy in the white hat behind the grill serving up dinners on the counter. Juri with part of his attention on another table swung by and picked up all four hot plates in one trip. He then hustled the warm meals over to the table in the dark corner. Most people, if they had ever spent long periods of time in the ocean would know that sometimes, sinuses would fill up with salt water. Multiple tables needed his attention and trying to save time, he cut corners. As he carried out the dinners, three of the customers were still in deep conversation with the one other lady watching the approaching waiter. Instead of stepping next to each seated patron and placing their meal in front of them Juri, being in more than one place at a time, stood at one of the corners of the table and leaned over to deliver all three New York's and one lobster. When the long downward reach got below a 45-degree angle his sinuses unloaded all over the entrees in an uncontrollable, continual stream of saltwater. Not once but twice. The look on the woman's face was one of abject horror. She was stunned silent. The other three diners were so wrapped up in their discussions they hadn't noticed. Juri quickly said…*"excuse me I think I have the wrong table"* and scooped up the plates and returned to the kitchen. *"Phil…I need three rare New York's and a lobster as fast as you can get them up"*. Without giving Jack, who was working the section of tables next to his, a reason for the switch he said, *"you gotta trade me tables and take over table #5"*.

Juri surfed with Jack before their waiter shifts at the Ancient Mariner for over a period of a decade. On more than one occasion they rode waves with Jack's friend Billy, legendary Hawaiian big-wave rider Laird Hamilton's stepfather. Juri was definitely the one watching better surfers in that trio.

Consuelo was the new cocktail girl at the Mariner. She had taken up an offer by one of the owners when he was on a ski vacation in Aspen. If she ever found herself in Newport Beach, she had a job at the restaurant. All the waiters paid close attention. When the dust settled Juri was the novelty left standing. They meshed well together. She got points for being well traveled. Her family owned a golf course in New Jersey, which didn't figure into the equation very much. She ventured out to San Francisco to put flowers in her hair and then to the mountains. Both pluses. Consuelo was a creative committed to weaving and other crafts. Big bonus. She was good with her hands, the icing on the cake. They rented an upstairs apartment on 36th street together. It was good times. They shared interests and had free time for the beach with evening work that put money in their pocket. They were part of a bigger social group at the Mariner and with their work mates journeyed extensively through Mexico over the course of the next 3 or 4 years. Camping, surfing and the beach with a little bit of art all became part of the family.

Origins

CHAPTER 11

She was very supportive of Juri taking up some of the financial slack during his final year in graduate school. After getting his master's degree they decided on Europe. They planned reunions with both of their families; Consuelo's in the Garden State, on the way to loading the Volkswagen Camper on the boat in Elizabeth, NJ. He must have been the only insane person in the world to ship a VW *to* Europe rather than *from* Europe. And then they would visit Juri's relatives in Slovenia. Two things he had to do first. Confirm with the Yugoslav consulate in New York that he wouldn't be conscripted into their military when he entered the country. Slovenia, where he was born, was still part of Yugoslavia. And second, he had to surf the Jersey shore.

The van was driven, loaded and then shipped off across the Atlantic three days before they flew to Reykjavik. He was asked by a stranger at the airport, while holding his surfboard in a white board bag under his arm, why he brought his ironing board along with him. He didn't have an answer. Besides the surfboard wasn't meant for Iceland. It was too cold. Instead, it was aimed at France one of their primary destinations. They landed in Frankfurt and took a train through Nancy to Le Havre. They tasted three countries in two days and were still on the run without one day of touring. They had a boat to catch or more precisely a VW Adventure Camper to unload. It had a permanent fiberglass bubble attached that offered the occupants plenty of vertical standing room and lots of additional storage space on top for a surfboard. That left the living quarters outfitted with all the amenities uncluttered. This version was much roomier and upgraded with all the bells and whistles. It was certainly a step up from the VW Westfalia, its German counterpart. And it had California plates, which paid dividends as an icebreaker at many campgrounds along the way.

The camper was on the road to Paris, a destination at the top of most everyone's list that was in Europe for a second time. All the perfunctory sites lived up to expectations. It was selfish of him but he had Biarritz on the brain and all he wanted was to get the board lashed to top of the camper and in the water. He relented enough to consider his travel partner and they spent the next week taking in Paris' top ten. The Louvre and Notre Dame were culturally gripping and he was irritated with his shortcoming. All the Art History exams he took were right there in the flesh. The flying buttresses of the great cathedral reached out to him. Versailles transported him into history much like another Kubrick film, *Barry Lyndon*. He enjoyed the company and midnight in Paris with her.

The rolling hills south of Bordeaux were *"irie"* cornrows of grape vines. Much of the wine they served at the Ancient Mariner came from this region. Bayonne a considerably sized city that stood between him and the waves was where the bayonet, something he trained with, was invented.

They rolled into Biarritz, recently cultivated, eager to see the ocean again at the Bay of Biscay. Seventeenth century architecture clung to the rocky crags and coves of shoreline. House of Bourbon castles doubled as casinos. The buildings were old and historic. The experience was new and novel. And for miles there was surf.

They stood out. They had smaller blue plates with yellow numbers while everyone else had longer horizontal white plates with black numbers. Every morning's drive to Grande Plage was to conclude where they would choose to ride waves that day. It was the closest beach to the campground and there were always surfers in hoodies standing by the low wall in the parking lot checking out the early conditions. Depending on the direction of the swell and its size they knew to go north to the beach breaks of Hossegors or south to Guethary, the point at Lafitenia or the harbor jetty at Saint-Jean-de-Luz. The surf got big; Hawaii big. One day just for the sport of it Juri paddled out at Grande Plage in small shoulder high-waves when the swell started to pick up. In the span of an hour, it was up to 6 ft and then by the afternoon it was huge. The waves were exploding over the lighthouse. Juri had never witnessed such an accelerated increase in size over such a short period of time. It was one of those swells that came along maybe once in 10 years. Lafitenia was supposed to hold any kind of swell but for three days surfers were driving up and down the coastal road from Hossegor to the Spanish border in search of waves they could ride. Everywhere along the Bay even Lafitenia was closed out. For surfers the sight of massive swells so big they can't be ridden smacks of forbidden fruit or a fruitless waste of time. Not because they don't have the courage but because it would be impossible to negotiate the green part of the wave when the monsters crash over themselves all at once creating nothing but whitewater closeouts.

After three days the swell dropped to a "manageable" 20 feet plus at the crowded point. Lafitenia was going off. There was an aggressive tenacious group at the takeoff spot on the right side of the cove with two story high green walls stretching across the span of the bay. Sitting in the cluster waiting your turn wasn't going to happen. In frustration he paddled deeper into the wave towards the rocks. He noticed that every once in a while, a wave forming near the boulders would push extra water towards the takeoff slightly delaying the peak to break. On one fortunate wave he stroked as hard as he could diagonally towards the crowd occupying the regular take off position. As he hopped up to his vertical stance it started to break over in front of him. He was smacked in the face by the force of the lip but shook his head and hair to regain his vision. Launched airborne between the thin front part of the wave and the enormous back wall he dug in the right rail of the board to grab the face of the wave. The rest was instinctive and just as thrilling. He carved a line as if he were drawing on the water. He negotiated his sightline and direction to maximize speed. It was an express train going all the way across town. On the paddle back where most everyone was jockeying for position he got a few hoots. Buzz and Craig, two East Coasters he met in the water a few days earlier, paddled over to talk about his wave. Buzz was originally from Cocoa Beach but had just set up shop in the Outer Banks. Through conversation, one of those bizarre coincidences, it turned out Buzz's brother worked at the same restaurant where Juri's sister Sonja waited on tables in California. Buzz shaped surfboards and named his enterprise *IN THE EYE.* He superimposed the letters over a graphic image of a hurricane. Buzz was graceful, fluid and creative in the waves and definitely not a crazed surf Nazi. Craig's style was strong, assertive and athletic. Something one might expect from someone from an ocean city in New Jersey. Both of them got their share of respect out in the water. The crowd in the water was humming. Nerve endings were bare. On the horizon a monster set was approaching. They made like covered wagons racing after a land grant. There were lines in the water. Lines from the white trails of big wave boards rushing out to sea. Lines of white water from the previous shore-bound breakers, but most importantly, the multiple towering green lines approaching from the open ocean that was threatening to have them all for lunch. It was a furious abstract watercolor. Juri was paddling in the middle flanked by Buzz to his left and Craig slightly ahead of both of them to his right. This wasn't winner-take-all typical of trying to be the first to catch a normal wave. This was blatant all-out survival. Dire circumstances weighed heavily for those who didn't make it. The first wave started to show a feathering of white at the top signaling it was starting to come over. Paddling faster than they could possibly go they arched their head and neck back in order to see the top of the breaking wave. They were caught dead-to-rights in the impact zone. Being tossed by waves this big was serious. The explosion of waves this size could hold someone down for seemingly longer than they could hold their breath. The classic analogy was being in a washing machine with the door slammed shut. Somehow all three made it in one piece through the first wave. The turbulence of the white water tossed them through both the heavy duty rinse and spin cycles. They yanked on their leashes to recall their boards and began the rabid stroking towards the next even bigger wave. Completely exhausted, this was literally do or die. They looked up at the mountain of water coming down on their heads and dove off their boards to get as much distance away from real danger. Avoiding getting hit by the fiberglass blades strapped to their ankles was the first order of business. The fundamental priority under these circumstances was to get as much distance as possible from their surfboards. There it was the moment of truth. Juri took one last gulp of air and dove as deep as he could go. Even before he could let out the end of his leash the mass of water came down on him. It was underwater pinball. He was right side up upside down. Tumbled and forced down to the bottom he needed more air than he had. The rubber leash was playing tug of war with Juri and the surfboard. Later that evening he surfaced, or at least that's what it felt like. He was held under for an impossible amount of time. In the weightlessness he couldn't figure which way was up. His gasps for air burned at his lungs when he came topside. Getting oxygen was a visceral reaction. Buzz and Craig were 50 yards in either direction. They had both snapped their leashes and their boards were being swept towards the rocks. Juri summoned his board by a quick tug of his still attached leash and paddled in their direction to see if he could help retrieve their boards. His chances at first glance were better than theirs. In hopes of making up lost ground, he held on and lay prone on his board. The next rush of white water sledded him forward as he tried to catch up with their surfboards. He could see them both careening off the boulders in front of him. Craig's light-colored board was in two pieces. Buzz wasn't much luckier. His surfboard was rebounding off the rocks with each successive wave. Enormous dents were visible on the deck and rails and by the time Juri arrived on the scene he was too vulnerable to make a rescue. It was too dangerous to get between the boulders and the oncoming waves. Salvage was left to chance. When the board finally drifted away from the rocks it was nothing more than a limp battered piece of fiberglass.

Kicking back in beach chairs next to the camper in the parking lot at Grande Plage, Consuelo and Juri struck up a conversation with an older couple. She was a typically attractive older woman from Paris and he was an ex-marine officer during World War II and an ex-pat who had met during the war. They were married in Biarritz after France was liberated and made it their home. Consuelo and Juri were invited to dinner at their flat overlooking the water on a couple of occasions during their stint in Biarritz. The California plates caught the captain's attention and he came over for a salute. The license plates on the van turned out to be a conversation piece on many other occasions.

On a tasty sunny afternoon Juri surfed crispy little offshore waves at Hossegors just north of Biarritz. From his location in the water noticed numerous beachgoers clad in bathing suits going into an area that was ringed by high temporary fencing. There was a busy flow of revelers coming in and out of the enclosure and you could faintly hear music from the water. Curiosity got the better of him. He paddled in to see what it was all about. It was France and it was hedonistic. He left it at that.

Immediately south through Basque country, they took a hard arid swing west. Coruna was Consuelo's families' ancestral home. They approached Portugal from the north via the Spanish plain. The van started running roughly. It got worrisome and they limped into Porto on his birthday. They walked the steep roads of the functioning fishing village with open shops and markets, relaxing in the outdoor cafes. The waves next to the breakwater at the entrance to the harbor were huge but he had a slight fever. They searched for a mechanic and decided to take a room. They were road-weary and in need of rest. After dozing off for a good portion of the afternoon they went by the shop to see how the VW was doing. The mechanic, a roll-up-your-sleeves kind of guy was on his back on a dolly under the back of the van. He had disconnected the gas tank and it was disassembled all over the floor and he was cleaning it out with some sort of mineral spirits. The diagnosis was that they had taken on some watered-down gas somewhere along their journey. Juri intuited immediately where it might have been. A year older, he was driving down the west coast of Iberia headed for Lisbon the very place some of the best-known historical explorers set sail from.

Refreshed and re-energized, they headed for Peniche one of the more bizarre surf spots on the planet. They drove a few miles out to the end of a long narrow peninsula where the Atlantic was visible on both sides of the road. At land's end there was a circular spiked hub of land shaped much like a mace, a weapon of medieval times. The options available in the 360 degrees of a small number of tiny coves and scalloped bays were strangely like a sampler of waves at each little separate beach. A choice was made at one of the compact inlets that sported really fine four-foot peaks that half a dozen foreign intruders were helping themselves to. When the wind picked up and shifted onshore, they all paddled in and ran across the road to the beach on the other side where the prevailing wind was now offshore. It was one of the stranger phenomena Juri had ever witnessed in his surfing life.

On the drive through Seville and then on to Cadiz gradually the size of things started to increase. In Portugal Juri noticed that all the dogs were only two feet tall, the suits of armor in the museums were three feet tall and people were all four feet tall. It wasn't an understatement to say Portugal was a small country. In Spain sizes seemed normal. In Gibraltar the apes were taller and Africa was in plain sight. They met up with Buzz and Craig again who were ticketed to the Canary Islands and Fuerteventura for more surf. It was her vacation too. Consuelo and Juri had a private discussion and Juri told his two most recent friends that he and Consuelo were headed to the Riviera and points east. Part of him wanted to go south with them but for now the compass heading was in the direction of Madrid and Barcelona. The border between Spain and France was Pablo Picasso's territory. Even he wasn't clear on which country he was part of. Nice was on the French Riviera and the Palme d'Or and Gran Prix awards at the Cannes Film Festival generated the kind of films that Juri gravitated towards, cinema with a message. The gambling houses of Monte Carlo were out of their league but certainly interesting from a distance.

Sanremo put them in Italy but in the dark it felt just like an extension of the French Riviera. Extensive surfing in France and Portugal took a bite out of their allotted time. They had to choose between Florence and Venice. Juri's past and his extended family were in Slovenia across the border to the east. Venice was a more direct route. It was the first real cold weather they experienced on the trip. Somewhere packed in the duffel bags were down parkas. They needed them. The centigrade thermometer read zero.

Everything was a dull grey, the sky, the statues and the pigeons. Venice brought out the vagabond in him. It brought out the historian and the artist. He was soaking it in on multiple layers. He was a rolling stone and maybe an onion.

They kept running into the same people. The couple they had coffee with in Porto, then seeing them again in Madrid. If he thought about it, it wasn't so unusual. They were all on the same time frame, with similar interests headed generally in the same direction. Besides, all roads led to Rome.

Fourteenth century Venetian Gothic architecture, canals, arched walking bridges, gondoliers and the bronze horses of St Mark, it was all he expected to see but much like a chance face-to-face with a celebrity. Once dialogue was initiated it became more than a cliché. They got a sense of Venice the guidebooks couldn't give them. Consuelo was in her element in the arts and crafts shops off St Mark's Square. She purchased a bag of African trading beads hand-blown out of glass where Marco Polo played as a boy.

Trieste, historically, was part of Austria Hungary then Slovenia and now Italy. Multiple languages rooted in those cultures were still spoken. On the street Juri's ear heard his first language, Slovenian, spoken for the first time since he left his parents' home. The road to Ljubljana, the city where he was born was roughly 95 kilometers… "down the route on Highway 61. Man, you must be puttin' me on."

After a quick stop at the Postonja Caves, they drove the van displaying their California plates into the capital city. At Njegoseva 9, the house he spent the very first days of his life, imagining how it might have been before his first memories. In the small rooms upstairs now occupied by family members, he knew it was different. That house was the genesis of everything. From the beginning all the experiences that shaped him started here. It was ground zero for his DNA. The house stayed in the family all this time after two wars and three generations. His mother's family was not in the political hot water his father's side was. They were allowed after the war by the new authority to retain the home that was confiscated earlier by the Third Reich before their defeat. His father and the rest of his family were not as fortunate. Boris, Lija's brother and Juri's uncle, was the current head of the household on Njegoseva. Makika was the real matriarch. She had the air of composure and uncommon intellect to carry the family through the turmoil of the war and the decades after it.

Though everyone was well versed in English, Consuelo was at a distinct disadvantage when conversation became intimate. At the dinner table the nieces and nephews tried to keep her abreast, happy to exhibit their command of her language. Juri and Consuelo on a visit to an upscale department store were obviously American tourists speaking in English. Two professionally attired women behind the cosmetic counter were comfortably chatting in Slovenian about the foreigners, nothing bad or malicious, more just a curiosity. It was a delicious moment of having the upper hand. Like holding aces against kings. The audible super power of being in on their conversation without them knowing was literally exhilarating. Juri let them go on. He gave them rope. Then in his first language he said… *"kako si"…zelo dobro, upam"*. "Rdeca" was the color of embarrassment. In a heavily accented and broken English one of the sales clerks asked him…*"how to you speak good Slovenian"?* He didn't tell them the truth. He said he studied it in school. They probably knew the public school system in America doesn't teach Slovenian.

Ruli, Juri's cousin was a French language professor at the university and an avid and expert skier and mountain climber. He had summited Triglav the highest peak in the Julian Alps on a number of occasions. The apples don't fall far from the tree. He had a vacation home in the Alps at Gozd Martulijek.

They ventured to Koper and Portoroz, Slovenia's little slice of the Adriatic. In the summer the area attracted sun worshipers and tourists. Tomaz, Ruli's brother shared a story about a young woman, a family friend that was fatally attacked by a shark, just offshore from where the family was having lunch. Back in Ljubljana it was time for robust familial good byes. Consuelo and Juri considered Greece but serious civil unrest vetoed that as part of the journey. Instead, they turned the camper around with the surfboard strapped to the top and slushed through the winter roads back through the tunnel at Mt. Blanc in the direction of northern France.

The VW that originally came from Germany was now making its way across the Atlantic for a third time.

It was Juri's turn to take care of finances. Consuelo was now free to take weaving classes and become skilled with all sorts of ethnic fabric making processes. She joined a renowned group of weavers and fabric artists in Costa Mesa. She thrived in the innovative environment. They shared their esthetics as peers even though their expressions were very different.

The weaving studio presented an opportunity to go to China. It was shortly after Mao's death and the People's Republic was still immersed in the little Red Book as the Cultural Revolution was coming to an end. Nixon had yet to make his historic visit. The roadways were absolutely choked with streams of bicycles and with the exception of a black Mercedes here and there most vehicles were either two wheeled or human powered. It was a risky venture to try to cross the street unless there was a uniformed policeman directing traffic.

They came in under the cover of darkness. Beijing in the dark was not as exotic as Beijing in the misty hazy fog of a winter morning. Their hotel was a suite of three high ceilinged rooms furnished with turn of the century antiques and relics from a seemingly endless array of dynasties. The watercolor view outside the window was just like all the landscapes in the museums. The architecture was unmistakable. Up the street and across from Tiananmen Square and the Forbidden City were mile-long lines at the mausoleum that housed Chairman Mao's body. It was on display for all to see and by the looks of it, all showed up. They waited quietly, for an excruciatingly long time and with respect, the only way you were allowed to view the body. Everyone wore Mao suits in a choice of two colors, military green or navy blue with the typical red star emblazoned on the cap.

Shanghai was a city apart. It had, if not a European flavor, certainly an international flair, more so than any other port in China. One of the major port cities on the eastern coast of Asia, historically it harbored galleons, brigantines, caravels, clippers, junks, frigates, schooners and tramp steamers. All this traffic brought in goods. Goods were the currency of trade. Everybody wanted in on the action. Juri walked the street alone one day, something that never happened intentionally. Without their assigned guide he stepped out into the street and ducked into some shops without thinking about it. A grandfather clock in an antique store caught his attention. It was the identical twin of a German clock he purchased for Consuelo last Christmas except for the fact that it was hewn out of black ebony instead of golden oak. Except for the type of wood and the color all the intricate detail of craft and facing were absolutely identical. The original clockmaker was without question the same individual and from the same shop in Schwenningen. The current walk along the harbor exposed more modern ships bearing flags from even more nations and a mixed bag of architecture not only influenced by successful merchants from a variety of countries of the past but from today's more contemporary Chinese innovation. Shanghai, because of its economic history based on trade, was a precursor to the whole of modern China today.

They boarded a train to Nanjing. Crossing on stone trestles over an enormous dry riverbed that seemed to go on endlessly to the vanishing point. If it had been possible to look directly in the direction the steam locomotive was headed, they probably couldn't have seen the other side. For a span of 15 minutes all they witnessed was sand and more sand. Then as the tracks gradually curved to the left the view unveiled hordes upon hordes of workers in conical straw hats wearing pajama like clothing. There were thousands upon thousands of laborers. They had bamboo poles slung over their shoulders carrying baskets full of sand strung to each end of the bamboo. Their short choppy running stride revealed the weight of their load. As the train continued the crossing, a panorama of epic proportions unfolded into a saga that might give Cecil B. DeMille another nomination. The sheer number of humans was mindboggling. Counting on their resources, this was heavy equipment at its primordial.

In Nanjing there was a very large image of Mao hung on the opposing wall of the terminal. As they approached closer the painting became sharper. The clarity of edges was masterful. Standing under the monumental portrait and arching back to look up at it, it astounded Juri that what he was viewing was, in fact, an embroidery. A team of seamstress artisans apparently had used the infamous *"blind stitch"* to render the Chairman. After Mao's death that particular stitch was outlawed in the factory workplace because of its severe detrimental effect on the eyesight of the seamstresses.

Guangzhou, one of the larger cities in Southeast China had the reputation as the commercial trade center of the People's Republic. And for their troupe it was a shopping spree on the contemporary version of the Silk Road. Exotic bags had to be purchased to hold all the goods that weren't shipped.

Crossing over to Hong Kong when it was still a crown colony was definitely a case of east meets west. Chinese junks superimposed over glass and steel high-rises. One culture sailed past the other. The commotion of the financial district contrasted the muted ambiance of residential Repulse Bay. Little did the queen's subjects known that time was running out.

Newport Beach

CHAPTER 12

With every return from a trip, LA felt a little different. But it wasn't so much SoCal as it was Juri. When he traveled to different countries, he saw different people doing the same things he did, differently. That played over and over again in his head.

They started to drift. It probably had more to do with Juri than Consuelo. She never talked about wanting to have kids but within a year after they went their separate ways, she had a son.

Juri shared another three-bedroom upstairs apartment on River Avenue with Skip from the restaurant and his closest surf buddy Jack's brother Stymie. Assorted visitors filed in and out at all times of the night and day. Typically, they began with an early morning surf check and if the waves were working, they would surf through the afternoon until the on-shores blew out the conditions and rendered it unmanageable. Then after the wetsuits came off it was straight to the Mariner for an outdoor shower. From there the routine was to fold napkins for the setups for that night, wait tables and then unwind. Waiters, cocktail girls and bartenders were all pretty much poured in the same mold, young, bulletproof and willing. It was always happy hour but it was pushing midnight. Whatever social arrangements were made were played out. Then it would start all over again with the dawn's early light surf check. It was cyclical and it seemed never to end, certainly at least not during the summer. After the Corona Del Mar Volleyball Open, one of the two major Orange County tournaments, the winners Ron Lang and Ron Von Hagen came into the Ancient Mariner. Juri waited on their table. He rubbed elbows with the very players he was in awe of. That personal connection with world-class athletes energized him. On days when the waves were flat and even on days when it wasn't, Juri ventured to Corona Del Mar where volleyball, not surfing, was central to anyone's standing at the beach. Hierarchy was a strange unwritten rule. Most knew about the obvious alpha male but where you stood in the pecking order in those days was dictated by how you performed during the weekend tournaments. There were all levels of play from Open tournaments in which professional and Olympic players competed all the way to novice tourneys. AAA ranking was the highest you could achieve, with AA tourneys still a very high caliber of play a slight notch down from the name players. With A tournaments it was mostly young up-and-coming contenders contrasted with a mix of older players who were in it mostly for the love of the game. Juri once played in an A tournament in Santa Monica where one of the competitors was Wilt Chamberlain of NBA fame who could spike the ball without jumping. B and Novice tournaments were a hybrid bag of pretty much anything. Always fun, the mixed tournaments with one male and one female partner were usually a social game at the lower ranked events and sometimes a strange blend of serious and not at the higher ranked events. Less frequent four-man tournaments were specialized events where specific skills were at a premium. In the traditional two-man game overall skills with ability in all aspects of the game were critical to make it deep into the draw. In the current version of the game with the AVP and the FIVB, there are fewer overall opportunities as participants for a larger group of non-tournament weekday players. This makes it less obvious for those who don't compete to earn an accurate measure of their capability.

At Corona Del Mar State Beach the elder statesman on the courts was Bob Wetzel one of the pioneers of the beach game along with Gene Selznick of Santa Monica and Dick Davis of Laguna Beach. The alpha dog at Corona was John Vallely, probably the least known winning beach competitor of all time. John was an All-American basketball player for John Wooden at UCLA. Coach Wooden called Vallely the best jumper for his size that he ever coached. That was high praise. John Vallely was drafted by the Atlanta Hawks and developed shin splints that prematurely ended his career. One season earlier in Juri's pursuit of volleyball, John teamed up with Ron Von Hagen to win seven tournaments on the tour that year.

The Easter A at the Santa Monica pier traditionally inaugurated the tournament schedule for the year. Juri gained currency among his circle when he won the tournament and earned his AA rating with John Cummings. They both noticed that returning to the courts at Corona on Monday, there was a revised air of regard. The new notches on their belt earned them a place higher on the ladder. John Vallely and Juri became good friends the remainder of that summer. John took him under his wing and they mutually talked volleyball for as much time as John could tolerate. The local crew consisted of other recognizable and established players with AAA and AA ratings. Woody Brookes, Brian Lewis Sr., Tom Bryan and Bill Imwalle were other triple-A competitors at the beach. Woody's sister Karen worked with Juri at the Mariner and Brian's son Junior was to later be one of the top AVP players. Juri teamed up with Woody at the last moment to win the Half Moon Bay Open before big money and sponsorship were part of the game. They came home with state-of-the-art televisions that weighed a ton and made the drive south cumbersome.

Woody had a remarkable focus on the court beyond that seen in most athletes. What Juri appreciated about him was that he was an ace storyteller. During down times in tournaments there was plenty of time for exchange. Some used it for strategy, and theoretically cleaning up mistakes in their game. Woody used it to spin yarn. He seemed to have a lot of Ron Lang stories. Apparently, the legend had a winning record against him in their many encounters that offered up lots of "Woody" interpretations. There was the time when on nine consecutive plays in a row Lang "cut" the ball in front of Woody. A "cut" shot was a delicate slice of the ball depositing it in the short corner of the court. It was considered finesse rather than attack. Consensus had it that to be effective you had to mix it up with your opponents to keep them off balance. Most would weigh the predictabilities and proceed in favor of the numbers. In chess you assess your position and go with the unpredictable. Each subsequent play Woody would tell himself that this time his opponent was going to go deep with the ball. Ron Lang was creative enough to go against the grain and obstinate enough to keep embarrassing Woody's ego over and over again. On another occasion as the story goes, teamed with Von Hagen, Lang reacted to a high velocity carom off of his partners chest directly into the net. A thunderous spike turned into a semi-accidental rebound that paralleled the sand into the top of the net. In the time it took to blink, Lang was on his back, like an Angel or a Dodger sliding into second base, to receive the ball. In an artful and effortless all-in-one motion, he handled the ball in a manner reminiscent of a sleight-of-hand master. He set the ball with his hands perfectly for his partner who put the ball away. Those who know volleyball realize that setting the ball with your hands was one of the most exacting skills in the game, hard enough when upright.

At the Corona Del Mar Open in July, Juri teamed with Bill Imwalle to defeat two volleyball icons Jim Menges and Ron Vogelsang and his best finish in an open tournament to date. The finals of the tournament lasted well after the setting sun. At dusk with the light dimming a number of 4-wheel drive pickups positioned their halogen running lights trained on the court to allow for the continuation of play.

Laguna Beach
CHAPTER 13

Gravitating to Laguna Beach was a natural fit because of its reputation as an art community. Laguna was esthetically more appealing and at the time a more progressive town which suited him just fine. The politics were more traditionally conservative in Newport. Laguna had a certain village charm with its town center and most the population residing in the hills above and around the restaurants and shops concentrated in the few blocks adjacent to Main Beach and the landmark Hotel Laguna. People gathered in the distinctive town center. The ambiance was one of café culture. Juri exhibited at the Laguna Festival of Arts in the canyon. He also displayed at the New York Art Directors Show in the Big Apple. It was a busy time for him. He was teaching in the art departments at Cal State Long Beach and Chapman University. The last few years he lived in Newport he would ride his motor bike south, which seemed to be his preferred direction, to spend time in Laguna. Juri was soon to be a department head at the Laguna College of Art and Design. He was playing volleyball at Main Beach. And he was surfing at new spots like Rock Pile and El Moro more often than he was at 56th Street and the Newport pier.

Main Beach was high-density people watching territory. There was a spot affectionately called "the bench" right in front of the volleyball courts where you could station yourself down and watch the parade go by. The leisure pursuit of checking out the tourists and locals was always fascinating. Not so much a judgment than it was a peer review into human nature. The young athletic physiques on the sand tended to draw those who liked to scrutinize anatomy. It was a case of the ladies checking out the guys and the guys checking out the ladies. And Laguna being accepting of alternative lifestyles, there were good people of many persuasions. The female version of the game was always the cash cow for televising women's volleyball. The crew rode the bench with Chip the unofficial greeter manning the right flank.

The top volleyball dog at Main Beach was Pete Ott who marshaled the ground rules with sarcasm and a fist full of irony. He had a strange sense of humor and a powerful build. His upper torso was that of someone that might be 5′ 6″ with long arms and legs of someone who might be 6′ 6″. Pete's dad, a renowned sculptor had a home studio in the canyon. Peter was an accomplished naturalist who ran nature tours to the Baja Peninsula. He took his father's lead and pursued creating wildlife art. The snake man was quick to adopt any and all discarded exotic animals that were injured or unwanted. He was the sole proprietor of an unofficial wildlife sanctuary. When stopping by his place for a game of horseshoes or some serious table tennis, your new companions were pythons, a variety of chameleons and red macaws. Peter was especially hard on volleyball out-of-towners who journeyed to get in a few matches with Laguna players. On one peculiar occasion two very strong competitors from the South Bay waited to challenge Peter and whoever he was holding court with. When their turn came up and after only three points into the game Peter and his partner, saying nothing, walked off the court and just sat stone-faced on the edge of the boardwalk. The visitors were dumbfounded. Volleyball could be as territorial as surfing. It dawned on Juri he didn't go to school in Laguna and was a recent transplant himself yet seemed immune from the wrath of Ott. He thought it might be because they both had art in common that Juri had an exemption.

Local Laguna volleyball numbered many other players with strong finishes on the tournament circuit including Phil Anderson, Danny MacFarland, Bill Imwalle, who migrated south with Juri, the Dvoracks; Dusty, gold medal Olympian and his two brothers Rudy and Drake, Mike Floyd, Rick Edwards and Marty Gregory. With the later advent of the AVP the next generation of Laguna players included such notables as Leif Hanson, Scott Friederichsen, Mike Garcia, Mike Minier, Justin Pearlstrom,

Neil Riddel, George Carey and Mike Stafford. They were on a list too long to note. Competition during the week was keen. It amounted to practice. Protocol dictated winners stayed on the court to be challenged by the next team. Especially on weekends, if you lost, the waitlist backed up for hours before you might have your turn again on the winners' court. Infractions and line calls that were on the honor system in non-tournament play made for interesting and sometimes contentious conversation on the court.

The middle of the following summer Juri was on the top of his game. Against stronger opponents, strategy became a chess game, even an art form. Committed competitive athletes are always in a race to grasp an understanding of the game before their physical bodies are past their prime. The alignment in the sky was perfect. The Laguna Beach Cuervo Open, a designated major on the tour schedule was also home court advantage. Marty Gregory, one of the established players from Laguna Beach was Juri's partner over the last few seasons. The day before the tournament Juri was quoted when asked by a reporter from an Orange Coast area newspaper where they would probably end up in the draw. He was on the record as saying...*"we probably won't finish in the top four"*. In the first round they drew a team that included Mark Barber, who would later turn out to coach Olympian Gold Medalist Karch Kiraly on the sand, and whose father Bobby a volleyball hall-of-famer was the oldest player to earn a AAA rating. In the next round they defeated a strong local Laguna team of Craig Kiernan and Ron McElhany and in the third round they won in a dramatic defensive match over Olympic Silver Medalist Mike Dodd and former AVP president Jon Stevenson. Saturday's play would end in a victory over Don Shaw and Skip Allen, the only team to defeat the eventual double-elimination tournament champions Dane Selznick and Andy Fishburn. Here they were still in the winners' bracket with their next match slated for the tournament quarterfinals of a 32-team tournament on Sunday morning against the two most recognizable names ever to play the beach game, Karch Kiraly and Sinjin Smith. It would be the last season those two would play together as a team. For Juri the anticipation was a rush, a feeling of pride and satisfaction to compete at this level and hold his own.

Sunday morning brought a mass of onlookers who were already situated in their beach chairs crowding the main court. Laguna had a reputation for its large raucous and fun-loving crowd. One small *"Lagunatic"* contingent pre-deposited a couch with 15' high Eucalyptus branches planted next to the sofa's armrest. The temporary foliage occupied by a pair of macaws had the obligatory keg buried next to it with a barely visible spigot in a beach bucket. Some of the tribe wore remnants of volleyballs over their heads like skullcaps and fine satin smoking jackets. The stage was set. While Marty and Juri lost in a good match, they were not embarrassed. They had just gone toe to toe with a superior championship caliber team. They were still in the double elimination tournament and now in line to play for fourth place against Randy Stoklas, a beast of a player and maniacal bad boy Steve Obradovich. For the locals it was a mundane ordinary game that they lost in undecorated fashion. They took their acclaim from the crowd and became spectators to watch the semis and the finals. While Juri would go on to win his share of more minor tournaments, as far as competing at the highest level of elite players he was more than happy with the outcome. As he predicted in the newspaper article, they didn't end up among the top four teams but taking home fifth place in such a major competitive tournament ended up being a badge of honor regarding his volleyball career.

Sitting on the bench he noticed an athletic looking lady with more than her share of good looks. They say that subconsciously we pick our volatile relationships. Consciously he had no way of yet knowing her eruptive personality. He found out soon enough but couldn't completely chalk up his losses. With passing time, she had a way of not bringing out the best in him. The angst of the on again off again was torturous. They decided to take a trip to see if a change of geography might help the discord.

The itineraries were separate vacations. Edie went to Mendocino to visit a pot farmer and he went to Metatantay, Rolling Thunder's encampment outside of Carlin, Nevada. The camp didn't belong to any one specific tribal group. It was a bare bones co-op retreat open to anyone that was of the right mind and spirit. Juri wasn't sure where his "head was". At the entrance to the camp a sign read, ...

NO DRUGS
NO ALCOHOL
NO FIREARMS
NO VIOLENCE

The weather didn't listen. He was pelted by huge stone sized hail. He worked with the animals even though they talked back to him. In this territory he was low man on the totem pole. The pecking order turned him into a go-fer. As the novitiate he was told what to do. Juri was the novice and it infringed on his feelings of independence. He had shaped choice and freedom into important necessities. Being ordered around was submission. It created an uneasiness he hadn't felt since the service.

His first conversations were with a long-braided Oglala Sioux with a particularly red headband. American Horse, for his part on the Six Nations Council, actually carried one of their passports. For Juri that was a paradox for a Native American. One day when he was helping repair wickiups, American Horse rolled a cart stacked with carpet remnants and scraps of a white woven synthetic material with brass grommets minimally riveted on the larger pieces. Juri sewed the pieces of fabric to some carpet remnants then inlaid the covering between the woven willow branches of the domed hut. He was asked by his workmate if he knew what the white material was. They had shared bits and pieces about each other during the course of their chores after the morning circle. Juri was from then on referred to and tagged as *Coyote.* Turns out the fabric was donated to Rolling Thunder by Bulgarian born artist Cristo from the groundbreaking *Running Fence* project in Northern California. Juri immediately asked if he could pocket some pieces of the art relic. The conversation flowed both ways. What was more significant than the fragments of the famed art installation was that American Horse's wife was run over and killed by a military truck at the infamous occupation of Wounded Knee.

Rolling Thunder was in San Francisco with his daughter who was diagnosed with an extremely rare disease. The specialist confirmed it was tuberculosis of the spine. Pott's disease commonly found in mummies of ancient Egypt is almost non-existent today.

On his drive to the airfield at Elko he reflected on his expectations prior to arriving. The experience was contrary to his preconceptions of what Metatantay would be. It dawned on him that visualizing an image before painting it; the outcome would always be absolutely different from the original incomplete mental picture.

Back in Laguna his relationship was in the off mode again. Then one evening when Edie showed up at his door he didn't have the heart to reject the sure path to oblivion. He was a candidate for amnesia. Hindsight with a smattering of emotional disconnect was easy. What was unfeasible was "no".

Assessment of past follies was a folly in itself. He was beating himself up and raking his self-esteem over the dying embers. Understanding would come in time but he was only half way through his melodrama.

Sandinistas

CHAPTER 14

It was time to get out of Dodge again. Juri was playing summer slow-pitch softball when the manager, or to be more specific, the guy who put up the cash for the team, ran out on the field and yelled at one of the players for some minor gaffe. It dawned on Juri that the players on a co-ed team on the adjacent diamond were having way more fun. One gal had just hit a lethargic blooper that landed just inside the foul line and spun crazily off into no-man's land. As she waddled around first base, she stretched out the paltry single into a double. Two of her male counterparts sprinted out to second base with beers in hand as her reward. It was a no brainer. It was easy to see who was having the most fun here. Something reminded him of his situation at home. Something correlated with a relationship gone "north". He ended up doing the right thing. He switched teams. Not at home. But for the last two games of the season, he had a ball.

Randy, a teammate on the co-ed squad had accidentally run into Juri at the Tahoe airport when at the last minute he was asked to do a children's benefit. Juri was in Tahoe because his plane was diverted from Reno to Tahoe because of a summer storm. During this chance meeting in the passenger lounge, they concocted a trip to Central America. He and Juri hashed up a plan to go to Nicaragua as observers during the Contra War. A contingent of artists organized through an international group that Juri and Randy joined as a seemingly political gesture, which in truth was just another excuse to travel. Not a particularly insane thing for a Vietnam vet he thought.

Daniel Ortega's Nicaragua didn't distinguish itself much from many Latin American countries Juri had traveled. Even though there was a guerilla war going on, people were remarkably gracious and affable. Managua was excessively rich in graphics. Murals were abundant. Political billboards and revolutionary graffiti were everywhere. Juri started a photo series, a visual essay. Pictures were speaking louder than words.

Conversations in the street were easy and often, even though 14-year-olds in olive drab had automatic weapons strapped over their shoulders. In contrast, Randy and Juri played some basketball with the local kids in a park. Nicaraguans were capable of exacting the difference between American citizens and the American government. But then little things like a population armed to the teeth became more noticeable. One day they were returning to Managua from Esteli, where Ortega himself attended the massive 5-year anniversary demonstration rally in the hillside township as a show of national unity. Their transport came over a mountain pass down into the valley. They noticed figures coming out of the jungle to their right dressed in paramilitary trappings making like black ants. The illegal army cautiously shuffled in migrating lines down into the valley. In front of the bus was a semi-rig that hauled petrol in a shiny chrome tank a couple of hundred yards ahead of them on Highway One. Off in the distance Juri spotted one of the combatants kneel with what looked like a rocket launcher over his shoulder and fire at his target. The missile hissed like a dragon hitting the tanker dead on exploding all over the highway. Our driver stomped the pedal, swerved through the debris and put all of it behind us. As they corkscrewed through the twisted skeleton of the semi, Juri could feel the centrifugal force torque left as he scanned right. Past the window and through the blur of smoke, flame and ash he caught a last moment glimpse of distorted shapes of dark clad mercenaries. There they were. The *contras*. It was simply his tax dollars going to work.

Wartime culture in Managua turned out to be an evening concert in the bombed-out music hall, under the stars and bats buzzing the orchestra. The musicians packed up their instruments in the middle of the concerto as the rain started coming down. The next afternoon the group visited with a collective that met with a Guatemalan women's co-op organized by Rigoberta Menchu who would eight years in the future be awarded the

Nobel Peace Prize. Hand woven fabrics, clothing, blankets, bags and purses were spread out on tables in the studio. Large looms and weaving tools on display underscored the origins of ethnic cultural expression. Juri's personal interests in indigenous crafts were piqued. Informal conversations with the advocate director explored connections with his academic and artistic contacts. Proceeds from the handcrafted goods purchased at this impromptu market went to the displaced refugees in Chiapas on the southern Mexican border. Rigoberta Menchu was a sole public voice for that supplanted group.

At the Masaya Volcano there was enough activity of spewing steam that you couldn't see the opposing rim of the crater. An adjacent inactive crater was lush with vegetation while the active one was barren and rocky. Before they were visible, Juri and Randy heard the squawking of a flock of brightly colored lime green parrots flying out of the white billowing steam. Their color only divulged, as they emerged contrasted by the massive white cloud. The sound of spewing steam took wing.

Matagalpa in the mountainous central region had an old historical flavor and, because of the topography, more susceptible to the clandestine war. Vulnerability to the mercenary tactics of the *contras* was statistically borne out. In the plaza Juri spotted a Nicaraguan photographer trying to earn his living with a crude, primitive box camera vending portraits in the street. It was grassroots entrepreneurship at work. Juri was in a sit-down with some students when Randy informed him that Manny had been detained. The 65-year-old joined our group two days after we arrived in Nicaragua, had been missing for six hours. The militia had stopped him and confiscated his film for photographing for what they said was a security building. Another political incident intruded on their peace of mind. Naomi's husband who was flying in to join her and the group after the fact was detained for a short while in a stop-over in El Salvador. The politics of that authoritarian government were definitely on the record with El Mano Blanco and the death squads of Jose Napoleon Duarte and Roberto D'Aubuisson.

Granada, south of Managua, had a distinctly Spanish flavor in its strong colonial architecture, cathedrals and plazas. There were prominent symptoms that the conflict had ravaged the area on Lake Nicaragua. Bullet holes decorated the adobe walls of public buildings on busy avenues. Common people in the street slung rifles over their shoulders. Whitewashed structures had rough brushed slogans painted on them. *"NO PASSARAN"* became the rallying cry of choice. Maybe it was ironic that this pre-historic inland sea once open to the Pacific Ocean had large predatory sharks still cruising its waters.

With two days left in country, Randy and Juri decided to take some R and R on the beach. They rented a car and headed south. Pochomil was a small backwater coastal road stop somewhere between a village and a town with an ample amount of charm. They parked next to a palm-thatched beach bar with a triangular Campo sign slung above the door. Juri spotted a derelict long board with a big fat skeg laminated to the bottom of the deck. It was leaning against the palapa looking like the lone stranger. One cold Victoria and a tepid inquiry and Juri paddled out in the water. While the wind was calm, conditions were sloppy. The water had a reddish-brown tinge that mimicked the topsoil all around them. They probably rode in on the heels of a rainstorm. The waves were barely negotiable, but Juri got in a cheater five and the chance to surf Nicaragua.

The drama at the airport was unexpected. It ended up being easier getting into the country than it was to get out. A number of flights had been mysteriously cancelled and in the lobby a din of would-be passengers were negotiating their plight with all sorts of uniformed authority around heavily armed military. Randy and Juri managed one confirmed ticket between the two of them until they stumbled onto an out-of-place Bolivian with an extra ticket. He was willing to do a two-for-one trade plus a few cordobas.

Passengers on the first stopover were treated to a dose of unwarranted tension as Salvadorian military personnel boarded the plane armed with automatic weapons. They walked both sides of the aisles as if they were looking for someone. It was short-lived and the plane took off without incident. The remainder of the flight back through Houston was uneventful. It was a good time for introspection. Juri used it to reflect on the politics and how information shapes conflicts. Lives are affected. He always felt most places he went people were people. There was always this thread of attainability with common folk.

The incentive for uniqueness came from variation. Plurality brought us to choice and collectively those choices became the components of a living record of human expression. When we didn't have a view of what the world was really like we tended to retreat into homogeneity, looking alike and thinking alike. The lack of tolerance for differences came from this denial of the planet and its diversity of cultures and ethnic variations. What always struck Juri about travel was the sensual ocean of texture, pattern, color and form particular only to the place that you were. This was not just a visual experience. The senses were charged by the novel, and the exotic. Keenness preceded awareness.

Octavio Paz, Nobel Prize laureate wrote...

> *"what sets worlds in motion is the interplay of differences, their attractions and repulsions. Life is plurality. Death is uniformity. By suppressing differences and peculiarities, by eliminating different civilizations cultures' progress weakens life and favors death. The idea of a single civilization for everyone, implicit in the cult of progress and technique impoverishes and mutilates us. Every view of the world that becomes extinct, every culture that disappears, diminishes a possibility of life."*

The world we share and the world we keep privately to ourselves contained these possibilities. We needed to enjoy them, to celebrate them. Held in those connections were the impressions and effects of global tribes that influence us all. As we continued to proceed in our world could we afford to be threatened by ethnic diversity and native migration patterns? If there were any answers to those questions they have always been there in the differences of divergent cultures and ethnic variation. As an artist and a teacher, Juri had a priority in his philosophy: to ask others to speak to concepts and images regarding their backgrounds and their experiences not as spectators but as participants in what had been passed on to them.

He needed to teach. It provided him with a certain pleasure and a way to help other people. In teaching others, he found the road to his own learning. The problems of others, he recognized as his own. The compensation became some resolution and clarity in an all-too-narrow realm of swirling personal experience. Travel continued its magnetic pull.

The cabin lights dimmed and he fell asleep. Back in Laguna the world didn't seem quite the same. He felt he expanded a little bit and the pull of travel was spilling over him like water seeking its own level.

Art Market

CHAPTER 15

He was grateful for the day shortly after graduation. In his total cluelessness he went right to the top without paying his dues. It was ridiculously naïve and without a shred of decorum to show up at the Westwood offices of the National Football League's creative division without an appointment. He walked in off the street with his portfolio under his arm. He had not yet cut his teeth on a body of experience. He was straight out of Art School with maybe one or two magazine editorial commissions under his belt. The sharp, graphic, professional impact of the lobby with its three-dimensionally sculptured letter forms casting a checkerboard of shadows on the tastefully-tinted walls made him take note. The fonts were cast in a variety of typefaces he recognized. Letters became art without saying a word. He was starting to feel a little in over his head. The receptionist asked if he had an appointment. His response was short, small and to the point. *No.* He felt like his pants had just catastrophically dropped to his ankles. At that exact moment a young associate art director came out of one of the side doors and overheard the word *"portfolio"* and asked if he could browse through it. They walked over to the table and couch for a sidebar, putting the receptionist's query to rest. After flipping through a few pages, he asked if he could take the portfolio back to show to some other senior people. What Juri had no way of knowing was the office's schedule had only one or two days a month of down time. The myriad of projects and commitments to deadlines for media, television, books, magazines, programs and public relations demanded a large staff to coordinate with writers, photographers, artists and designers before everything went to print. He had the sheer dumb luck to walk into this frenetic timetable on that one fortuitous day without a scheduled appointment and the unimaginable good fortune of the timing of that junior art director's entrance into the lobby at the same time Juri was standing on the precipice. Not yet aware of the many key factors in the timing of all the minutiae unfolding in front of him, he was grateful and elevated. He was accompanied into chambers with anticipation. The layout of the inner workings of the creative team aroused his interest. He was on their turf but he thought he belonged.

Dave Boss had a reputation that preceded him and it was absolutely earned. He ran the shop with a trust in a creative staff that showed him undeniable respect and he had the ability to get more out of them than they expected. Over the span of Juri's career Dave Boss would turn out to be one of the most admired art directors he worked with. Juri was not just an extension of the hand of a competent director but he was given free rein to interpret the subject in his particular charge. Dave's standing in the industry was unquestionable.

The viewing of his work bolstered Juri's self-regard. His replies turned more confident and more open with approval. Praise from potential employers of this caliber was heady stuff. Dave offered him a commission to do an editorial piece called "Rolling Man" about a paraplegic athlete in a wheel chair right there in the office to take home with him. After the submission and publication of the artwork in *Pro* and *GameDay* the official programs of the NFL he received a signed letter on league stationary from Dave Boss that amounted to a big pat on the back for doing a good job. That letter and maybe the painting led to a 10-year relationship with the NFL. The work included program cover artwork for multiple teams until Dave Boss retired when the new director now in New York changed direction and emphasized photography over artwork.

Juri hit the ground running. His exposure through the NFL led to an early client list that included CBS, Honda, Yamaha, and Princess Cruises. His commissions came from the US, Europe and Japan. And his work was in public and private collections and exhibited nationally and internationally in places like Los Angeles, New York, London, Paris and Auckland.

After graduation he chose to continue to pursue a master's degree, not because he wanted more schooling but because he felt the need to be around his mentor Dick Oden who had opened him up to his art.

He remembered as a graduate student responding to a survey asking if he ever considered teaching as a profession. Starting after his first year in college then the year in Hawaii followed by three more before Vietnam. It took another three semesters to get his degree and now he was in graduate school. The years were mounting up. A big bold 'no' was scrawled into the negative column. He knew he didn't want to see the inside of another classroom for quite a while. His preferences after his second graduation were art, surfing and volleyball. Not necessarily always in that order.

Dick Oden mentioned he needed someone qualified to teach a particular class at California State University Long Beach. It was one of the classes he took from Dick as a freshman some years earlier. He didn't have the heart to say no to the mentor he owed everything. There he was, teachin' the golden rule. At first most all teachers operate with some degree of fear in front of the class. When they do it long enough one of two things happen. Either they get bored or they learn to give what they have. Those that get bored either quit and take on something else or continue teaching and chase the paycheck. The teachers that do it with passion discover ways to become good at it. Some do it for what it gives back to them. It was somewhat stunning and absolutely more than unexpected when he realized how well he fit in on the other side of the desk.

Chapman University in Orange California had an opening in the private school's small art department. After a candidate review Juri was hired to teach a variety of courses over the next few years, one at a time. During this period one of his colleagues, Richard who taught the sculpture class, became a trusted friend. His personal work played and experimented with installation and public art arenas. His wife Sylvia headed the dance department at Rancho Santiago College. Through Richard, Juri met Paul, a philosophy PhD originally from Texas, turned mountain man teaching at Idaho State University. Paul was a consummate scholar yet a dedicated outdoorsman more than capable in extreme conditions. Deborah, Paul's wife, was an especially delightful friend and ally to Juri. She had the ability to make the air around conversation sprightful and uplifting. Richard, Paul and Juri grew tight. They spent quality time at campfires in the mountains, deserts and beaches talking deep into the night. They were all in academia now but they lived in the world. Richard and Paul met as postgraduate Fulbright Scholars in India with Richard doing postgraduate work at Michigan and Paul at Yale.

One of their treks took them down the Snake River in Idaho on a rafting trip. Paul checked out a small three-man raft from the university and they headed down the river. In two vehicles they dropped one off at the takeout point and drove back with the raft to where they planned to put in. At a particularly vicious class-four rapid with a mean reputation at the end of the run, all three were dumped into the bitter cold. Thrashing through the standing waves and rapids they scrambled to gather their oars and other gear. Once retrieved and inside the boat, they portaged to attempt the "widow maker" a second time. On this approach they strategized with a plan to enter the chute. At the last second before dropping into the hole they would rush to the front to balance the tipping boat at the exact right moment. This time they rode it out, a little wet but all in one piece. "Hoorah...that was a piece of cake" was Juri's cry. His raft mates both turned to him with a cold-shouldered stare and exclaimed... "Really". Juri replied, "That was so easy I could swim the rapid..."Oh yah"..."for sure" ...and the challenge was on. There was no backing out now. He strapped on the helmet and life jacket and in his running shoes walked into the water up stream about 50 yards above the rapid. Paul shouted instructions showing his concern. The steep gorge downstream from the churning rapids presented a problem. Its high walls without a beach made landfall more than difficult. The only choice was a small patch of sand just past the rapid on the east bank. If Juri was swept past that small excuse for a beach it was a runaway train down the canyon for at least a mile to the next possible exit. As he inched his way into the main stream of faster flowing water, he would soon be in deep over his head. This was real. He had surfed big waves all over the world and was a solid swimmer but this was nature showing her brutal and frenzied rage. With his feet up in front of him to ward off rocks below the surface, he was swept up in the current, a small cork in a hurricane. Going through the waves in the rapids was almost familiar. Big waves had a degree of respect that was required for their sheer mass. This rapid was something like that but not as predictable as an ocean swell approaching a shallow reef. Juri started to become unsettled as real estate started to rapidly get chewed up by the river. He was running out of territory to make landfall. It was a video on fast-forward. His swimming aim had to be far to his left to make his target section on the shore now almost directly in front of him. In the water he was quickly losing ground. The movie sped up and he had to find a way to slow it down. He grabbed at a rock jutting straight up above the surface of the water. His forward velocity spun him around violently as he grasped at the vertical bolder but he managed to hold on. The pause enabled him to catch his breath and take measure of the situation. He had one last chance. Swim diagonally against the current and he might still make it. Taking a few last deep breaths, he swam in a northeast direction to reach southeast. It looked dire at the last minute as he stabbed at some bushes at the end of the sandy shore. It turned out he had a handful of twigs and one sturdy branch of a sapling growing right at the edge of the water. He could breathe easily. He made it. From Paul and Richard's vantage in the truck on the dirt road paralleling the higher banks of the river they partially lost sight of Juri's position in the water because of some trees and the embankment. He caught a partial glimpse of them through the branches and could tell they thought the worst. They ran for the truck and raced down the road in the direction of the high walled canyon. Juri thought about ignoring them but decided against it. He let out a shrill whistle as he climbed up to the road.

The next rite of passage was a thousand-foot-high pinnacle spire that rose high above their tented campsite. Richard and Juri were novices at rock climbing having never done more than scramble up a few boulders at Joshua Tree National Park. Their trust was in Paul's hands. Juri told himself Paul would never put his and Richard's well-being in jeopardy. He boulder-hopped up rock faces before that weren't necessarily tactical but this time they were decked out in harnesses and helmets. They had coils of climbing rope and other small aluminum cast gears and cogs because it was vertical. He asked himself if this was going to be hard-core. Juri didn't come close to having Paul's experience or expertise but surely, he was a stronger athlete than Richard so as long as there was someone under you on the pecking order, you'd probably be ok. The way he should have thought about it, the climbing team was only as good as its weakest link. They free-climbed the first leg of the assent without complication and then belayed the next reach that was quite a few degrees steeper when they came to the granite chimney. There was only one direction, straight up. The slender tower had a depression running up the exposed face. The plan was to 'sit" in the crack with their butts backed up to one side and their feet opposed on the opposite side. The heel of the left hand pressed against the left inside ridge of the depression and they "spidered" their way up inch by inch. This leverage technique was actually relatively easy if they didn't attempt to gain elevation too quickly. Strenuous on the muscles but you could rest simply by leaning back. Slow but sure.

The payoff came by way of the sheer exposure of the granite needle. The view on top, which was an area about the size of a card table literally made you hold your breath. It was like hanging on a glider. They catered lunch with a view. At the campsite thousands of feet below the tent seemed smaller than the toe pad on a tree frog. The background music was whistling in the wind and the million-dollar view crested the snow-capped Sawtooth Mountains.

Later in the afternoon, dropping temperatures acknowledged it was time for the descent. Because Paul was the only one experienced enough to collect climbing gear left on the mountain, so on the way down he had to go last. He designated Juri to be first man on the rope. The strategy was to rappel down to the first outcrop mimicking Army Rangers or Navy Seals. As Juri prepared the rope around and through his harness he had to be looped to a suitable anchor on top. Juri looked around, no trees…no fence posts. All that was available was a rounded nub of a rock about three to four inches above the granite and dirt surface. He murmured under his breath, "are you friggin' kiddin' me". There was no way he was going to step off that edge backwards entrusting his very existence on that loop not sliding off the rock that was about the size of a Botts' Dot raised pavement marker. As he became the subject of ridicule for not manning up, he was getting frustrated. Juri would bend down to do his best to secure the sling on the end of the rope to the rock, take two steps backward and STOP. Despite Paul's reassurances, it was a no-go. It was like a Plexiglas force field that wouldn't allow for that final backwards, precipitous step. It became a *Groundhog Day* rerun attempting it over and over again. Finally, peer pressure and embarrassment tipped him over the edge. As soon as his weight put pressure on the line the loop grabbed and took a firm grip on the rock. The actual act of rappelling was radically adventurous and energizing. Belief was a powerful concept, a transformative concept. Richard held up his end of the bargain harnessed to the middle of the rope. Dinner tasted really fine that night.

Wet Vices

CHAPTER 16

He had loved the ocean from the first day his dad dropped him off on the way into work and picked him up on the return home. It was freedom all day long. The water held his imagination without limitation. The ability to be independent didn't require a coupon. Surfing's appeal took hold from the beginning like it had always been there. A phantasm swallowed him. It was the ocean covering you up and spitting you out. The myth of Jonah would understand. Something about it was inexplicably difficult to put to words with any meaning. Most surf conversations are trite. Hanging with surfers you hear the same dialogue about the waves caught that day. The same stories will be told over and over again in places like California, Hawaii, Indo, J Bay and many more. The list can be from a Beach Boys song. Not much is divulged. The truth was that talk is cheap, not that these dudes didn't know what they were talking about. Words were not the experience. The sensation under his feet was like slipping on ice with some hope of control. It was at all costs a shot in the vein, something you had to do. It was something you couldn't be without. It *was* the first "lifestyle".

He remembered coming in out of the Mazatlan lineup. The January heat on his shoulders and the powder blue board under his arm, dripping salt water, he turned to check out the point break for one last approving look. The ocean was going to do it to him one more time. A small wave washed gently between his feet and as it receded it deposited a small jewel. A *Jenneria Pustulata* lay propped up on dry sand between his leashed ankle and the other foot. A cowrie shell with a brilliant dark blue background and raised reddish-orange spots, something spectacular had popped up out of the rabbit hole. A gift from the ocean herself had been offered up. He stared down at it without any knowledge that it would drive him to many more remote tropical destinations in both his immediate and distant futures.

In those early days, Mexico seemed much farther away, much more remote than its true proximity. It was like visiting a distant country. Mexico became his quick fix. 3 M's and Shipwrecks, surf spots that don't exist anymore, were altered by progress and time. A fish factory was built at 3M's and its effluence brought in the sharks. The shipwreck, that shaped the waves, eventually eroded. As ritual demanded, they downed shots of tequila at Hussongs and then shot off Mexican skyrockets they bought in the street. The four of them were high school buddies and it would be the last time they would all be together, not for any grave reasons but simply because sometimes friends fade away. Juri lit the rocket on a stick with a short stubby brown cigarillo and charged the three of them in the dark on the cliffs above 3M's. He tossed it side arm as it chose its own erratic path three or four feet parallel to the ground. It lodged in the belt loop of Jack's Levi's still smoldering waiting to go off. The three clearly heard Jack running haphazardly towards the cliff's edge after a big bang, seemingly propelled by the missile itself. They heard a curdling, howling scream from the darkness and sprinted to the steep face of the rock to see if Jack had gone over. Instead, what they found was Jack face-planted into a hefty fat cactus in the star-lit night.

Baja was close enough for the short haul but the mainland became a steady diet of nine Januarys in a row. The working crew at the Ancient Mariner, the restaurant where they all worked, would juggle their shifts to free up a minimum of three weeks at a time. In between semesters they would caravan in VW buses and pickup truck camper rigs and head south of the border. The drive would usually begin before dawn in order to hit the border at Calexico and cross into Mexicali at dawn's first light. Driving in Mexico at night was considered *"muy peligroso"*. It was a daisy chain of campers, surfboards strapped to the top in pairs taking turns on point. The procession would blow through the villages on Highway 2 paralleling the Mexican side of the Sonoran Desert stopping only at Pemex. They were seasoned travelers and knew enough to stay vigilant making sure that the attendant cleared the previous amount on the meter before dispensing gas from the red pump. With an AAA map on the dash, they knew their way by heart. The road went through Hermosillo, a hard town even before the days of the cartels. Then south to the coast at Guaymas they pulled into the one campground in San Carlos for the evening. The embarcadero had a distinctive, idiosyncratic mountain peak silhouetting the bay that they designated the "Castle." A walk on the beach called for a local bay-front meal. Golfo de California was tranquil and quiet reflecting the lights of the harbor on the surface of the still water.

Mexican food wasn't the same as food in Mexico. Mexican cuisine in the continental US never compared to the real thing south of the border to Juri. Whether it was stacked plates of lobster in Puerto Nuevo or sierra *a la plancha* in Puerto Angel or deep bowls of ceviche served barefooted at your table in the sand in Cabo, it just tasted better. He didn't know if it was the proximity of the sea, or the natural ambience that wasn't staged, but *mariscos* were to die for in good ol' Mexico.

In the morning the highway opened up to vast empty kilometers through Ciudad Obregon, Los Mochis and Culiacan the last pitstop before Mazatlan. On shorter trips she would be the terminal destination. Mazatlan had a more open feeling than other Mexican cities. Its newly constructed *malecon* arcing from the town center all the way out to Lupe's and the campground across the street. The point break with its red rocks and Isla de Venados and Isla de Pajaros just off shore painted a scene straight out of Surfer Magazine.

On longer more adventurous treks, Puerto Vallarta and even Manzanillo were on the itinerary. Manzanillo with its epic giant green wave was legendary but Vallarta, Punta Mita and especially Sayulita became the secret they guarded with their lives. Sayulita was a quiet quaint village on a beautiful small crescent bay. Dotted with small simple casitas, it not only had style, it had surf and it was only a short drive around Punta Mita to some of the best Mexican waves Juri had ever sampled.

Juri found himself on a flight to Oaxaca with one crazy angry lady and that was not even the scariest part of the venture. From Oaxaca they waited to board a DC-3 to Puerto Escondido and a wave of ill repute. He had logged enough international experience. Juri had cut his teeth on surf in Hawaii, Peru and France and he was ready for another challenge. As they waited to board the prop-driven plane, the delay became one hour, then three. Something was amiss. The airplane was visible on the tarmac but there was a hoard of officials around the aircraft and at least half of them were dressed in suit and tie. Not a good sign at all. Some bozo had refueled the DC-3 with jet fuel. Surely this was a recipe for a sizeable explosion. As "el *jefe*" and his entourage endlessly discussed the options, Juri and his companion grabbed their board bags and with four other passengers hired a van to drive the 250 some kilometers to Puerto Escondido. The road from hell took seven and a half hours on a corkscrew winding path with drop offs that made one swallow especially hard. They were totally exhausted and at nerves' end with no patience to try to find their lodging of choice at 3am. They had the driver drop them at the first place they came across on the edge of town. Walking into "reception", they had to bang on a desk bell to finally get someone's attention. By the looks of the place, it didn't have much in the line of amenities, *maybe* two stars. Even though it was only a handful of hours before sunrise, the heat was stifling and all the two of them wanted was a bed. Juri turned the ceiling fan on full throttle and they were out like a light.

He didn't know if it was the morning light or his sketchy partner who woke him. It was probably the roosters but nonetheless there it was. The ceiling fan had dropped down out of its housing hanging only by three electrical wires millimeters from his nose and still spinning at a serious rate. Had he gotten up in the middle of the night to take a piss, something would have certainly shorted out.

Breakfast found them relocated in their preplanned courtyard with a beachfront view. There was a sense of urgency to finish the outdoor meal because there were 6-foot, paper-thin waves going off. It turned out to be an energizing session. Both of them were reinvigorated and the recollections of the dust from the road were washed clean from their memories. Walking, lounging, reading and exploring Puerto Escondido did wonders for their enthusiasm. The next few days were relaxing. All you could hope a vacation south of the Tropic of Cancer could be.

He really screwed up this time. Without getting a fix on the local ground rules, he suggested they walk the beach to the south in search of new waves a couple of miles south past the point. Boards under their arms they hiked with their valuables, money, passports, airline tickets and camera in his daypack, not trusting to leave them in a hotel room that had no safe. Two wonderful hours later in tropical waters with the sun pleasantly toasting them to a nice winter tan, they paddled to shore and toweled off. It was then that cooler heads needed to prevail. Down the hillside and out of the bush, two young hombres hardly more than boys, sporting a shiny silver pistol, marched toward them. One already had a brown paper bag with eyeholes over his head and the other was pulling on a pair of white briefs to mask his identity. Juri's mind raced. He needed to stay between his hot-tempered companion and the young boys who were at least as scared as they were. Chances were, her volatility would ignite the situation so that the perpetrators would do something stupid.

"*Su dinero rapidamente*". Again, his brain went into overdrive. Which wallet contained the least amount of cash? His response was, "*poco a poco*" …trying to diffuse the situation. To this day he doesn't know why they just didn't grab the whole backpack. As he quickly searched for something to give them, with his hand in the zippered compartment his fumbling started to make them nervous. It was a juggling act. He had to keep himself between her and the *bandidos* and grab the smallest bankroll. Thankfully there was a light breeze blowing when he threw the bills at their feet. The wind scattered the paper money and they scampered after it. He grabbed her by the shirt, scooped up the pack and said in a muffled tone from the back of his throat without moving his lips… "W…A… L… K". They didn't look back. With a brisk pace they mulled over possible outcomes. This turned out to be a best-case scenario. It was the first and only time Juri had a gun pulled on him in Mexico. He now had a story he could write about some day.

Rivers of Wind

CHAPTER 17

Marty read a historical account of some of the explorers that first set foot into the Wind Rivers range in west-central Wyoming, located in the upper spine of the Rocky Mountains. Their descriptions whetted his appetite for isolated natural beauty at elevations as high as 13,000 feet. Would Finis Mitchell's accounts turn out to hold up with time? On a warm July day, the four of them, Marty, Christina, Edie and Juri outfitted with a week's worth of rations set out from the trailhead at the St Lawrence Ranger Station. A full day's hike to the first of the Wilson Creek Lakes was mostly uphill all day. It was one of those days where the work was worth it. Back in Lander before they initiated the climb, they were required to get a hiking permit because the trail was on Shoshone and Arapaho land. This was a much less trafficked area for backpackers that kept the crowds at a minimum. Marty and his friends would find out if their experience lived up to the author's words. It was a tough trek up some switchbacks, fording a shallow part of the creek and over some loose boulders in the riverbed. Then the path funneled into a bottleneck over a high pass where they got their first real lay of the land. Before them was a string of lakes named after somebody called Wilson, probably no relation to the character in the Tom Hank's movie *Cast Away*. The diamond faceted surfaces of the lakes led to an absolutely awesome and spectacular cirque of Rocky Mountain peaks all above 12,500 feet. Juri dove headfirst down a snow embankment on one of the glaciers. They selected a campsite between two of the lakes that were connected by a stream that carved through a solid granite table of flat rock. The small rivulet supplied easily accessible water for cooking and cleaning. The smooth hard shelf provided a perfect place to warm up after a cool dip in glacial water. Each lake had a small island but without a boat, was just enticingly far enough away from shore to be explored. Juri did a solo hike up to the glacier at the foot of one of the peaks. He scrambled straight up a steep incline to get a view looking back down at the dozens of lakes below. When he reached the top ledge of what was a flat meadow, a hummingbird buzzed him and hovered a brief moment then darted off. On top of the outlook on the topographical continental divide he got a dose of the great outdoors. In front of him, frozen in surprise for an instant, was a herd of elk. Both were caught off guard in a momentary staring contest before the herd scrambled off. Marty snagged dinner on the end of his fly rod, a few cutthroats and a couple of browns. Whatever they were they certainly tasted good over the fire. The following summer the same foursome tried to replicate the previous year's trek. On that repeat visit they started the second venture up the mountain later in the summer on Labor Day with a thermometer reading of 82 degrees. The trail felt familiar and they saw things they missed the first time around. As was the case at these altitudes weather could change quiet abruptly. You could see it coming. A massive cloud low in the sky was threatening to grey out the blue. It was the underside of a great big drawer being pulled out along the sky's edge. As the sun was blocked out, the temperatures plummeted. From walking shorts and tank tops to beanies and parkas in the span of an hour, 80 degrees turned into snow flurries. Making haste was a necessity and they picked up the pace considerably. Juri was perspiring under the parka. They stopped to take a break and he grabbed at his beanie, unzipped his parka and sat on a cold boulder. Now he was going in the different direction. He was chilled then shivering. He had displaced a whole lot of heat through his uncapped head. He bundled back up after losing too much body temperature too quickly. As he rose to hit the trail his head hung heavy. Juri lost a notable amount of heat and energy and now had the onset of hypothermia. They were almost where they wanted to be a couple of hours from their intended campsite, but he couldn't go any further. They pitched their tents right there off the trail and told Juri in the morning that he slept 16 hours straight without waking even through the loud bugling of an elk herd during the night. He was starting to feel more himself and in two hours they were at the lakes. Before pitching camp, Marty unpacked his fishing rod and headed to his favorite site. Juri unpacked the bottle of Pinot he smuggled in his pack without listing it on the menu. He leaned it against a sitting log next to the tent. Marty was showing good form with his casting technique and after a solid night's rest in winter-rated sleeping bags Christina and Edie went for a hike around the lake. As Marty hooked another keeper, the snow began to fall. It was starting to blanket the ground. They were at higher altitudes and this could become serious. The sky was a solid pallid grey without any form to the cloud cover. The light snowfall turned to flurries. The trail was being covered beyond recognition. Not staying on the predestined path could be dangerous. It was time to retreat. They decided to make a hasty departure. Shoving their sleeping bags into stuff sacks, they dismantled the tent. It was a race to the bottom before the trail vanished in the snow. Fortunately, they were able to use landmarks on same trail they recently negotiated last season. Juri thought the lucky stiffs who trekked in the following spring would be wined and dined to a bottle of California Pinot Noir complimented by Wyoming frozen trout.

After the ensuing summer solstice, Juri headed for Wind Rivers again, this time with Paul. It was Paul's initial trek with that particular "tope" sheet. But instead of Wilson Creek Lakes they compassed south to Raft Lake. It was a much longer trail and took 11 hours. Exhausted from the grueling inroad, they mainly sat and caught up with their absence and kissed the past's ass by the campfire. The plan was to then drive to Utah and meet up with Richard on BLM land somewhere between the rocky crags and slot canyons of Zion, and the hoodoo spires of Bryce Canyon. They parked the vehicles and walked a fire trail up a spiral path to higher aspirations. At one point the trail came within reaching distance of a Golden Eagle aerie. The startled raptors struggled out of the nest, pounding their wings to gain altitude. The pair of Goldens circled the conifer voicing their protest. The three amigos got the drop on a waterfall from the top of the precipitous cascade. Standing on the ledge of a bluff looking down on the white ribbon of water they felt superior. Being on top of the world felt just fine. It was Sunday and time for an appropriate sacrament. With some herbal assistance, a pinch of psilocybin, Paul and Richard wanted to revere the forest around them. Juri chose to climb closer to the sun and scrambled up some rocks to view the valley floor. The sense of communion was personal. He wondered if his ancestors in the Julian Alps had similar feelings when they strapped on their sheepskin rucksacks. He caught the eye of an eagle soaring midway in the valley directly across from him. This was reverent. It was an understanding of his surroundings. He had an attuned heightened sense of vision that came not only through his eyes, but seemed to lift him to a vantage where he observed himself. The eagle noticed and they acknowledged each other. Juri was overjoyed. He was in a timeless space. He occasionally had glimpses and a taste of this awareness in tournament competition where time was a viscous slow dance and he knew where the ball was going before it was struck. But that was more fleeting, more temporary. This was the place to be. He wished he could bottle it. He just knew. His soft, muted chuckles literally turned to tears of laughter. It was a warm place of understanding. He had no idea of how long he had been shirtless there in the sun propped up against the rocks. He blurted out in an audible anticipation ... "Paul is coming". He had no clue as to why that idea popped out of his mouth. It couldn't have been more than three minutes when Paul appeared over the boulders standing there like an apparition. They stood there speaking without saying a word, and then they talked. They walked back to the waterfall where Richard was lying in a fetal position, curled up in a reptilian posture. It didn't go well for him. Paul and Juri consoled him. They comforted him with support and camaraderie. He explained that he had been going through critical misgivings about his work and his status as an artist. It was a productive and necessary assessment for him but a difficult one. Juri was sensing some of Richard's angst but still holding on to his bliss.

Baja Peninsula
CHAPTER 18

In hindsight, he was fortunate to be able to say he traversed the peninsula before the road was completed. That put him among a select few who drove the 1,000 kilometers, the length of Baja, without the benefit of pavement. A small band of brothers who experienced what it tasted like off the beaten path. From TJ to just south of Ensenada was the typical one lane in each direction and from there on the road dropped off the face of the map. It was now as close to an expedition as the two could get. Daniel was a tall, lanky adventurer whose head barely fit inside the 1951 Catalina green Ford panel truck mounted with four extra tires on the roof rack. The spares were accompanied by six Jerry cans to accommodate the long distances between topping-off the tanks. The coastal towns of San Quintin and El Rosario had some supplies that reached from the northern towns closer to the border, but once they swung onto the Catavina Plateau with its unique indigenous ecosystem, the pickings were slim. They learned the meaning of *llanteria* pretty quickly. Before reaching La Paz on the gulf side, they had to eventually replace, trade or purchase eleven tires beyond the original four on the truck and the four tied down to the rack. They dealt with those concerns at bends in the road, barely more than sparse wood shacks and 50-gallon drums of petrol. The cacti were a huge problem. It got so thick slaloming through the Saguaro and the Chollo that it not only scraped the side of the panel truck to shreds it picked off the tires seemingly like some giant desert dart game. La Paz was a refuge, and eleven days later it came out to an average of a tire a day.

They regained their humanity via a cold shower and a warm meal. They chilled for an extra day and then glided on a hard packed, dirt road into Cabo in about five hours. Cabo San Lucas and the East Cape at the time already had an infrastructure that catered to sport fishermen and tourists. They were back in the Twentieth Century spending serious beach time at Land's End. In a few days they boarded the scheduled weekly car ferry that in those days went to Mazatlan. It was Juri's first time to Mazatlan and in many future visits he would see the town grow into a city and then into a world resort. It was the same as watching a friend's child mature into a young adult.

Daniel decided he was going to sell the panel truck and crew on a boat to Panama. Juri needed to get creative and find passage back to California. Surfing at a local beach break, he met Craig and Drew who were from South Bay. They were returning in five days, which let Juri unwind from the severity of the road. They charted the pavement of the mainland by way of highway 15 and Nogales, then through Arizona and on to California. Manhattan Beach was some 40 miles north of Newport Beach and right on the way home.

Kayaking in Bahia de Los Angeles years later, a group of people from Laguna Beach claimed spots on the more-secluded north side of the campground. In the late afternoon they paddled two kayaks around the headland, leeward of the wind. As they turned the corner one of the women shouted, "…what the hell is that?" On the deserted shore miles from the campground where sound traveled like an echo chamber, a black SUV with two individuals in black paramilitary gear were loading duffel bags off a *ponga* into the vehicle. Juri didn't think it was wise to engage in any conversation.

The narrow beach at low tide became the route of choice for Lee, Juri and the Dalmatian. Lee and Juri had built tree houses together as kids before they were transplanted by the construction of the new freeway to San Diego. They saw less of each other, even though their new homes were both in the same city. Lee and Juri would grow into artists and professors at CSULB by distinctly different paths. They cruised in a yellow VW Thing along the spit of land at Santa Maria that ran perpendicular to San Quintin, where the westerly's usually came up in the afternoon and trashed any chance of waves at most beach breaks. Because of the unusual orientation of this particular spot, the constant steady wind swell would wrap around the point of land and transformed the waves into perfect little offshore "A" frames. With the presence of a permanent sandbar, there was a small precise location where the wind swells generated waves that broke consistently into the face of the local prevailing wind, usually a bane to surfers at other beaches where the orientation was in the opposite direction.

A year before, Jack, Bill and Juri had camped here at the same spot when a parade of cars full of *Federales* appeared while they were in the water. Twenty minutes earlier, two tall lanky gringos were digging in the sand dunes 100 yards north of them and then ran back to the campground with a sense of urgency. The Mexican authorities were a response to the discovery of two skeletons buried in the dunes in their sleeping bags. Most likely, because of the isolation of where they were found, they were probably surfers much like Jack, Bill and Juri, unfortunate to have a shiny new truck, unlike Bill. The tragedy turned out to be that they probably didn't spring for the security of the campground half a mile towards the main road.

Juri, Lee and the dog checked out this spot on the more current edition of dawn patrol when they noticed they had a visitor. A dolphin shadowed the car. As they got closer to the end of the beach, at the tip across from Bahia San Quintin, the dolphin got increasingly closer to shore keeping pace with the VW Thing. At one point before they turned the Thing around, the bottlenose swam in such shallow water that half his body was exposed above the water line. They retreated to the waves and at one count between the dolphin, the seal and the dog there were more animals in the surf line than humans.

For a number of years Juri never partnered with a solid player in the Estero Beach draw tournament. The beach just south of Ensenada was littered with volleyball courts as far as the eye could see for the annual event. The beach was the arena for all that was to happen over the weekend. This time he was matched with an unheralded young buck from Santa Cruz that played beyond expectations, leaving them undefeated the first day of the tournament. That night a bad batch of shrimp fajitas left Juri with an excess of down time on the commode. In the morning he tried to make a go of it but ended up having to bow out and hold that position for most of the afternoon. Thankfully the discomfort lasted for only that one day. On Monday he and his friend Donna, who accompanied him to the tournament, went kayaking to a remote beach where there were no roads and the shore was littered with whalebones all the way to the next headland. On the paddle back they were startled when a large pilot whale projected vertically out of the water 10 feet from the boat.

They went with Wade and Linda to the Seven Sisters, a series of surf spots on the Pacific side of Baja, halfway north of Punta Santa Rosalillita. Then they drove along the coast to Punta Maria, a sand dune spit. Juri didn't have 4-wheel drive so they camped as far on the beach as they could go. Wade went out to a spot on the sand dunes. They would take turns paddling their kayaks to each other's camp to visit. On a new-moon night after the meal, he and Donna had to paddle back in absolute darkness navigating only by the sound of lapping waves they knew were on the beach where they pitched their tent. As they paddled towards the sound, every time the blade hit water it dripped gold phosphorous and drew concentric circles of liquid fluorescence. This light show triggered their wildest imaginations and fantasies. All around them was translucent and incandescent calligraphy as elegant as any of the Japanese masters.

In the village of Juncalito at Eric's two-story palapa just south of Loreto, Juri was snorkeling off a small island out in the bay when he found himself in the middle of an enormous bait ball of fish. Unexpectedly from his underwater vantage he saw, or more precisely felt, dozens of pelicans repeatedly thrusting into the mass of fish like silver spears at break neck speeds. For a moment he worried about his safety but became more comfortable after engaging in this underwater choreography, realizing he was not the target. The effect was nothing short of hypnotic.

South of Mexico

All his travels in Mexico prepared him to be a better communicator in Central and South America. The deeper he got into Mexico, the more the impulse to keep heading south seemed to drive him. He was always pushing at borders, wanting to know what was over the horizon. He had read about history and Simon Bolivar and passages about archeology and adventure in the Amazon, and pyramids in Central America claimed by the jungle. Those readings conjured images of what he could do. They spawned wanderlust, a vice to be proud of. Landing in Belize City was harsh. It was a hard town with its share of gangs and drugs, but departing the capital city out on the cays there was a change of attitude. Whether it was the gentle breezes or the hammocks strung to swaying palms, he wasn't sure. What he knew when he saw it was laid-back and kicked-back. This stretch of coastline was part of the second largest barrier reef this side of Australia. Ambergris Cay was the largest island in the chain and had all the tourist amenities, maybe too many for Juri and his companion. They negotiated for a place on a little known out of the way tiny islet called Tabacco Cay. The ponga was crewed by a Spanish speaking Rasta with dreadlocks encapsulated in a tam with the appropriate red, yellow, green and black colors of the Caribbean. With a crunching, sliding, grading sound, Manny beached the boat. Juri, in ankle deep water, jumped out holding his running shoes. The island was on the small side. He figured he could throw a small coconut the entire length of the island. The weathered two-story structure under a stand of palms took up a good chunk of the shoreline. The beach intruded into the downstairs kitchen with its sand floor and an outside staircase led up to a simple room with a queen size bed draped by a soft white mosquito net. They walked the whole island in about 15 minutes but the water was another story. It was why they came. A small crystal lagoon between a crescent shaped reef and the beach was more than a welcome sight. Clear waters exposed underwater coral teeming with sea life. They agreed they could spend a whole lot of time exploring. They changed into their beach gear and dove into the shallow blue. Without mask and snorkel, for the moment they would save the up close and personal for later. Warm water was always welcoming in the winter months especially after some accumulated hard miles.

A basic picnic table under the shade of palm trees served as the outdoor dining area. Lunch was served. Their choices were lobster tail or ital. Juri filled his plate with both under the watchful eye of one of the natty dreads. Was he just observing Juri's insatiable appetite or was he lifting an eyebrow at the adulteration of his epicurean vegetarian entrée? Snorkeling in 15-ft of water just off the beach Juri had an uneasy feeling of being watched. As he turned his head to look over his right shoulder, there up on the surface was a gathering of barracuda floating silently still. The only perceptible movement Juri could see was the rapid scanning of their eyes checking him out. Barracuda, usually solitary creatures, were so thick they looked like an endless repeating pattern of wallpaper. On the terminus of the reef where the pass allowed compact boats to enter the east side of the island, he noticed a small swell with steep little lefts starting to break off the coral. He grabbed his fins and got in some fun. Body surfing Belize was not on the itinerary, nor was it something he expected. That night there was a full moon that lit up the water. Manny told them to put on some reef shoes and grab a flashlight. They got in the dingy and cruised out on the reef at low tide where parts of the coral that were exposed. Manny pointed to roiling of the surface and quick splashing movement on the water. The entire reef revealed spiny lobster foraging for their meals on top of the barrier coral. He carefully guided the craft, using his gloved hand to fend off the sharp reef and used it as an anchor, to station the boat in the middle of the largest number of crustaceans. By shining his "torch" he enticed the lobster to his pail and then with a quick deft scoop collected the next day's dinner.

They woke up with two frigate birds hovering over their balcony, almost stationary in the sky right above them. It was a display of a magnificent weightless ballet for their morning benefit. Soaring freely on wing and wind was enviable. There was something in the lagoon that had not been there the night before. A huge white catamaran with a large trampoline was moored out in the water. It quickly became the topic of discussion at breakfast. It turned out to be on the afternoon excursion plans, sailing the Belizan Reef. Plans for above water and underwater odysseys were in store for them all day long. Because the wind was at bay and the catamaran was using mostly motor power, it was wonderfully calm and transparently blue. Water visibility was easily fifty feet and the surface was like a mirror. The warmth of the sun felt good on Juri's shoulders. He sat there, reflecting on his good fortune, holding on to a lanyard.

Toweling off on deck, having just come back on board from a snorkeling session with the visionary sea world under the surface, he heard that sound, that particular guttural resonance that had haunted him before. It was the unmistakable drone of an attack helicopter. Coming down at them from the southeast, it clearly had the bulls eye markings of British military and had them in its sights. It was in a steep downward tack headed right for the mast of the catamaran. The pilot was beading in on the boat and pulled up into a severe anti gravitational 360° maneuver, a precise and complete vertical circle directly above them. After the completion of the second approach at the mast, the helicopter then circled the boat one more time close enough for the crew and all on board the boat to see the pilot salute them in an incongruous greeting. The speculation on the catamaran was possibly the helicopter was part of an anti-drug smuggling patrol and waved off after confirming they were just a boatload of tourists.

In the coastal city of Placentia in the south of the country they came across a weathered old bar right out of a spaghetti western. It came complete with a set of swinging slatted doors and a raised wooden walkway. It was high noon when they ambled in. Juri took a step, crossed the portal and paused. He assessed the situation. It reminded him of the bar scene in *"Star Wars"* or maybe more like *"The Magnificent Seven"*. As everyone's head turned to gaze the new customers, an uneasy feeling came over him. The cast of characters sporting an assortment of paramilitary fatigues staring him down were all mercenaries, soldiers of fortune and ex-contras. This former jungle fighter had walked into the lion's den and he felt like new meat.

Land of the Inca

Landing in Lima would be his first experience in South America. He thought it was easy for many Americans to culturally lump all Spanish-speaking countries as roughly the same. Juri distinguished New Englanders and Southerners as different from his own Californians and they all lived under one flag. The other Americans came from regions and countries that were under a variety of *"banderas"*. They had the inalienable right to be dissimilar, as was their history and culture. The Museo Larco and Museo de la Nacion both attested to Peru's ancient pre-Columbian civilizations.

He knew enough about surfing in the country through Peruvians he met in Hawaii. Herradura was probably the premiere wave in the Lima area. It was a cold hollow left that broke off a reddish-brown bluff at the south end of the beach promenade. The Humboldt Current kept the water cold and the fog engaged. Wetsuits were mandatory. The wave was fun and the locals were generous. His little bit of Spanish helped but when two English-speaking Peruvian surfers paddled over he felt even more at home. They suggested he check out a party that was being thrown that night so he could get to know more of the local group. That evening looked much like any gathering in SoCal, attractive women, sun tanned beach dudes and an assortment of conversations. He spotted the only other gringo in the room. Jackson came up and greeted him *"hello"* before Juri could say *"where you from?"* Turns out Jackson lived in Peru and was employed by a mining firm. Originally from the Santa Barbara area he lived in Peru for two years and was involved big time in onsite troubleshooting. He was a fixer. Juri plied him with quarries about the land of the Incas and Jackson asked how things were in the Golden State. They talked at length about Peruvian attitudes and politics. Juri factored in the industry's point of view and they got around to discussing the better surf spots in the rest of the country. Jackson's opinion was that they were all a couple of days drive to the south. He mentioned he had a few days coming at work and if Juri was up to it they could pack up his truck and point the compass. There was little hesitation on Juri's part so in midweek they cast off on a road trip in that inescapable direction. Aiming south in the southern hemisphere meant going against the grain. It didn't mean warmer temperatures, but quite the contrary; it brought in colder water with each and every mile. They caught a good little day at Punta Rocas on the way to bigger things. There was a very special spot that

Jackson said he had surfed only once before because it was so remote. It took two days to reach, had a good southern exposure and proved to be worth it. They arrived at a large sweeping bay with a bold rocky point on the southern side of the beach. The swell that originated in Antarctica was mammoth. They caught it big and monstrous. Jackson was putting on his wetsuit and waxing up while Juri was already making his way out through massive surges of water. There was a very light touch of offshore wind holding up the shape of the waves. As Juri paddled over the top of the first wave of a big set he became aware of the power of this swell. Cresting over the top he looked down the back of the wave and with the next oncoming breaker ahead of him it looked like a giant green U-shaped glacial valley. He was in a deep trough pointing straight down and then paddled up ferociously to make it over the top of the next wave. What was out of the ordinary was the sheer scale and volume of water he was immersed in. He couldn't relax. Being in unfamiliar remote waters, his tempo had to be quick and urgent to make it over the subsequent walls of water. Then as he paddled up over the top of the next wave he saw the unmistakable black and white harlequin markings of an orca. The blunt rounded nose of the killer whale had breached the low surface of the trough at a distance by the rocks toward the other end of the bay headed in his direction. This was not SeaWorld. This was the tempered Pacific in the middle of nowhere a hundred miles from the closest medical facilities. The smartest, meanest alpha predator of the entire ocean ecosystem decided to show up at the same beach for some fun and games. Fight was not a good option. Flight wasn't much better. With an overabundance of newfound vitality, he turned the board for shore and grabbed the board with both arms and hung on for dear life. He imagined there was no way he could outrun the killer. He remained prone on the board and in a moment of fortunate chance rode out the first wave all the way to the beach. It was walking on water while clutching his surfboard. Jackson was just starting to enter the water when Juri waved him off. Juri's urgency made its point as he hustled to stop Jackson from paddling out and explain the situation. They sat there for twenty minutes trying to catch sight of a telltale vertical fin without any luck. The dilemma was that they had invested time and effort to get there and they were watching premium waves break right in front of them and as surfers tend to do, chose to paddle back out. It was scary good.

Back in Lima it was time to set out for one of the wonders of the world and the UNESCO World Heritage Site of Machu Picchu. Juri arrived in Cusco a town of classic Spanish influence with a mix of Inca ruin. On a winter morning he climbed the higher hills above the city center, took off his parka in the warming sun and simply listened to the drifting sounds coming from the plaza with its columned arch walkways down below. If he was quiet he could make out the words of the songs being played by musicians in the square. The panpipes were undeniably Incan. He had settled himself against the mysterious stonework ramparts of Sacsayhuaman. Here was another one of those ancient sites with inexplicably colossal stones that were carved so fine you couldn't slide a piece of paper between the cracks. Juri wondered who built this edifice and how did they do it with the technology available. Much of whatever stories this fortress held remained a secret. He boarded the train to Machu Picchu that paralleled the Urabamba River. The lush jungle views out of the window fascinated him with rip-roaring rapids and colorful hanging orchids. He caught glimpses of the ancient Inca Trail carved out of the mountainsides with fedora-topped, poncho-wearing foot traffic still attesting to its viability. His momentary thoughts drifted to reports he had heard about Sendero Luminoso, a leftist group of guerillas commonly referred to as the Shining Path. Most of their territory was in the jungles. As the train lumbered up the valley past minor stops, the anticipation of sighting the Incan city built on the side of a mountain needle was in play. The canyon was getting steeper and deeply hollow. Space was getting cavernous and the rays of light were more pronounced. The perspective of colors created severe depth. There was a deep purple blue cast to the void between the spire and the ring of mountains that surrounded Machu Picchu. It was obvious there were certain places on this lonely planet like Machu Picchu, Everest and the Grand Canyon that sensitized you to the sheer volume of space around you that overwhelmingly reduced one to such a miniscule and insignificant dot on the landscape. It was an outdoor cathedral in all sense of the word, a place of worship that quietly welcomed a pilgrimage. It stood alone with its narrow tracks, obvious why it was chosen as a citadel, one that was never pillaged by the Spanish Conquistadores. Juri showed his respect, walking lightly over its cobbled stones. The layout of the granite water system caught his attention. It was ingenious how gravity was used in providing the community with both drinking water and water for agriculture from a spring higher up on the mountain. Self-sustainability would be a necessity in a state of siege mentality. He saw the pictures a thousand times. The iconic panorama in front of him was so much richer than any photograph could provide. Right there and then it was the truth.

At the first short stop on the train to Puno, a few backpackers disembarked at Aguas Calientes to hike back and approach Machu Picchu from a different perspective. Heading west toward the Pacific, the tracks tended to get steeper over mountain passes and snow fields of the Andes. They rolled into Puno on the eastern shore of Lake Titicaca. Food vendors bundled in indigenous clothing hawked their wares as the train labored to a stop. It was a bustling train station with people walking in all contrary directions. Juri inquired about lodging in an out-of-the-way place on the lakeside and drew a warm bath to thaw his bones. In the morning he went out on the lake to the floating islands of Uros. It was an artificial community that was as real as you could get. Built solely from reeds harvested on the lakeshore, bound together to create floating mats that were then added to, to make floating islands. The feeling underfoot wasn't the most secure at first until you got used to it. It was mushy and spongy especially the bigger you were. The scale of the islands was large enough to support a population of approximately a couple dozen full-time residents. They imported soil from the surrounding countryside to grow cash crops and sold crafts from their woven shops. Even their boats were constructed of the same reeds. Juri continued on toward Bolivia and the ruins at Tiwanaku and the Sun Gate where tradition says was the cradle of civilization. In La Paz the most elevated capital city in the world, the wealthy buy homes at the lower altitudes and the rest of the common folk live in more available land at higher less oxygenated highlands.

Again, it was time for the turn-around. A backtrack by train to Puno and then Arequipa where he would purchase a return flight to Lima. He was worn down from travels and bought a first-class ticket that assured him an overnight lounge seat on the midnight express. Sitting in his assigned seat just prior to the train pulling out of the station in Puno, he counted his blessings that the seat next to him was the only one vacant in the entire car. Just as the engine started to roll and recoil in a negligible clash of whiplashing, Juri grabbed at his armrest to see a behemoth 300lb caricature of a man struggling down the aisle in the direction of the one remaining seat. Juri was at the window and the aisle seat was now occupied by a human being who spilled over not only into the aisle but also pinned Juri against the glass. The travel gods were once again disfavoring him. The rotund man was not only taking his unfair share of the ride he started to snore at ungodly decibels. Forceful elbow jabs did little to quiet the situation. It was a long night and Juri slept most the next day at his hotel to make up for lost time. He woke in the late afternoon and took to the streets of Arequipa for an early dinner. The cosmopolitan city was a major hub at the base of the Andes located in a low valley ringed by huge mountains. Juri was seated next to an Australian couple in their late twenties with a young boy. They got into conversation about everything but kangaroos. They were all headed in the same direction and agreed to meet up at the Lan ticket office in the morning.

Juri was an experienced traveler and reflected on the pluses and minuses of traveling alone versus journeying with friends. Having a travel partner prompted sharing the special moments on any voyage but it colored the experience through the eyes of your friend. Traveling alone was lonely for most but the encounter was pure. He also felt one was inclined to meet more people on a one-to-one basis when you traveled alone. At the airport office he kept a tight grip on the bag containing his valuables. While the mother watched the excess baggage and her child, the husband and Juri went up to the ticket counter with their passports and cash. Out of the corner of his eye, Juri saw a man pick up the couple's child and go out the door with him. Juri charged after him and as the man turned left down the sidewalk he gently let go of the child. Juri turned in time to see another man with two bags that didn't belong to him turn right on the sidewalk. One was Juri's and the other was the property of the Aussie couple. Coming to the assistance of their boy, the couple was hysterical. Juri shouted a minimal explanation as he took off running after the second man. The diversion tactic worked perfectly. It was a skillfully carried out con job. The boy's father quickly got wind of what was going on and joined Juri in pursuit of the culprit. They rounded a corner and up an alley into a courtyard just getting a last glance of a figure ducking into a housing tenement carrying two familiar pieces of baggage. They sprinted up the stairs and in an elevated atrium in limited Spanish Juri asked the woman on the landing... *"en que direccion se fue el hombre."* As she was about to answer they saw her attention drift over their shoulders to another man behind them who was shaking his head in the negative. She never replied. Juri and the couple had what was most important, their passports, their money and their health. What he didn't have was his camera and hundreds of photographs of Machu Picchu and the rest of the images of Peru including all his surf friends and the waves at the gigantic secret spot. When he got home it would all just be talk.

Sitting on the plane waiting for the flight to Lima, he was taken by the height of the steep mountains surrounding Arequipa. Juri loved flying. He once spent a whole day at Honolulu International simply watching airplanes and travelers. He had boarded aircraft hundreds of times before. But out of nowhere, there was a premonition. Not necessarily of fear but of an acceptance of the knowledge that the airliner was not going to make it gaining altitude over the summit of those tall mountains. It felt like a certainty. He actually thought of disembarking, but there was a morose sense of being ready to accept his fate, a ritual of preparedness that he had never before or since experienced. It was a willingness to accept his mortality.

In Lima he picked up his surfboard and paid his goodbyes to Jackson. When he arrived at LAX, he was unkempt and tatted. He sported a beard from a couple of months of travel. The immigration authorities asked where and how long. They asked him to step into a private room where he waited for over an hour. His ride thinking, he had missed the flight returned to Orange County. The room was completely white with one security camera mounted to the ceiling. After an infuriatingly long wait, two uniformed officers entered with his luggage. They produced a large labeled white plastic jar of Trader Joe's vitamin C crystals that was part of his health regimen on long trips. The immigration officials citing his prolonged stay in Peru and the crystalline white powder in the container as questionable. He tried to reason with them asking if they would put a taste on their tongue and verify that it was actually vitamin C. Another hour and corroborating lab results freed him to find his own transportation home.

Circumnavigation
CHAPTER 19

Business was good. Juri had just finished a series of large paintings for a theme park in Japan with a Jack Nicklaus-designed golf course at its center that encircled a conical hill. The park was partitioned into sections based on western cultural myths. Camelot, Atlantis and Olympia, all individual components, were created and contracted by Landmark Entertainment. He bought himself some time. Time to do a major trek. Never mind his self-employed small business had built up momentum over the last four months and was on a roll. He decided to do some major traveling. Besides, he was ready to take a sabbatical from teaching and his relationship needed some fine-tuning. Or was it the other way around, did he need to take a leave from the relationship and tweak his teaching a bit?

They contemplated geography, trying to rationalize traveling together one more time for the good of their alliance. It was just another excuse to hit the road. Regardless, they purchased a pair of round-the-world tickets with combined carriers Air New Zealand and British Air. That meant they could fly to any destination those two airlines serviced as long as it was basically in one direction without backtracking. The plan was to inaugurate the journey going west from LAX, the same compass heading taken by James Cook. They arranged not for around 80 days, but were prepared to take up to six months to experience the Seven Wonders.

They boarded with appetites, carry-ons and big eating grins. The two of them stowed away a couple of duffle bags, two surfboards and buckled up. It was clear sailing as Juri looked out the window seat to get a glimpse of the equator. He never spotted it. First stop in the South Seas was Papeete on the island of Tahiti. He had experienced parts of Polynesia before but this was to the power of ten. Literature, film and the travel industry had not prepared him sufficiently for what was right in front of him. Arriving at most tropical destinations, that first step exiting the aircraft onto the gangway was always an assault on the senses. It began with a whisper of warmth in the trade winds on a February morning. On the breeze, soft fragrance of plumeria caressed like gentle sweet, scented fingertips. Disembarking at island destinations was usually not directly through an enclosed walkway to the terminal but down an aluminum gangplank, then across the tarmac to baggage piled up on the ground. Instead of those automated conveyer belts, their gear was transferred by tractor out from the belly of the plane in full view of the disembarking passengers filing across the runway. In plain sight across the narrow channel was the spired island of Moorea with its jungle-covered limestone crags. The island, only 30 minutes away by ferry, looked further away as the salt air muted its contrasting outline. The hotel for the first night was a three-story job on Boulevard de la Reine Pomare IV, the main drag on the bay front. They deposited their bags in the hotel room and grabbed a sidewalk table at a café with a harbor view. The aerial roots of a huge banyan tree near their corner table encouraged that out-of-doors feeling. She ordered a baguette sandwich and a Mai Tai. He sided with the shrimp ceviche and a Hinano. Just before crashing from the long travel day, he took the elevator down the three floors to get a bucket of ice and some drinking water. Returning to the room he pushed the big #3 embossed on the domed copper button. As the doors parted in the middle, he knew he was in Tahiti when the elevator occupied by young Polynesian launderette with a red hibiscus cradled above her right ear, sheets draped over her shoulder exposing her breasts carried the rest of the wash bundled up in front of her. He gave her a polite and nonchalant *Ia Orana* and then the only other Tahitian word he knew, *Maururu*, he used to thank her on the way out.

Before Edie and Juri had the chance to explore the main island, they booked a morning passage with Aremiti to their lodging at Cook's Bay on Moorea. Crossing over from Papeete and coming in to the docks, they scrambled to get the best possible view on the top deck. The drive from the ferry landing was awesome. It was a slice of true Tahitian life with people going to market on the roadside. The road was always the one universal gathering place anywhere you went. The main road that ringed the island was scattered with manicured South Seas homes leading first around Cook's Bay, a tourist enclave and then Opunohu Bay where more locals lived and Captain Cook actually anchored. There was no suitable answer to why he didn't choose the bay that was named after him. Island smarts had it that Haapiti on the southwest side was where the waves were. On consecutive days the drive came up empty. Unusually calm open oceans rendered zero waves so they drove around the island for other diversions. Waterfalls, jungle treks and outrigger paddling made up an impromptu itinerary.

On return to Papeete, they booked passage on the Temahane, a cargo-passenger ship leaving for Huahine the next afternoon. They walked the harbor area around the boats and after a bite to eat hopped on a *le truck*, the traditional Polynesian flatbed transport with parallel benches and roll-up tarp in search of a welcoming beach. Edie spotted a friendly-looking island snack bar with sand floors, a thatched roof and beach umbrellas flanking the area between the bar and the lagoon. They sat down and noticed a sign next to a shattered and splintered fiberglass beach lounger in both French and English that spelled out an ominous warning...*DANGER FALLING COCONUTS*...Juri was reassured. They were watching out for the tourists. Further up the road they unassumingly passed up Teahupoo a sadistic surf spot that had not yet made the map but they did stop off at a location that did. The Gauguin Museum was clearly marked on their excursion charts they handily picked up earlier at the hut marked *VISITORS*. He was disappointed. The understated structure had plenty of Gauguin artifacts but little in the way of his paintings. Let the man speak. What is a Gauguin Museum without one of the master's pieces? Coming almost completely around the island on the east side they paid homage to the black sand beach made famous in Bruce Brown's classic surf film *Endless Summer*.

The cargo vessel was a tramp steamer out of a 40's movie with local Tahitians towing their rice sacked belongings slung over their shoulders and strings of brightly colored parrot fish just purchased at the public market. Some were carrying chickens in wire cages along with breadfruit and green stalks of bananas. Backpackers in search of bargains slept on the deck under a row of portholes. Those wanting a real bed signed up for modest cabins just on the other side of the windows. The quarters were sparse and the boat was slow but the destination was Elysian.

The Temahane took its sweet time to reach Huahine. It also took everyone else's time. They sailed from Papeete in the middle of the day and reached Fare in dark hours of the morning so they would have to wait until sunrise to see what they got out of the deal. If sighting land in the daylight was preferred, then they should have left Tahiti sometime after midnight. Juri and Edie grabbed their stuff and disembarked in a village that was dark and locked down. With no reserved lodging and nothing open, they found a stack of 50 lb flour bags under a corrugated roof dockside and made their bed. Waking to the roosters rattled their senses and all around them was what a South Seas Island should be. A warm pleasant trade wind aroused them to get the day going. Exotic vegetation blanketing the topography of eroded limestone urged them to explore green and the blue lagoon called for snorkeling the reef. Juri could see about a direct mile out from the center of town were small silhouetted figures surfing the reef. All around them was what they wanted, the South friggin' Pacific.

First things being first, they referred to their Lonely Planet Guide to find a place to stay. How long? They had the luxury not to be sure. They walked past the post office and into a bakery where the aroma of fresh baked coconut bread slapped them silly. She ordered a slice and some hot coffee and he decided on two slices and some spice tea. The bakery was one of the many shops attached to a covered wooden walkway that had the feel of an old western novel. Instead of six-shooters the patrons carried mangoes and papayas. Further down Main Street where a big banyan tree rooted itself on most of the corner stood a big grey three-story colonial with a sign that simply read HOTEL.

Polynesians can be laid back without making it a chore. They for the most part are light hearted and playful because somewhere at their core they know what they have. People from all over the world come to them. Juri was told a story about a Tahitian chieftain who was invited to the states by an American doctor who had visited. Tahitian royalty arrived at LAX and boarded a limo that was reserved by their host. As the driver pulled out past high rises in the business district of Century Blvd and onto the frenetic traffic of the 405, the elder Tahitian requested the driver to turn around and return to the terminal. The couple checked in and boarded Tahiti Nui and returned home. They did the round trip in the span of a very long day.

The wooden-slatted deck of the local eatery overlooked the reef and the pass into the lagoon. There was an obvious group of seasoned adventurers seated at an adjacent table. Their surfboards leaning against the railing, they were comfortable and casual with their surroundings, signaling that they had been here a while. Juri's enthusiasm was hard to hide. Barely visible more than a half-mile out on the reef and towards the horizon, the outlines of wave riders against the sky gave a perspective as to the size of the swell. There it was again. Bryce was from Newport Beach and knew some of the same people back in California that Juri did. He even knew Dick Oden's son Noah. How was it possible to come halfway around the world to have a conversation you probably should have expected to have back home? Chad had only met Bryce here in Huahine after making the longer trip from Virginia Beach. Chad always carried his Nikon and a waterproof bag of lenses with him even out in the skiff anchored on the reef. A third member of the group, Bjorn was a tall slender Norwegian and the only non-surfer of the five. But he was game. They all geared up and took the skiff out for Edie and Juri's inaugural surf. They anchored a couple of hundred yards from a beautiful paper-thin right breaking off the far side of the pass and an equally fine left invitingly closer. First out of the boat was Bjorn. He was already snorkeling in the crystal, clear lagoon before the rest of them had waxed up their boards. Chad, a goofy-footer, and Edie chose the closer break. Bryce and Juri headed over to the right. Juri was just ending his first playful engagement with what Huahine had to offer by kicking out over the top of his initial wave when he noticed Bjorn hyperventilating and frantically streaking on the water back to the boat.

Snorkeling face down on the surface he was startled by a shark about his size that swam from behind and under him in a graceful glide. Black Tips were not aggressive and the reef sharks were common and not much of a concern unless you cut yourself on a rocky ledge. Bjorn's performance was the topic of debate for the next few days.

Bicycles available at the hotel were basic transportation for exploring the island outside of Fare. Most the roads outside of town were crushed coral and made a tire sound reminiscent of driving your car across gravel. Black coral slab *marae* were monuments scattered across certain historical island sites. These were formal gathering places in the past for ancestral rituals and still revered in the present. It was most important for visitors to show respect.

The family that ran the hotel was opening a small upscale resort on the other side of the island. They asked Edie and Juri if they would be willing to pose for a few photos to promote the new vacation destination in exchange for credit towards their mounting invoice. Sounded like fun to be counted among the glitterati. And having your room on the house wasn't bad either.

When he surfed alone and didn't have access to the skiff, Juri regarded the venture of the long paddle out as work ethic. The waves were clean and a bit scary on the takeoff because of the coral shelf under your feet. Bryce and Chad were already out as well as a small tight group of Tahitians. The ground rules said it was the Polynesian's wave. They had priority until you were deemed to pass muster. The cardinal rule regardless of where you surfed was home field advantage went to the locals.

There was another American in the water who seemed to be chummy with the Tahitians. It turned out he was praising the word of God on Huahine. As a missionary for the last two years somehow, he didn't preach the golden rule. On a one-man wave he was a shoulder-hopper. He took turns jumping the waves in front of all the visiting surfers. His etiquette was of no interest to the locals while at the same time he was a cretin with everyone else. This man of God, Juri thought didn't have a Christian attitude in the water. On one particular wave Juri dropped in deep and started to lean into his turn on a sucking right-hander. When for the umpteenth time the apostle got the jump on him and cut him off, his trail in the water caused an otherwise perfect wave to crash down on Juri. He was dragged across the reef as the dipstick gauged the finish of Juri's wave. It took a set of five waves for Juri to gather himself in the roiling inside section over sharp coral and paddle back out. He was beaten between a rock and a hard place. Infuriated, he wanted some measure of satisfaction. He had a dilemma. Anger the Tahitians, who were now between him and his bone of contention, and for the remainder of the trip be in their dog house or just suck it up like the waves were doing and let it be. Juri, letting off steam, paddled right up next to the goon inches from his rail and said nothing. Juri shadowed him for a while until he cooled down. The waves were fine and the view spectacular and Juri wasn't there. He was in his head. The next day out in the water there was no missionary but the Tahitians were exceptionally friendly. He guessed that his handling of the previous day passed muster.

Chad wanted to do some surf photography so the next day they all put on their Sunday finest, rented the skiff for a session out on a further reef in the center portion of the lagoon that Juri hadn't surfed before. Some fine sampling with the camera behind him, Chad bagged his equipment in the boat, grabbed his board and paddled out with his subjects. After a couple more hours of satisfaction they all stroked over to the boat. Totally alarmed when they got to the skiff, it was half-full of water and in danger of sinking and they were well over a mile off shore. Someone had forgotten to replace the rubber plug in the boat after cleaning and draining it the day before. They forced the sleeve of a neoprene surf shirt into the hole and bailed the skiff with the hopes it would hold until they made it to shore.

The next morning Chad was visibly upset that in the middle of his working vacation salt water rendered his camera equipment inoperable or in other words…useless. In a protracted period of morbidity, he decided he would check out and head home. He asked Juri one favor. He was supposed to hook up with Brett, a friend from San Diego, who would be arriving on the Saturday boat and asked if Juri could explain what happened. Cool. No problem. They manned up and bid their goodbyes.

On the weekend at the dock, he looked for someone who fit the description. Mostly locals on the gangway, then he spotted two possible suspects. Most surfers look alike. That's not true, but on that day it was. One guy had an oversized backpack and the other was carrying a surfboard. It was an easy guess as to which one Juri called Brett first. The other guy's name was Bill and he was from Wisconsin. The two of them had just met on the boat and struck up a conversation. Befriending strangers was one of the fortunate perks of world travel. With the identification complete, Juri started explaining to Brett that Chad had emigrated earlier in the week. Then it happened again. Bill spurted out... *"You gotta be kidding me. You know Chad E. It's a damn small world. I met Chad at an event in Madison last year when he was on a photography assignment."* So here they were two total strangers linked by chance and circumstance and all they had in common other than a ticket to a remote destination in the Pacific was a close mutual friend... *"Wow...!!! What do you think those odds were?"*

On the return leg to Papeete the Taporo took a wide swing through the pass as he actually spotted familiar faces surfing off his port side. All sorts of hand gestures were exchanged as they pulled away and entered deeper water. The color mutated to a deep purple cast. Something the artist had only seen in paintings. Their timing was good as they arrived on the big island just in time for a bite to eat, pack, and hit the rack and in the morning head to Faaa International for the next leg on Air New Zealand to Avarua.

Rarotonga, the seat of government and the largest of the Cook Islands, was another gem in the pool of Pacific islands. Most tropical islands tend to have one main island road circumscribing the outside perimeter of the atoll. They took the opportunity to put a little distance between them and the airport and stowed their bags at a small Muri Beach bure. Their view on the other side of the island of a crystal blue lagoon with a very small islet, called a motu, with nothing but a few coconut palms and plenty of white coral sand. The plan found them boarding the typical de Haviland island hopper propeller driven aircraft capable on especially short runways. The next destination on the puddle jumper was Aitutaki, 262 kilometers due north on most maps. Arutanga, the only village on the island, was just a collection of a few Polynesian homes, a couple of shops and a post office. The only pavement on the island was the tarmac where the de Haviland refueled. The permanent residents loved to chat up the visitors. In a way it was their Facebook and Twitter before Facebook and Twitter. Fast traveling news is relative.

Aitutaki has an encompassing exposed ring of coral protecting the island from storms. These flat low-lying coral atolls were different from most of the Society Islands. In Tahiti most of the geological formation was by volcanism. The twin basalt and lava peaks on that island stand well above sea level. Mont Orohena ticked out at 7,352 ft. For Aitutaki the lack of elevation posed an eminent problem. The politics around rising sea levels means something close to home when the 7.1 square miles of your flat island averages an altitude of just under 50ft above sea level. It was odd in some places to be able to eye the horizon on the waterline both in front of you and behind you at the same time.

The Cook Islanders are Maori people, a constitutional monarchy and in a 'free association' with New Zealand. What that really meant was they administered to all their own affairs but they are granted New Zealand citizenship. Holding New Zealand passports made them kiwis, legally capable of living and working in places like Auckland and Christchurch.

Melody was typical of young Polynesian men from this part of the Pacific. He had labored in New Zealand. Not excessively tall but built solidly. He had a stocky torso and massive powerful legs. His calves were bigger around than Juri's thighs. And he had that look in his eye, especially when he had a Matutu or two. They seemed to be always bloodshot. Juri had a vague feeling there was trauma in his history. He was a salubrious fun-loving maverick, always his own man and no one person was going to tell him what to do. Maybe it was the strong streak of independence that brought them together. Whatever. An undeniable chemistry or resonance bound them to the same moment. They spent time, all three of them in each other's company over the next month. Edie surely attracted all sorts of male attention but Melody always steered the conversation Juri's way and always with a baying humor. He was one of those waggish people who made Juri more comical. It struck Juri odd that underneath all this Melody would every once in a while, sneak in questions that could have heavier overtones if one chose to take them a particular way. Quarries to his 'haole' friend were looking for answers to two questions at a time.

Save lagoons in Bora Bora or Moorea, Aitutaki had unmatchable water qualities of anywhere in the tropical world. Words couldn't match nature's color and clarity. Aitutaki was a stunningly beautiful backwater island off the beaten path and it was precisely the water that made it hard to leave.

Their first venture to Fiji would be short-lived due to cyclone Hina, a category-five that reached wind gusts of over 220 kph. They took a place a bit south of Nadi at Seashell Cove close enough where they might negotiate for a boat and lodging on yet-established Tavarua. That first late afternoon they understood how their beach got its name. The unusual phenomenon of the ocean receding out a couple of miles prior to a coming storm bared the ocean floor to pedestrian traffic. Locals out in the mudflats gathered floundering fish for the taking and Juri netted specimen shells in his t-shirt.

Mother Ocean was loading up to gauge her tidal bore at Viti Levu. As cyclonic storms rotate, the winds and tides do strange, alien things. The whole ocean seemed to vanish in biblical proportions. Like harnessing the energy of an archer's bow, water was pulled back only to be released as a massive tidal surge on the shoreline. Ken, in the adjacent bure, was headed to the Philippines to find a wife but in the meantime was concerned about the cyclone headed their way. Stories of all the tenants gathering in the only two-story structure on the property during last year's storm season were flying freely. The surge was high enough to reach people standing on tables on the second floor. Water was waist high before it started to subside.

Edie and Juri boarded the windows and set up camp in the windowless lavatory of the cinderblock structure. They took the mattress off of the bed and threw it against the inside of the bathroom door. It was to say at the least, a long night. The windows shook and the door rattled. Seventeen hours of gin rummy later the sound of the storm abated. They cautiously rolled away the ramparts and carefully pried open the door. They didn't recognize where they were. It was still intensely windy and raining. Calm blue water roiled muddy brown and choppy. Lush green coconut palms were stripped to wooden spikes. The high chain link fence of a tennis court was lying on its side but a chestnut horse tethered to nothing was still standing. They got the brilliant idea to put on their masks, snorkels and swim fins in the dark and waddle over and visit Ken to see how he was doing. He answered the door with a blanket wrapped around him and shivering. He was so traumatized that he didn't notice what they were wearing. Edie and Juri were disheartened that their wardrobes didn't make a bigger splash.

Plan B had to be enacted quickly. They asked if there was anyone available that could drive them to the airport as soon as possible. It was obvious that public water would not be potable for an indefinite period of time and that swimming in bacteria laden lagoons was not preferable. When the ocean calmed and all people in the big hotels finished packing, they would become potential passengers and there would be no seating available to get off the island.

The sun was starting to come up and they had a driver. Pronto was in order. The orange and beige van had a high ground clearance that made fording all the flooding in the road possible. With all the weaving and dodging a 12km-drive became 17. Try holding your breath for that long. In the terminal they knew they had a chance when there weren't yet throngs of people at the airport. They had responded with foresight and moved quickly and with due diligence. Air New Zealand was very supportive, not having yet faced the oncoming onslaught. Two ticket agents found them a flight leaving for Auckland in 45 minutes and booked them a window and an aisle seat; no matter they were in different rows.

Auckland was the San Francisco of the southern hemisphere. A mighty bridged city, it had 2 harbors open to ocean on both sides of the North Island. New Zealand's population deemed nature and the environment a national treasure. Every road-stop along the way had a boarded handicap walk of minimal distance, partnered with medium intervals mapped out for more vigorous hikers and for the dedicated, there were official treks that required signing in for overnight huts. The out-of-doors was in New Zealand. The countryside was nothing but green, it had more sheep than it did people and birds that don't fly. Up the coast at Bay of Islands, they passed through a time warp. It must have happened on the ferry from Paihia to Russel. Straight out of a collective childhood memory, it was a water crossing that led to a simpler time. Cottages lined the waterfront in plain view of islands that dotted the bay. Residents put glass milk bottles in wire 4-paks with cash out there in the open. Right there on a wooden platform attached to the white picket fence ready for the milkman's morning delivery. Juri thought raising kids in an environment like this would be healthy. Not many places left today where you could trust leaving money out in the open.

On the west coast swing back down the north-south road was a place aptly named 90 Mile Beach that conjured up everything the name might have suggested.

Raglans made world famous by Bruce Brown, Robert August and Mike Hynson was a few clicks below Auckland. It was the height of the surf season and it was flat. The travel gods were probably offended by something. Juri had no idea what it might be. At the entrance to the batshit crazy glowworm caverns in Waitomo Edie had a meltdown. Neither of them remembered what it was about but she walked off like he wasn't going to come after her. Like he was going to leave her stranded in a foreign country. She was not going to get into the vehicle.

On the drive south they were aiming for Rotorua and found themselves in a Vauxhall Camper somewhere between Matamata and Papatoetoe. Located near the Bay of Plenty, Rotorua was a Maori stronghold. Geothermal activity dominated the region with spewing geysers, frapping mud pots and glazed sulfur deposits. The indigenous people of New Zealand were there long before any Europeans set foot on the territory. There was a striking awareness of Maori culture for anyone observing the tribal ritual prior to any All Blacks rugby match. Players squatted in a Haka war dance chanting with their tongues out in a display of threat that their opponents would soon be eaten. It could be argued it was a subliminal transfer from cannibalistic time to the playing fields of modern sport. A scary prospect if you were the opponent.

At Wellington they boarded a very seaworthy ferry for the passage to the South Island. Hemispherical conditioning made it confusing whether going south meant variant conditions. Was a directional shift north to warmer climes preferable? The bounty that lay to the south was going to be a panorama they had yet to feast on. From Wellington across the Cook Strait and through long-fingered inlets to Picton where they unloaded the Vauxhall Camper, getting a footing on South Island. One-way backpacking treks were rare. In their experience most hikes required a return leg but at Abel Tasman National Park on the Tasman Sea there was one available. On a two-day coastal hike Edie and Juri enjoyed a forest walk along the shore with no time restraints. Whatever pace suited the moment dictated the stride. With lots to observe, there was wildlife everywhere. Fur seals were easy to spot and small blue penguins claimed a lot of attention. They pitched a tent right on the sand the first night to a sky where there were so many stars you couldn't distinguish the constellations. In the morning they tested the adage that food always tasted better when you were hungry and in the wilderness. They hiked out to their furthest southern point on the trail and planted a big red flag in the sand they found in a bin along the edge of the beach. Exhausted from the miles, they took off their boots and faced the sand, taking in a warming sun. Juri awakened from a well-earned nap by a nibbling pair of wekas between his toes. Unlike the national symbol, the better-known nocturnal kiwi, also a flightless brown rail, the wekas were active during the day and the two tended not to compete. Good timing. Around the headland a canopied boat was motoring its way towards the embedded red flag. The water taxi assured that they wouldn't have to double back on foot to where they left the camper. At that moment on the boat, it was luxury, high-end trekking.

South along highway 6 on the west coast of South Island at Punakaiki they ventured onto the unusual geologic formations called Pancake Rocks. Strange limestone pinnacles, while solid and stable, looked like they were individual stone slabs stacked precariously one on top of the other. When the enthusiastic blowhole did its thing and spewed saltwater across the bow it was the perfect time for an orchestral crescendo. At a rest stop they took the time to hike up a conical peak that had been inverted upside down by volcanic activity in the distant past. It was Disneyesque. A manicured green spiral staircase of ferns twisted up over steps naturally created by the roots of trees. As they climbed further up, a veil of miniature rifleman birds magically appeared. At less than three inches, they were New Zealand's smallest birds. They flew, trifling between the climbers' legs, to pick off insects stirred up by tramping boots. The hikers thought of it as animation in real time.

Franz Josep Glacier sounded like family to Juri. They used their influence to helicopter up the summit and put on ice spikes. Tethered by a climbing rope, Edie, Juri and the guide gripped their ice picks and stabbed their way up the slope. The guide issued a caution as they approached the crevasse. The drop off was deep-deep blue.

The Southern Alps needed to be circled to approach Mt Cook from Lake Pukaki. It was the only way in. In front of them stood seven or eight expansive snowcapped mountain peaks rising well above the clouds that were all over at least 10,000 ft. And looming over them all was Aoraki as the Maori who were there first called it. Mt Cook was a grand natural gesture measuring in at 12,218 ft. Even without fast-forwarding the video, the clouds poured over the tops of the peaks in a kind of stop-action motion. Majestic was a cliché. This wasn't. It was the mountain that Sir Edmund Hillary, the first of European descent to summit Everest, trained on before his historic climb. In that cluster of rock was Mt Sefton, the fourth largest mountain in New Zealand. Edie and Juri trekked a couple of hours up to a promontory directly across from the granite peak. It was carrying the burden of massive glacial ice. Edie repeated suggestions of wariness about his progress out to a small jutting rock. The concerns were delivered in a high pitch tone. On the precipice he sat with his legs dangling over the ledge that opened up a void of about a vertical mile down and a horizontal mile straight across from a prime alpha mountain. Avalanches calving off the glacier were rare events to witness. He sat and watched from his position on the precarious rock. Juri used his eyes to first scan for any movement of white and then seconds later he could expect a deep basso grumbling that reverberated off the steep granite faces. The sound came out of the bowels of the valley. The resonance left a tingling feeling.

Sutherland Falls, three times the size of any waterfall in neighboring Australia, was a remarkable quest that required two days in and two days out. He turned over a couple of rocks. Under the first one was an Aussie and wedged under the other a German. Those two cultures exported the hardiest of travelers not shy braving the remotest of places. This was their chance. They were only going to be there once, on this trip. Photographing something special should never be put off until you swing back to capture it. When you do, it will be gone. The light will be different. Will it be raining? Reaching a unique place was the same. Don't count on it a second time. The second time may not come. It was a grueling hike that made the payoff even better. Coming over the ridge and seeing that long thin veil cascade to the valley floor some 1,900 plus feet down was whatever one wanted it to be. They earned it.

They had anticipated and talked incessantly about Fiordland National Park, which was in the very lower southwest corner of South Island. The Park consisted of multiple-fingered tall canyons jutting into the interior from the ocean. They were actually mountains rising off the sea floor. A maze of channels, bays and sounds with tributaries that fed waterfalls that you could boat under. Glaciers had carved its deep U-shaped valleys. It was the yang of Norway's yin in the Southern hemisphere. It also had a cold reminiscence of Cat Ba in Vietnam.

They jacked themselves up by viewing slides and reading accounts of previous visitors. They did their homework. Weather was going to be a make-or-break deal. They were there in the wrong season. With an average of over 200 days of rain a year, chances were, they would need their ponchos. Good fortune for the pristine condition of the region was the challenging weather that was responsible for the lack of logging and mining in the area. Mitre Peak was the crown jewel of Milford Sound and it reigned over the inlet resembling a bishop on a chessboard. Taking a seat on small watercraft in the protection of the fiords was a ticket to somewhere most haven't gone. There were over four dozen full time resident bottlenose dolphins that called Milford Sound home. Riding a watercraft under a rainbow waterfall with dolphins splashing their flukes to all kinds of high-pitched squeaks and whistles may have smacked a bit of unicorns. It was a haven and a sanctuary fit for anyone doing some away-from-home soul searching. They had the travel gods on their side. It was all a crapshoot anyway. Good fortune had offered up great weather, especially during the rainy season.

Queenstown was about adventure. Out of doors was a prerequisite if you wanted to enjoy Queenstown to the fullest. If you could dream it, it was probably available. The mountains, the forests, the lake, all were accessible venues. Outfitters were abundant on South Island. Edie and Juri grabbed the end of a paddle, latched a carabiner to a rope, hopped on a mountain bike and hitched a ride in a gondola to the top of Bob's Mountain to catch a glimpse of the Remarkables. Then needing another fix, they jumped a raft on the Shotover for a run of the rapids just a little under 9 miles long. Shark Fin was a rapid just below a big hole that pinned their boat like a taco wrapped around a blade of granite. The rush of brutal current made it nearly impossible to unpeel a raft bent in half. It took 6 people and 2 ropes 20 minutes to free the inflatable. Mr. Toads' wild ride ended with a traverse of an old 170-meter-long abandoned mineshaft. There were places in the dark where they were advised to keep their head down. The light at the end of the tunnel brought them to the terminus of the ride. They spilled out of the shaft over a cascade of boulders that shook them to their molars. But they were pre-warned and prepared to meet their adversaries. The run ended in a large basin of flat water much like an aquatic amphitheater. They were told a jet boat would also be coming from the other direction on the river. The speedy craft with 10-12 passengers would be braking in a spinout, trying to douse them with their wake. Their group was in three small rafts. The red boat could outrun them but the rafters could outflank them. The pilot of the speedboat could have been a blackjack dealer with the slicked back Elvis look. He was a prime target. They kept their buckets under wraps especially the one with fish innards until the exact right moment.

The swing up the east coast was pastoral, with lots of farmland. It was sheep country. While the first breed in New Zealand was the Corriedale, the Romney and Merino breeds became widely popular. Not that Juri was a sheep farmer but sheep shearing demonstrations armed him with a lot of trivia.

Christchurch was the main administrative center on South Island and the largest in population. It was a university town having multiple educational institutions with the University of Canterbury topping the list. There was a lot of culture for a mostly-rural island. A big deal Juri thought of a city with three major cathedrals, one of them bearing the same name as the grammar school he attended, Blessed Sacrament.

Once they got back to Picton, they retraced their steps to Auckland International Airport and set in motion the next leg of the journey down under to Oz.

Sydney's iconic Opera House, its present-day sentinel, was Australia's branded version of America's lady of the harbor. Juri and Edie gathered their luggage and for lunch they compared apples and oranges in lieu of Tim Tams. It was over 800 km southwest to Melbourne, the next-largest city in Australia. As most avid travelers knew, the continent's population density was in a ring around its coastal perimeter, definitely a country of people who lived at the beach. The interior was the outback. And there were stories to back that up. Juri chatted it up with a mate from shark-netted Bondi Beach. Over a Fosters, an incident was related about driving cross-country. It was the fastest direct route on red hard pack of the deserted noncoastal road. Straight as an arrow for kilometers, he was driving down the center of the country on the left side of a dusty road surface. Hypnotized by the repetition out his windscreen, his eyes were at half-mast. Monotony lulled him to that state of half sleep, half wake. Then an anomaly in the road presented itself. There was a large shrub of a tree dead ahead as the road curved left, a monumental shift in the way things were going. He slapped himself in the face and ratcheted down on his velocity. He hit the brakes hard. There in the middle of the road was a kangaroo taking a doze in the only shade for kilometers. His back tires lost traction as he sideswiped the dim form in his path. There was a disgusting sound at the moment of impact. He skidded to a halt and assessed the damage. He ran over the Quantas logo. He felt unpatriotic and a little depressed. To make the best out of a bad situation, he propped it up against the grill of his car and put his jacket over the kangaroo's shoulders. He then placed his sunglasses over the snout, stood back and snapped a pic for posterity. As he was trying to review the photo, the kangaroo shook violently and jumped to its feet, apparently only dazed. Not only did the jacket, but also his passport that happened to be in the breast pocket hop off towards Darwin. Juri had a hard time imagining this storyteller applying for a duplicate passport and filling out the reason in the replacement box. And he also made note to make sure he hung on to his documents the next time he saw a roo.

Not being fans of major metropolitan areas, they booked a flight that was in the opposite northerly direction towards the Great Barrier Reef and its 900-some scattered islands. Brisbane was at the southern-most terminus of the reef that extended close to 2,300 km almost to Papua New Guinea. It was definitely a water wonderland. Boaters, divers and adventurers sought out the Great Barrier Reef as a destination from all imaginable places on the globe. Further up the coast out of Yeppoon they arranged for a week out on Pumpkin Island. The private island was about the size of a small aircraft carrier with a few rock islets sprinkling its shoreline. There was a bare-bones hut with a bed and running water and a canoe but no electricity. On the mainland with a week's worth of perishables, they were taxied out to the island by the couple that held the deed to the sparse slice of paradise. Juri and Edie were given a specific time when the boat would be back, barring bad weather. It was right out of the pages of R. L. Stevenson, a hybrid of camping and survival. Getting the lay of the land took about 10 minutes, paddling around the island about twice that. Having no neighbors, they could do what they wanted and wear what they wanted. The boat ride back to the mainland was into a brilliant orange and purple sunset and they felt like they were going into the closing scene of a magnificent film. In the boarding area for the Brisbane to Perth British Air flight, their names were announced over the p.a. system. With some concern, they walked up to the agents at the departure gate and were asked if they minded being upgraded from economy to first class. This time the travel gods were good to them.

The flight from Brisbane to Perth took the same amount of time as one from LAX to JFK or MIA to SEA. So they buckled up in their XL posh seats, kicked back with prawn cocktails and champagne in clear plastic wine glasses and savored the good life. Approaching the west coast of Australia was otherwise known as flying dark. There was absolutely no sign of light or life under them all the way across the center of the country on the night flight. John Glenn on Friendship 7 orbiting over Perth, with all due respect to Paris, proclaimed it the *'City of Light'*

Edie hailed a cab and they asked the driver to take them to a tidy little hotel, any neat little motel would do. The response dampened their spirits. The U.S. Pacific Fleet was in town. Grey Battleships were stacked up in the harbor. Naval games were in full force. Not a room in town was the battle cry. They managed a to find a bunk in a seedy little place on the sharp edge of town.

Juri, despite their lodging the first night, made a mental observation that Perth, at least in those days, along with Auckland were among the cleanest, unsullied major cities he personally experienced. Having amassed his share of road weary miles meant a lot. To feel clean and unsoiled when traveling was reinvigorating. The Swan River flowed to a small world-class harbor that would soon be hosting the Americas Cup. The sidewalk cafes and restaurants were fine places to sit and watch Aussies, the river traffic and have a sip of Swan Ale.

Stevie and his brother Barry teamed in earlier years with Juri and his brother Frank on a champion recreation league basketball squad back in California. They had all played at the same high school but not necessarily at the same time. Stevie, who was four years younger than Juri, had met Linda while traveling in Europe and then migrated to Western Australia to get married. Good thing he knew what direction he was headed. She grew up in Perth and Stevie was committed enough to pack it all in for family life in Western Australia. The four of them strapped their boards to the car a couple of times and drove down to Margaret River to catch a few choice waves on the Indian Ocean. Back at the Perth beaches, they played at milking less consistent waves. They actually had more fun on a couple of sneaker days bodysurfing south of Freemantle. Edie and Juri went out to Rottnest Island on the 10am ferry. The island got its name because early sailors mistook the hordes of quokkas, tiny marsupials that had free range of the island, for rats.

Time in Perth with Stevie and Linda went too quickly. A few days turned into a week and then after two weeks it was time to go. Juri had read an obscure book that mentioned a remote place in Western Australia where dolphins in the wild made contact with humans. After the hair on his arms stood up it captured his imagination. Before widespread use of Internet, he researched Monkey Mia's exact location. He thought he had enough information to track it down. They took a bus to the end of the line that took them a little more than half way. Perth was the most isolated capital city in the world. They took a bus to the end of the line and they still had a couple of hundred kilometers left to go. There was a point when the bus they were on met up with an on-coming bus with the same markings going in the opposite direction. The drivers both acknowledged each other with a casual gesture then pulled over to the side of the road. They both exchanged places behind the wheel of each other's bus then drove it back to where it came from. It was a novel and ingenious way to assure they slept in their own bed on any given night. Kalbarri, a timeless fishing village had a vicious entry in and out of the anchorage. Vessels attempting the open ocean past high pounding surf on the breakwater, all approached the challenge with the same tact. Edie and Juri hopped a small Cessna carrying pitmen to a gypsum mine outside of Denham. The owners of the fish camp at Monkey Mia switched to 4-wheel drive for the last 26 kilometers to the remote beach that Juri had read about those few years before.

In today's world there is a new asphalt road that transports tourists into an official park with a designated ranger and an entrance fee. In those days when Edie and Juri visited, it was free range, open and wild. A dirt road served only a portion of the route in. It was a basic and ageless fish camp with barely two or three well-worn trailers. The most common form of transportation for fishermen was by boat. Other than the owners of the camp, an elderly couple well versed and weathered, there were two young scientists from the states with a National Geographic grant to study dolphin acoustics and two other venturous women in their late twenties from Melbourne. Besides Jen and Nancy, Juri and Edie were the only other people at the camp who weren't after creatures with fins or at least not the kind you wanted to catch on a hook. They rented one of the small caravans for a month.

It was absolutely a life-changing experience for them. It was one of those pages in his travel journal that deserved the bookmarking of a fine silk ribbon. The bay expanded across uneven, uninhabited scrubland. The surroundings had an enormous empty presence. The waters had a blue teal cast and definitely were not troubled. Dolphins were common near shore. The guy who went out in the mornings in his aluminum outboard and submersed a microphone into the water said there was a resident pod of about 18, sometimes supplemented by other visiting pelagic individuals. They had occasion to count as many as 30 Bottlenose in a relatively tight area all at once. As they spent more time, they grew to distinguish many of the dolphins by their uniquely marked and scuffed dorsal fins. The matriarch of the group, Holey Fin, mothered three generations living in the pod. She had a small concentric cavity visible on her fin, most likely from a bullet or a large hook. Puck gravitated to spending time in Juri's company. She would swim up to him with a flat blade of seaweed and offered it for him to drag across the surface while she feigned snapping at it. Her intentionally slow and inaccurate chomps at the target were like someone clapping on the surface of the water. One time when Juri held the reed away from her behind his back, another dolphin swimming by scooped it away and swam off. Puck in two quick strokes of her fluke overtook the other dolphin and snatched back the flat reed. Every morning Juri had an early ritual. He would walk out knee-deep at sunrise, pat his open hand on the calm morning water to summon Puck. Usually within a few minutes she would show up with her muzzle open and positioned up in his direction. He would cross his hands behind his back and bend forward to receive her high-pitched squeaks and whistles. Boy, could the girl talk back. She was a communicator.

A young boy and Charice, the other National Geographic researcher, were chatting with Edie in the usual meeting place with two dolphins. In knee-deep water the boy saw his father anchoring his boat in shallow water about 150 meters north of where they were. He ran up the beach to greet his dad, took a large snapper and walked waist deep into the bay, still at quite a distance away. He took the fish by the tail and slapped it on the surface a couple of times. He then repeated his action. The two dolphins gliding around Edie and Charice spun on a dime and turned on the afterburners. They stayed submerged just under the surface without breaking any whitewater. The dolphins left two smooth swells in their wake at warp speed in the direction of the boy. Their acute sonar capabilities acknowledged that the object breaking the surface was a fish, and by the shape specifically one of their favorites, as well as exactly how large it was. All of that was deduced in an instant with a natural, acoustic ping. Jurij asked Charice if she thought the dolphins tolerated people for the handouts of food. He asked if that was the tradeoff. His hunch, which she corroborated, was that it was not. Like a domestic cat a meal may be part of it but in the end, it seemed contact, communication and companionship were more relevant. A Bottlenose would be much more competent at getting enough to eat compared to the small morsels a human could hand out. Besides, there were more experiences that said otherwise that Juri had witnessed. The Bottlenose dolphins were there because they wanted to be. They were extremely intelligent to a degree that had only been measured by human standards. Those parameters were species-centric. The dolphins, by what he could see, were capable of mental tasks equal to and maybe surpass what humans could do. And their behavior wasn't necessarily compartmentalized like it was with their human counterparts. They could easily transform from one set of responses to another to resolve an issue. Their social life easily shifted from play, to dispute, to sexual foreplay and back to general amusement, all as one seamless continuum. Juri, Charice and Charlie, the handyman at the camp, were attending to a mother and relative newborn in the water. Though she was comfortable and trusted the three of them, she made a point of staying between the humans and her calf. A random fisherman walked up and immediately her posture changed. The angler, after small conversation, tossed his cigarette butt into the water. Alarmingly, she swam down to retrieve it and brought it back to him in her rostrum almost as if to say *'not in my house'*. Being around the dolphins on a consistent basis, Juri and Edie saw more and more that supported a need for significant reevaluation of cetacean intelligence and potential. A couple of weeks into Edie and Juri's stay, a string of three yellow 4-wheel drive school buses showed up at Monkey Mia over the western mounds from the direction of Denham. Privately, Juri was disheartened. The two of them had found what they were looking for and they had it to themselves. It was another lesson, one about selfishness. The kids had every right to enjoy the dolphins. The dolphins were friendly with almost everyone except cigarette smokers. For weeks now they were accepting and playful but when the children came something exceptional happened. The dolphins sensed the youthful exuberance and with the perspective of a little distance, Juri saw over the rise kids being kids scrambling in the water and dolphins frolicking and turning acrobatic somersaults and generally splashing around in a heightened unison with the children. How was this orchestrated? Somehow the dolphins picked up on the youthful abandon. The dolphins at some instinctual level were able to tap into the animated spirit of the children. Then an astonishingly remarkable thing happened. A family pushed a paraplegic boy in his wheelchair into the lagoon so half the wheels were under water. Immediately two dolphins swam up to the boy and faced directly at him, one at each wheel, arched with half their bodies out of the water. They were like two lion statues guarding a dynastic tomb. The two Bottlenose dolphins were completely motionless and somberly quiet for at least twenty minutes while the boy was writhing with giddy joy. Somehow, they differentiated something about this boy that was separate from the other children. It was obvious right there in comparison.

139

Juri witnessed the animated enthusiasm of the larger group on the right and the solemn muted posturing immediately in front of him. He was having a hard time wrapping his head around that one.

Their four weeks were up. The two friends from Melbourne tried to convince them to stay longer. Here was an once-in-a-lifetime experience presenting itself as a possibility. When an opportunity like this one stared them down, they had an obligation to oblige. They signed on for another 15 days.

Daily contact strengthened this interspecies bond. He was actually befriending a free animal in the wild. Puck and Juri invented all sorts of games. They challenged each other with creativity. The artist and the cetacean, the beast was free and the man was conditioned. Does the name Pavlov ring a bell? It wasn't research for Juri. It was even more than friendship. It was pure distilled unadulterated joy. Where was the pleasure meter?

He got to the point of absolute trust with Puck. She would swim up to greet him, roll over and Juri would stroke her stomach with gentle passes of his palms and then the back of his hands. Her lighter anterior surface turned pink. He'd never seen a dolphin blush. This wild creature had faith in him. The bond of trust would make it almost impossible to leave.

Asia

The flight to Denpasar marked a change, one that wasn't hard to put a finger on. They had gone from Austral to Asia. Culturally, this was one of the biggest shifts in their travels to this point. In Bali, the varied sights, sounds and smells had cultural elements that they never witnessed before. The architecture was peculiarly striking, with its multi-layered plum thatched roofing, the alphabet was indecipherable, the sounds of chimes and bells took their sweet time cascading to silence and the aroma of unnamed spices were in the air. Everyone wore flip-flops or some form of sandals. Balinese merged Hindu and Buddhist customs. The revered high cloth of ritual was a large black and white checkered pattern like the button-down short-sleeve shirt he wore in high school. He would have been a god if he had done his studies in Ubud.

Kuta was the main tourist beach. All sorts of world travelers filled tables at sidewalk cafes. Women in batik kamens with ceremonial foods balanced on their heads, paraded single file in the streets past outdoor shops. But the real beaches, the ones with the surf, were down the road a way. Uluwatu, along with Padang, had storied reputations from the surf magazines. International wave hunters stalked those two beaches in droves. Uluwatu posed for them from the bluff. At a snack stand table they looked down on the fabled wave. It lived up to its star billing. Waves like that had a way of making good surfers look like rock stars. To get to the water you had to take a path down into a deep gully and then through a natural eroded cavernous opening to the beach. The landmark back on top of the cliff was the significant Uluwatu temple. You didn't have to pray for surf.

In Bali, no matter what your occupation during the day, you were an artist by night. Everyone was a painter, sculptor, craftsperson, dancer or musician. And Ubud was the cultural center of art on the island. It was at the heart of the creation myth on *the Morning of the World*. They took lodging in the Monkey Forest. The name was apropos. Gibbons walked the streets with tourists. They were grifters pretending to be distractions. The monkeys bilked food and other shiny objects from the clutches and backpacks of the naïve. Juri tossed some peanuts to a mother and baby grasping at her fur. A doubly large male snatched the goobers away from them and put off Juri a bit. He tried to use his size to intimidate the large macaque and chase it off. But instead, the large alpha male bared his teeth displaying enormous fangs with an almost hissing sound. The hostile monkey turned and made-up ground towards Juri. The dominant male had turned the tables and Juri was now on the defensive. The next few evenings they went to the cultural center for dance, music, chanting and ritual performances that were an assault on the senses. Carved painted masks, colorful costumes and back-and-forth syncopation of gracefully contorted hands mimicked the dangling of marionettes. Traditional dances accompanied by percussion and metal instruments made for a sound exotic to the western ear. The Gamelan ensemble struck bronze bars with bamboo and metal mallets producing an uncommon resonant sound. The Barong paid homage to the big cat king of spirits. To Juri it looked like a Chinese dragon parade. The Baris was a male warrior that seemed to be performed by a mannequin-like dancer hinged at right angles led only by his rapid eye movements. The Kechack was staged on a dirt plot with a small charcoal fire ringed by the performers. The entranced meditative chant began with dozens of sarong-clad males rocking back and forth to a guttural drone that would start off with a low slow base sound and then pick up in pitch and tempo to become rapid, quite sharp and shrill. It was reminiscent of the gradual upbeat of a moving locomotive in American Blues music. But the high-water mark of the evening was the mysterious and dreamlike Wayang Kulit, a haunting archetypal shadow puppet play. Portraying elements of the Hindu Ramayana a master puppeteer, with a cast of leather puppets on sticks, would manipulate the characters against a plain white bed sheet stretched out in front of a coconut oil lamp. With an experienced deft of hand, the audience watched the shadows of forms and characters transmute between the hard edges of reality and the softer realms of the dream world. During the show the gods sent a sign. A shooting star drew a silver line in the sky between the sheet and the edge of the stage roof. And then to add to it all, on the way home in the dark as they turned the corner to the large cinder block fence that marked the perimeter of the rice paddies and their hotel lodging, nature had its say. A silent walk morphed into a deafening audible cacophony of frogs.

Candi Dasa was on the east coast of Bali. Not many Balinese frequented the beaches in this area. They believed a pantheon of dark spirits lived in the ocean so, except for fishermen, they stayed out of the water. They placed offerings of rice in small woven doilies by front doors to protect them from the underworld, but it was fine to sacrifice the tourists to the demons of the deep. Besides, the travel industry was a good source of livelihood for the locals. Edie and Juri found a newly built beach hut right on the water so everything was clean and functioning. Though it was tiny, it was comfortable enough and for $2 a day it came with breakfast. The chickens that laid the eggs woke them early to insure they got their money's worth.

Those first weeks were an introduction to the many rich layers of Asian culture to come.

With all due respect to Singapore, it brought him back to the familiarity of glass high rises and upscale malls. It was a shiny clean city not as novel as most other Asian metropolises. Basically, it was one of the premiere shopping centers on the biggest continent on the planet. Back home he had enough trouble being accompaniment at South Coast Plaza or Fashion Island. He wasn't about to devote time out of a trip of a lifetime to window shop in a collection of retail stores that reminded him of robo-security guards on two-wheel rollers. Their stopover would be brief. Just long enough to order two hand-tailored silk shirts.

The old airport in Bangkok was at least a half-hour taxi ride out of town. And the competition for fares was fierce. Hawkers and terminal vendors would all get kickbacks so it was profitable for them to line up passengers. Everyone knew the best drivers and the best hotels. It was an onslaught of entrepreneurship. An overly intense purveyor tried to get his hooks into them. He ignored the universal palms down back-and-forth hand gesture that said they weren't interested. He refused their plea to piss-off and continued to follow them wherever they went. His persistence was more than rude and started to make Edie uncomfortable. He suggested a blue cab but they jumped into a white one. As the cab pulled away from the curb, he hopped in the front passenger seat and in rapid Thai said something to the cab driver. They told the driver they didn't want him in the cab but the driver said it would be OK. In town they ducked into a hotel and told the front desk what had transpired. After a phone call a large security guard appeared and approached the interloper. Before hotel security could confront the individual, he deftly made a retreat. They had lunch at the hotel and then, just to be sure, waited and took a place a couple of blocks over towards the river and the Royal Palace. That seemed to be a good place to start their morning excursions.

The golden spire of the stupa at Wat Phra Kaew hovering above the skyline coaxed a closer inspection. It was said to shelter a relic from the Buddha himself. From the sixth-floor balcony dining area they could see most of the Royal Palace grounds and they discussed the anticipation of their imminent visit over morning tea and breakfast. The architecture made it plainly obvious that they were in Asia. Nothing in America, save a few immigrants, could ever dream of such constructions. Color, pattern and structure defined form that no founding father had ever thought of. It was utterly another world for someone from the other side of the Pacific. The tile work begged illusion. The design came from someone else's imagination. Asian form was a whole other branch of evolution. Darwin had no idea.

They had to build a separate structure to house the Reclining Buddha. A golden prone figure, roughly 50 feet high and 150 feet long, was so large it was difficult to get a decent angle of it inside the enclosure. The premium views were below the massive feet that were inlaid with mother of pearl. The foreshortened view from the heel played mind games with perspective in an Escher-like fashion. On the palace grounds there was an overload of the senses. Variety was the operable word. Contrast and variation were everywhere. The visual cortex was on hyper drive. Spread out across the grounds in front of the gates and portals were 12 colossal Yakshas or demon guardians, all approximately 16-feet tall. The monumental statues were embellished with reflective mosaic tiles creating a sheath of iridescent light that reflected from the forms. They were the brilliant defenders of an important place.

Immediately across the river was Wat Arun, the Temple of the Dawn. Basically, a stairway to the sky, the escalade up had a pitch so steep it was important to lean into each step with hands and body for fear of losing any of the already precarious footing. The view of the city proper made for a feeling of having reached the mountaintop. Down always carried more apprehension than up. The west side of the Chao Phraya River, the channel that divided Bangkok, had a myriad of canals giving the city its western reference as the "Venice of the East". Motor scooters and tuks-tuks frequented the avenues on the east side of the river. Long boats and barges cruised up and down the canals. Water transportation dominated the west side of the city. The floating market was an unofficial co-op of local farmers who sold every imaginable crop grown in this part of Thailand. Small boats of all shapes and sizes managed their way up the channels to specific locations and tied up to each other to create a massive outdoor-floating supermarket. For the stalwart shopper, hopping from boat to boat allowed for closer inspection of goods and produce. It was, not only weekend shopping, but also an optimum photo-op. The color and bustle of the floating market was an Asian idiosyncrasy. It was emblematic of how remarkably different things were accomplished, similar in purpose, yet an obvious contrast to America's supermarkets.

They took a water taxi back across to the other side and up a couple of blocks to Wat Traimit. Housed there was an impressive historical 10-foot Buddha. As the story went, during the Japanese occupation, the statue was covered in stucco and colored glass and placed out in the open of a city park to conceal that it was actually a national treasure made out of gold weighing 5.5 tons. With the top ten sites on the list checked off and their curiosity quenched, they had the luxury of walking the streets to simply see what else they could find. Some very scarce and unusual seashells in the window of a shop caught Juri's eye. Surprisingly in this back-alley shop, city miles from the ocean, there were a good number of rare specimen seashells. He bartered for two in particular. Conus Bengalensis and Conus Gloriamaris were premiere must-have shells for any serious collector. Chances like this didn't present themselves very often so he had to be careful not to show his hand to the store proprietor. He felt an urgency he needed to conceal. The Bengal Cone and the Glory of the Seas were packaged up and shipped home to avoid the possibility of road damage with half the globe still to navigate.

It was the first time in a while they paid attention to their time frame. A decision was made to save the beaches to the south of Thailand for a future journey and head instead in the direction of Burma, a forgotten land.

There was still dispute whether it was Myanmar or Burma. Whatever it was called, it was a nation kept in the dark with its isolationist policies.

Basically, run by a strong-armed militaristic regime, travel restrictions seemed to change by the hour. When they left Thailand, they were told the length of the visa would be for only seven days. On the plane Juri sat next to an American attaché to the consulate who was probably an intelligence officer. He was military in civilian clothes and gave Juri a business card which amounted to a 'get out of jail free card' in the event of unexpected difficulties. When they landed at Yangoon International, their passport visas were stamped for two weeks. The country that was passed up by time was, in turn, passing it out. The extra seven days was a gracious perk. It was a foregone conclusion more time was better. The country had been isolated from the rest of the world practically since its independence from Britain in 1948 and definitely since the military coup of 1962. The aversion to everything British changed any name given during Great Britain's rule. So Burma became Myanmar and Rangoon was officially Yangoon. For the western eye, vehicles from around the post WWII period gave the streets of Rangoon a classic film atmosphere. Juri and Edie treated themselves to a Grand Hotel with the same name. It was lodging straight out of a period novel with high ceilings, old hardwood floors and elaborately crafted decor. The lobby was an imposing gesture and the bar suggested the likes of Hemmingway and Mailer. It was time travel going back to the era of propeller driven airplanes and war rationing. Because auto parts were not available, people used Christmas tree lights on their dashboards to be visible at night, only turning on their headlights at major intersections to be seen and to save on longevity.

The Shwedagon Pagoda was a series of extremely eclectic temples and shrines in the heart of Rangoon. At its center, the 367-foot spire of the Golden Stupa towered above all the other structures. A local man asked Juri if he was Japanese because of the professional 35-mm camera around his neck. When Juri smiled, shook his head no, the man guessed maybe Russian. It had the air of an amusement park because of its variety of curious attraction, more like Madam Tussauds than Disneyland.

A boat excursion up the Irrawaddy River to Pagan, or again if you prefer Bagan, was another assault on the senses by Asian architecture unlike anything any westerner could prepare for. Sixteen square miles of individually unique and dissimilar temples spread out over the Irrawaddy River Valley. Marco Polo wrote about his visit to Pagan and the 10,000 temples in the Middle Ages, which he called "one of the finest sights in the world". They inquired about hiring a driver to explore finer structures and monuments instead of using an archaic hit-or-miss strategy. That meant a horse-drawn buggy over rough dirt roads. The cart operator doubled as their guide through the secret passages of the stone temples as they searched for the lost ark.

Back in Rangoon they partnered with a German couple they met on the plane from Bangkok. Searching out Rangoon with them put a different perspective on the experience. Sharing travel with others colors the encounter in a totally contrasting way, compared to traveling alone, or even with one other person. Unpredictable events are compounded to a factor equal to the number of individuals. Hannah had taken a hardcore malaria pill, a newly introduced pharmaceutical. A physician in the states had advised Juri, coincidentally, not to take that particular prescription. Hannah had serious heart palpitation reactions to the drug and had to be hospitalized for a day. Dire complications tend to become more serious on the road, especially in a country like Burma.

Juri contracted an automobile driver for more adventurous expeditions to out-of-the-way regions to the east of the country. Technically, they were restricted areas, but their driver assured them he did this all the time. The regime turned a blind eye to tourist money helping the economy of the nether regions. After logging a number of miles earned the hard way, it was time to grab a bite to eat. Tin, our driver, suggested a couple of roadside restaurants but they wanted a truly authentic Burmese meal. He said he knew just the place. The ancient brown DeSoto continued down a rural road for a while. A large representation of a dragon garnished in an array of mosaic mirror shards reflected the passing car a hundred times over. They pulled up to an enormous entryway gated by homespun planks that served as shelves for literally dozens and dozens of empty colored bottles. Looking into the setting sun it was literally an arched stained-glass window that the car drove through to park in front of a rather common residency of what might be a typical Burmese family. After genuine warm greetings between two cultures that were curiosities to each other, they were shown to a hand-hewn outdoor table under the shade of a cluster of trees. Between the table and the dwelling was a pond displaying a very disturbing green color. Tin was the translator, not only between the family and the guests, but also at the moment maybe more importantly, of the menu. They selected soup, rice and curried meats accompanied by multiple small bowls of dipping sauces. What was vague was what type of meat was in the curry. Not being one to be rude or unaccommodating, Juri tasted gingerly. The main course was actually delicious and he asked for a second helping. The adults did the cooking and the children the serving. The visitors helped themselves to a multi-course meal and they all communicated with universal hand gestures and body language. Tin translated in the empty spaces and it was all smiles. It was common folk and folk with something in common, learning and sharing. The children cleared the table, and with startling possible and immediate repercussions, washed the dishes in the urgently green pond scum.

The road trip continued to a British war cemetery in the middle of nowhere. Stories on gravestones told of pilots who had been shot down by Japanese invaders. His private thoughts made an unusual request. Find a grave marker dated on the exact day Juri was born. What was crucial about that imperative? It came out of nowhere, which was exactly where he was in no man's land. Was he blown off course to discover a lost spirit who might have crossed his path when he entered the world? With some soul-searching, he found him. A British chap who became a war hero on November 7 during the Japanese occupation. It seemed they shared something in kind and he had to go behind enemy lines to find him. Forbidden territory offered up a beginning and an end.

The narrative continued. Nepal, a Buddhist country was a federal parliamentary republic. Of those attributes, Buddhism had the most traction. Flying into Kathmandu required altitude. You had to get high to fly into the foothills of the Himalayas. Nepal being the birthplace of

Buddha had a rich spiritual tradition. Monks in saffron robes were everywhere in the streets and it was everyone's duty to supply sustenance. Customarily Juri shared his almonds with anyone in robes. Conversation over offerings of food was easy and convenient. Durbar Square was the heartbeat of Kathmandu. Historically it was an area of plazas and meeting places adjacent to the royal palaces of Nepal. Long the center of trade and markets, it still was the gathering place for most social life in Nepal. It continued that role to the same degree of significance for modern day Nepalese. Shrines and temples lined the streets with their distinct tiered and stacked roofs becoming landmarks and compass points in the layout of the city. Tourists, especially, identified their whereabouts by gauging those spired rooftops that stood above the skyline of Kathmandu. One's bearings could quickly be gathered by the identification of any particular individual temple. You could feel the altitude in the air. One had to work to get their oxygen. The atmosphere was thin and there was a lightness of being. At the basecamp to Everest, the popularity of the world's tallest mountain drew both the qualified and unqualified. Evident by the masses of foreigners who assembled there, the new influx of would-be climbers of dubious expertise endangered the Nepalese Sherpa who acted as guides to summit Everest. There were a growing number of tragic stories about failed attempts by people who had little more than money to prepare for the climb. When climbing permits were attained, because of the ability to pay rather than one's standing in the climbing community, there were going to be real problems. But taking it all in at the route to the base camp on a clear day, it was easy to see what all the excitement was about.

Sitting on the bus back to town, Juri spotted a local carrying a king-sized mattress strapped to his back, walking alongside the road. Then the ante was raised when they drove by a single man carrying the entire weight of a side-by-side refrigerator in the usual Sherpa fashion with a cloth sling over the forehead and the load on his back. The last few days they became more intimate with Kathmandu on foot. Juri spent those days negotiating for a very special Thangka with a shop owner over tea. It was a mandala painting with a silk border that monks used as a narrative object of meditation. The painting was composed of concentric circles and geometric forms. They were cyclical patterns representing different heavenly and underworld realms with small deities, god-like and demonic, depending on where you were in this spiritual world. It was a lasting impression he would take with him.

Paul, along with Deb, was in Sri Lanka where he was on a teaching Fulbright at the university in Kandy. Juri and Edie were fortunate to spend time with friends in the middle of their whirlwind world tour. Kandy was a historic city in the central highlands surrounded by a bio-diverse rainforest and situated on a grand lake with a promenade circling most of its approximately 4-kilometer shoreline. In view of the lake was the Temple of the Sacred Tooth, which housed the relic of the Buddha himself. The summer festival of the Perahera, where a nightly procession of elephants paraded around the lake in lavishly lit ceremonial garb, was one of those unique and remarkable ritual events only seen in a single place on the planet.

At the house Paul and Deb leased, a Toque macaque monkey reached through the bars of the upstairs window and absconded with Edie's camera. Fortunate to see the theft, they chased after the primate until it ran up a huge tree with the 35-mm Olympus. Acquiring a hose, they shot a bold spray of water aimed at the arboreal shutterbug. Thankfully the monkey dropped the camera as it came to rest on a heavy cushion of dried leaves. In the afternoon Deb took them all on a tour of the retail crafts of Kandy. Walking the back streets and alleys in pursuit of Sri Lanka's finest silks, rugs and handiwork was a pleasure under her expert tutelage. The next day, before they set out on their own, Juri went to the university and became part of the seminar in Paul's class. The students were surprisingly eager to collaborate and reciprocate with the newly arrived visitor's points of view on the many topics they discussed. It was unquestionably a form of foreign exchange.

They were traveling through Sri Lanka at the early onset of the Tamil Tiger civil war. The minority Tamil rebels were fighting the majority Sinhalese Army. The further North you went in country the more hazardous it was. The Tamil Tigers were carrying out exceedingly more and more violent actions. The farther one went up the road the more roadblocks and sentry posts they ran into. Juri and Edie were walking the sidewalks in Colombo when a huge explosion wracked the city just a couple of blocks from where they were. The force of the exploding bomb shattered windows all around them killing a number of people. A dismembered hand was projected three city blocks from the point of the blast. It was time to head south to safer ground.

They set their sights on the southwest coast. Hikkaduwa was a surf spot featured in some of the past surf publications, but when they bused through the town past the giant rippled Buddha, there were no waves. They decided on Unawatuna, a sleepy pastoral fishing village on the southern arc of the island nation formerly known as Ceylon and for its worldwide exportation of tea. Unawatuna had a wonderful laid back coastal town feeling devoid of many tourists. A large sweeping golden sand beach studded with coconut palms and a monastery was situated on the headland of the north portion of the bay. Shaved-head monks in saffron colored robes walked the beach as Juri surfed four-foot waves on a board that had a sisal rope tied to his ankle in lieu of a rubber leash. It was a surfboard he borrowed from a fisherman in exchange for the purchase of a few irregularly shaped pearls. The waves were transparent and the pearls opalescent.

Varanasi, the revered holy center of India, was in Uttar Pradesh on the Ganges River whose sacred waters flowed out of the Himalayas. This belief was sacrosanct and inviolate in India. It was at the heart of ritual in the Hindu faith. Pilgrims came from all over to bathe in the river's waters and use funerary pyres to ceremoniously cremate their dead. These rituals were at the core of culture in this ancient city. And unlike the United States where they went to great lengths to keep death away from plain sight, in Varanasi death was an integral part of life. Facing death, especially if it wasn't your own, was a remarkably humbling and quieting experience. The ambiguity of the process required self-reflection and focus on something other than self.

Air India carried them to Agra. They sprung for an upscale hotel with a hot shower, plush towels and amenities. As he was prone to do, Juri examined their lodging down to its finest attributes. It was an assimilated travel habit of getting the lay of the land. Next to the spacious walk-in closet was another door. As he turned the doorknob and opened the entry into an adjoining suite there was a shriek of sheer terror that emanated from the canopied bed in front of him. There lounging completely naked was a young Hindustani woman. The summoning screams brought on the hotel staff, the young woman's husband and assorted other onlookers. Fortunately for Juri, early into the apologetic explanations, the hotel manager assessing the damage took responsibility for leaving the door unlocked. Juri felt like tipping the man for his courage in preventing an international incident.

In the heat of the morning haze, Agra was home to the Taj Mahal, a UNESCO World Heritage Site. Water buffalos grazed on the banks of the Yamuna River in moments of frozen time. The Taj doesn't assault you like Las Vegas does. Its subtle lines were reserved and sublime. It was to be taken in slowly in a measured way, like vintage wine, it was best savored by the senses at a slow burn. To sit by the reflecting pool next to the Taj's mirrored image of white marble was a blessing bestowed by grace. Juri imagined the artisans who selected the specific-colored stone that was used to inlay the motifs of flowers on the internal walls. They were every bit as nuanced as any master watercolor. The muted transitions of colors were anything but accidental. If he was going to have an epiphany, it was because of the overwhelming attention to detail by the designers and builders of the Seventeenth Century Mosque. If not for the Taj Mahal, the Agra Fort built a full century before would be a major attraction for any city's tourism. A notable Mughal structure that walled in a large part of the old city was also a UNESCO World Heritage Site. Having two of those in its pocket made Agra a popular destination. It had a history of sieges and valiant landlords dating back to its erection in 1565. A deep red stone color gave the ramparts a throaty tone and easily transported its current visitors back to historic times. Walking the parapets of the fortification inspired all sorts of narratives of who might have stood that same ground those centuries before.

From New Delhi, the plan was to branch out over much of India. For that they would need more rupees. It was an era before the international availability of Visa and Master Card in India. American Express travelers' checks were tedious but guaranteed safe. The British left a legacy of cumbersome mounting paperwork. India had a bad-habit backlog of everything needing to be in triplicate. Standing in line to cash travelers checks and signing-off three times for each denomination took from breakfast to lunch. The thumping blow of every official hand stamp on each carbon copy became engrained like that familiar unwanted but repeated jingle trying to sell you something you didn't need. India definitely had a noteworthy paper trail.

Throngs of people pervaded Delhi's streets and alleyways. The heat was overbearing and completely stifling. They were there in the summer, an infamous time for traveling India. The only relief were constant cold showers and lying under the ceiling fans without completely toweling off. Venturing out to eat in the early evening became a popular pastime for searching out authentic Indian food. Spices played tricks on the palate. Color was part of the cuisine. It was part of the ritual. At India's Holi festival, tinted powder was sprinkled on everything including the participants in a riotous orgy of color. At the dinner table his tendency to prefer eating with his hands was the norm. He appreciated that best-intentioned etiquette, accepted rolling rice and curry between the fingers to consume exotic tastes. Many times, in his youth at the family table he was cautioned to use silverware instead of eating with his hands. Hindu haute culture, he thought, got it right.

The travel book on India was dire about contracting illnesses in the subcontinent. Stomach flus and diarrhea could be serious, especially with dehydration in the subtropical heat. Edie contracted something that might have been from the drinking water or from one of the many meals they recently consumed. Wherever she got it, it was serious. The medication she got from the clinic didn't seem to help much. She was spending an inordinate amount of time in the room afraid she would get caught without a clean restroom. She wasn't getting any better and it was time for a medical decision. The trip was cut short after a visit to the doctor who suggested they needed to hydrate her. Doing so in London would be easier than in New Delhi. It would mean truncating the journey and canceling part of the venue to the Middle East and to Egypt. But they both thought it was a wiser and more prudent option. Juri had family in England and considered networking more supportive if needed. Dora and Anka, his father's sisters were well established and worked for BBC. The comfort of family proved to help with a positive outcome for Edie and her contracted ailment. A few days after seeing a specialist, she was back on her feet and ready to hit the pavement again. They absorbed the British Museum and the Tate over a period of days. It was more of what they had learned in school but this time in the flesh. Dora lived in Cambridge and Juri was excited to see the grounds of the hallowed institution of higher learning. There seemed to be a subtle competition between the two aunts for their nephew's attention. Anka happened to live in Oxshott and wasn't far from Wimbledon. It was the first week of July and the tennis tournament was in full swing. They bought tickets and watched an 18-year-old Boris Becker unexpectedly take the championship as a bolt of lightning struck a cornice of the grandstand knocking off a chunk of the facade.

Time had come to ticket the last stop on British Air to Los Angeles. It was well past six months since they left the west coast for the South Pacific. His passport was so full of visas and stamps from the various countries they had visited that sometime during the trip he had to stop off at a US embassy to add extra pages. The addition of the accordion fold of blank pages were soon imprinted and confirmed he had out-traveled the average vacationer. Touching down again at LAX was ritually significant. They covered much on the path of Magellan or the flight plans of orbiting astronauts. Firsts were firsts and this was Juri's initial circumnavigation. He finished a lap around the block and the world wasn't flat. He'd had half-ass attempts at it before but this was a landmark moment. He was home and home couldn't be the same.

St Kitts

CHAPTER 20

The road belonged to the people. West Indians used the road for everything, for transport, socializing and connecting. The 31 miles of shoreline was an oval lap around the island. When he first lived in Dieppe Bay, some used it for an Obeah ceremony to cast a spell on newcomers. Some even used it for mixing cement to build structures. Because it was the only hard surface available, locals would create a ring of sand and smooth gravel from the beach, fill it with cement and buckets of water and toss it all together with a shovel right there on the edge of the road. Then in buckets, it was carried to wherever it was needed, to fill in driveways, build additions onto homes and even construct entire new blockhouses from concrete mixed on the pavement. But the whole island turned out when Carnival hit the road. After King Sugar and Crop Over on St Kitts, Carnival season was holiday season. Literally. Kittitians celebrated from Christmas Eve to New Year's Day. Each Caribbean Island marked their Carnival on a different calendar page. You could travel the Lesser Antilles each month and celebrate Carnival year-round. Christmas Sports were an overture to Carnival. An array of Masquerade, Bud Bull and Moko-Jumbies that included scratch bands, steel drums and Calypso. People were in the streets. The saturated color of Carnival rivaled Trinidad and Rio. People congregated in troupes that competed against each other. The ideal was to amass the most revelers of any group with colorful outfits, usually of a uniform color. The red troupe might have a flatbed truck loaded to the gills with giant speakers blasting the Carib sound. High celebration pulsed behind the music in a snake-like procession. The green troupe might have its players in festive costume following a parade float performing multi themed skits. "Jump up" morphed elements of a marching band into something resembling a Cotton Club chorus line. "Walk up" included anyone who wanted to shadow the person in front of them in archetypal choreography.

Leaning back against a block wall around the corner from the Circus on Church Street Juri was enjoying 'studying' two ladies that stood out outfitted in blue. The music was in rhythm. They were responding to the percussion. The driving beat was harder. Their infectious dance was taunting. Simultaneously they noticed him and altered their course. They were honing in on their target. Graceful yet primal they swayed him into a corner with their legs, both of them at least as tall as he was. At the wall all forward movement stopped but the dance continued in place. The blue dancers faced him with their hands canted against the side of the building, just above his shoulders. Cornered, he raised both arms above his head to gain some small advantage of leverage. The crowd, closing in, encouraged the repartee. When the display was over Juri stood alone, the stone wall a backdrop, with the residue of blue dye from head to toe. He had a big smile on his face.

To the end of the Southeast Peninsula, from Basseterre, was another 10 miles. Turtle Beach and the Monkey Bar, named appropriately for the free-roaming African vervet primates, welcomed visitors. The beach also counted as a full-time resident a 500 lb surf hog. The huge sow would lap up the garbage from the restaurant and cool off at water's edge. Juri and his teammates on the St Kitts national volleyball team played on the beach court there on weekends. The central part of the peninsula was the expat enclave and the location of most resorts on the island. Juri lived as far away as possible on the other side of the island from the Hilton.

St Kitts was a derivation of St Christopher. On his second voyage, Christopher Columbus named the island after his patron saint. Sir Thomas Warner established the next European settlement on St Kitts in 1623. His gravestone can be read on the St Thomas Anglican Church grounds in Middle Island parish. The island is part of the Leeward West Indies and lies generally west of Antigua and Montserrat and east of the Dutch island of St Eustatius. Formerly shared by both the British and the French, the federation of St Kitts, along with its sister island Nevis, gained its independence from Britain in 1967. Its history was entrenched in sugar, the plantation system and slavery. Shortly after independence the lion's share of the economy depended on tourism.

At some level, Juri was probably trying to balance the equation for time served in Vietnam, but on the surface the Peace Corps was just another justification for an extended vacation. It started with cultural sensitivity training in Miami and then a homestay in Barbados with Senator John Wickham and his wife Esme. Edie and Juri spent two weeks settling into West Indian life at their host's home on the south end of Barbados. John was a noted author and an editor at both BIM and the Nation Magazine. John and Juri would have long ranging conversations late into the night. After Juri moved on to St Kitts, they continued to correspond back and forth for a while. It was all too short a period of time and Juri wished it might have been longer.

The spectacular panorama of Dieppe Bay and the dominant cratered peak where the Atlantic met the Caribbean caught them unprepared. Out on the reef, the view clutched at them before they could drink it all in. They knew this was where they wanted to live. Dieppe Bay was an old French Fort with ruins of antique stone blocks recycled everywhere, probably quarried in the Seventeenth and Eighteenth Centuries in the British Isles as counterweight for the ships. From the promontory, the overview of town gave away secrets of plantation days. In the direction of the sea cliff was the skeleton of a time worn windmill that was used to grind sugar cane back in the day. Branching off from the main island road on one of the side streets that led to the landing and the one singular anomaly in the village was the Golden Lemon. It almost fit into the surroundings, being constructed out of similar large block stones that pretended to be ballast from the Middle Passage. But it was one of those resorts that would appear in respectable travel periodicals that had a flavor of bygone times of big estate houses with large crystal globed hurricane lamps on the tables. The trim, both on the place settings and the carved detail on the eaves, was a tasteful muted yellow. What he liked about the hotel was that it employed a number of locals. From its tables when the tropic clouds were favorable, you could see Mt Liamuga, the mother of the island, lying on her back, milking the sky. From the open portico balcony of the Golden Lemon, you could look out onto the northernmost spit of land on the island and be as far away from Basseterre as you could get. In the mornings Juri would walk past the restaurant of the resort on the beach path to gauge the swell crossing the reef, maybe 250 meters out in the bay. From there he could conclude which direction to go and which surf spots would be most advantageous. He even gave the reef at Dieppe Bay a go one time but it was kind of scary with a real strong rip that emptied out the little anchorage on the out-going tide. On a day after the surf season when the surface was totally calm, he went out snorkeling only to find giant antler coral sticking up in the impact zone, like punji stakes, right where he was surfing a few months earlier.

Going east was the bay at Saddlers with a semi point break that ended up in a playful beach break. It was right on the main road and often cars would stop on the embankment to watch the only two local surfers that he knew on the island. And hopefully, if the swells were big, mostly in winter and spring, they would head out to a concealed beach by driving through the sugarcane fields to an inconspicuous, unmarked spot bypassed by the main road that was home to a wave that was to die for. Somewhere south of Newton Ground and up and around Sandy Point was a reef break that you had to work to get to. One of his Kittitian friends told him about a former Peace Corps volunteer, a few years prior, who would walk to this spot with a surfboard. Luckily for Juri, Desmond followed the dude one day to get a shady glimpse of some of the interests of North American visitors. What he saw was a peeling reef break, one fine 15-ft "A" frame, makeable in both directions. And just to the north, a slightly smaller wave that wrapped around a small rocky bend in the beach that was rapid transit for much of its preordained long distance. It was a right-breaking wave and if you made it past the take off and the first large boulder, you were in for a treat. Juri was stupefied at his good fortune. Volunteerism had brought him to the Caribbean and an undiscovered wave worthy of all the surf magazines.

The first night, he slept in his tidily built cinder block and mortar rental on the main road that had been sitting vacant for a while. Before he could rig up the mosquito net and hang it from the ceiling, he woke with a strange stabbing pain on his thigh. It progressed to the point he thought about going to the hospital. Mostly, he didn't want to do that. While the private doctors were good, the facilities left a little to be desired. He described the severe pain as a throbbing toothache through his entire body. Sitting on the edge of the bed at home, then he would lie down out of pain, then sit up again, and contemplate the hospital. This dance continued through the night until the pain subsided. In the morning he went to see a doctor who spotted two tiny black puncture marks on his leg. By the looks of it, the doc said, he was bitten by an especially large centipede.

The green bananas hanging from the ceiling of the split-level kitchen were still not ripe, so he settled for packaged raisins on his cereal. Fruit that wasn't fresh and handpicked in the tropics was an oxymoron. When he cut papayas and threw the seeds out the slatted window over the sink, within days, there would be new fruit for the picking. The breadfruit tree in the back yard offered a potato substitute of fries and breadfruit mayonnaise salad. He would constantly mock himself for banging his head on the low overhead leading down to the split-level kitchen until he figured out tacking a small ribbon to the beam solved the problem of a squatting 6' 2" novice negotiating the cramped set of stairs. After a heavy rain, the tiny finger frogs would invade the downstairs through the open glass strips of the storm windows. Water and electricity for the last week had not been a hassle. The eight people next door, Vanta, her boyfriend Polo and six kids, shared a shed not much bigger than Juri's bathroom. They all started to stir. The naked body of an eight-year-old boy stepped away from their backdoor making wet patterns in the dirt. All of them shared breadfruit and vegetables from the tree and garden in his yard. It was much like living in a fishbowl. Keith Roy an adolescent boy from the village who had a crush on Edie, whom he called Lizbeth, would hang out in the backyard breadfruit tree. It was like having your own bird dog that visited all the time.

Juri decided to go into the office to take care of an administrative issue, to check on the status of the motorcycle that had been promised him almost three months earlier. There was plenty of frustration to go around whether it was then or now. He was a poster of *Easy Rider* staring down a deserted road waiting for a Japanese van, loaded with West Indians, speaking English harder to understand than a menu in a Greek café. *Yah mon*. He was rocketing through the villages like a giant green toboggan run. Called buses, they were more accurately minivans, operating under a different set of transportation rules than other vehicles. If he didn't look with a discerning eye, everything was clean and green. He loved the sights and smells of the developing world but some piles were esthetic and some just didn't make it. He sometimes thought the way people heaved trash around without awareness; you might as well be in a life size pinball game where litter buys you a replay. In truth, it all worked environmentally, before plastic packaging and canned food. Organic waste was tossed into the cane fields with impunity to break down and wash into the soil. Not too many cane cutters of old ordered at fast food outlets with their superfluous wrappings, although there was talk about a future KFC coming to Basseterre. Juri had a window seat when a local next to him finished his Coke, handed him the empty and asked him to toss it…*"No way"*. The guy had no clue as to what Juri was saying. The van slowed at a small one-room bank on the edge of town. The bus pulled over to get at least 2 wheels off the pavement as one of the larger ladies in the back climbed over people to disembark. Without a legible word uttered, she entered the building while the bus sat idling. She completed her banking in short order and re-boarded the van. No one complained. Apparently, it didn't inconvenience anyone. The bus deposited passengers next to a pier that had planks literally falling off it.

There next to the dock, only a precarious couple of feet from taking out the whole wharf, were the rusty bones of a beached freighter, a reminder of a summer storm with some Anglo namesake etched on its eroded stern. He turned the corner to the Ballyhoo, an upbeat restaurant in a two-story colonial on his left and the Royal Bank of Canada on the right in a neoclassical whale that housed his Eastern Caribbean dollars. On the next street over was Warner Park where the slave auction block stood. In the past, the shackled were marched directly off the galley ships and purchased there on the spot by their new masters. Abject humor became the sandpaper that scraped away the coarseness of bondage and its patina has lasted to the present day. Juri's next tack was past the Circus, a Rococo clock in the middle of an asphalt roundabout. Then he hung a right, ducked into an enclosed wooden stairway and into an office that looked like it was paneled from a salvaged trailer park. Isilin, the Peace Corps secretary, nodded a sympathetic expression. She was telling him not to waste his time asking. The current story was the boat from Antigua was not stopping at Montserrat where the most recent motorcycle he lined up was located. The previous volunteer went home over six weeks ago.

Walking down Bay Road in the oppressive heat with his black backpack and improvised duct-taped cardboard portfolio he could absolutely sense it working. He was using the least minimal amount of energy to move. The stifling temperatures that took their toll on him the first few months, he was now having some measure of success coping. He was experiencing the cultural meaning of *"cooling it"*. A couple of miles to the west and at the edge of Basseterre, he reached the triangular block created by the splitting of the main road that was home to the Teachers College. His entry, surrounded by a high stone block wall, presented the regal dilapidated remains of the former British hospital. The courtyard, in a state-of-disrepair, quietly stared him down. The jungle had breached down the mountain and somehow managed to crossover the fringes of town and overgrew the compound. King palms and mango trees helped transport him back to the narrative of a bygone time. But his movie, the one he was experiencing now, was just as delicious. There was a circular drive leading to what was the buildings' entrance. He took a shortcut through the knee-high grass path, past a fountain in the middle of a small entry plaza. The fountain was half full with water that was a green he didn't have to describe. Floating in it was a doll's head, half a door and one shoe. He plodded up the concrete stairs and into the structure where there was no floor, just a single board gangway spanning over the foundation about four feet below. He resurfaced in the back courtyard past old relics of Nineteenth Century hospital paraphernalia. There in sight behind a huge African tree with at least a 300-year memory was the two-storied u-shaped structure that was artfully labeled The Saint Kitts-Nevis Teachers Training College. The 'good mornings' coming his way were much more spontaneous and genuine than three months ago. Wednesday's group was dicey at the beginning of the term, but he had to say, were light years from when classes started. He couldn't have hoped for what they were achieving. Acceptance came with laughter and jovial enjoyment. Students from other classes would visit. Some even became unofficial regulars. Juri recollected that in plantation days the only forms of art that were tolerated were music and dance. And then, formally, only during Carnival, it was one of the only creative outlets available to those that didn't purchase passage to the New World. The newly generated art classes were something novel for them. Most of his students like Jasmine, Glenroy and Stanley had never had the opportunity to take art classes, not even in primary school. For people who couldn't brush a paint-by-numbers canvas, it was dramatic what they were doing with the nuances of color. At the beginning, holding their attention for the entire one-and-a-half-hour session was a challenge, but now it seemed like half an hour. This particular day he had to request they stop painting in order for him to be prompt for an appointment at the ministry. He had some space in his week because the editorial committee for the social sciences book *Our Country,* he was helping art direct, was in its last re-writes. Peter, a British liaison to the Ministry of Education, procured a grant to publish the book. In two weeks Juri would be buried with work. He contacted a printer in California he had a professional relationship with to bid the job competing with printers in London and Jamaica. He stopped in at Cultural Affairs to check on the proposal for a National Gallery and Performing Arts Center. Word was positive and now more than just an idea.

There was an occasion when he saw a rental car with surfboards strapped to the roof heading towards Saddlers on the main road from the landing of his house. He jumped on his newly acquired Honda two-stroke and chased the visiting surfers down. Company in the water would be a good thing for him, a far cry from crowded days at Church or Trestles, surf spots in California. Prior to the Floridians, the only other people in the water with him were friends visiting from home or the local kids he was giving lessons. Last week he was out surfing at the secret spot when a car pulled up the dirt road in the cane field. A guy in Speedos waxed up a yellow board and paddled out. In the surfing world Speedos weren't your typical surf wear, at least not without board shorts over them. He felt a little like Robinson C. when he first spotted Friday. Juri said… *"howdy"* and the dude responded… *"hola que tal?"* They spoke a bit of Spanish and then some English. Turned out he was second in command at the Venezuelan Embassy. He used to live blocks away from a good friend of Juri's when he was going to school in San Diego. After some friendly conversation he offered Juri his embassy's help with the proposed center. He said they could offer art and music exchanges and even some bucks. He mentioned that he used to book rock concerts in Caracas. This wasn't golf but it was good business negotiation in the water. His wife and two-year old daughter were both stunning and they all became best of friends. They had a car so reaching more remote spots was a little easier.

The only other consulate on island was the Taiwanese. After on a staff member's son, Eric a child prodigy, enrolled in Juri's adult art class at the University of the West Indies Basseterre campus. After Juri left Cultural Affairs to meet up with Marvene, a 61-year-old from Oklahoma for a bite to eat, they ran into Ron, another volunteer from Jackson Hole via Boston. A very energetic individual, he was an ex-ski bum, political radical. He also accomplished a lot with remedial reading and building up a library from scratch. They joined appetites at Jong's, one of three Chinese establishments on St Kitts, for chicken and potato roti with spring rolls. Juri guzzled two guava juices, Marvene a frosty Carib and Ron had a bottled Ting. At any given time, the evening class had an enrollment of about 25. Dennis, who had taken a computer graphics course in Toronto while visiting his sister, was one of the serious students. Being entrepreneurial, he started a silkscreening business. Juri helped Dennis with a project to produce beach towels for hotels in the Virgin Islands had consulted a personal friend from Laguna who had contact with a good field rep in the Caribbean. And Juri did some designs for a line of t-shirts for Dennis's retail shop in town. Dennis was a savvy businessman. His little retail shop was doing well selling to tourists and he was always looking to expand.

The facilities at the University Center were a little more contemporary. It was a more recent structure than the teachers' college where once on the second floor, the legs of a student's chair with the student in it, fell through the wooden floor down to the plastic seat leaving the pupil sitting at a right angle on what remained of the floor. The University Center however had modern administrative offices, about six classrooms and a small library. It faced Basseterre Bay adjacent to the War Memorial, a smaller version of the obelisk in Washington DC, and the tourist digs at Fisherman's Wharf. Class was out at 7:30 and before he had his motorbike, if he missed the last bus to Dieppe Bay he would be stranded in town and would have to stay with Andrew for the evening. Making it home, first thing in the door, he was greeted by two kittens. Sugar and Cane were found in the fields when they were no bigger than the size of his hand. When the sugarcane was ready for crop they lit fire to the fields to expose the bottom of the stalks to speed up cutting the harvest. Lots of feral wildlife, including mongoose, were orphaned. After acknowledging the cats, it was time for a cold shower. Hot showers were rare and in the same category as broccoli, art supplies and good books. It was a few years before much public use of the Internet and it was a long day.

The next morning was starting to make its appearance through the mosquito netting that draped over two single beds held together by a California King fitted sheet that came on the flight from L.A. Besides the residue of some vague dreams, he was aware of two things; that it was hot already and the sun wasn't even up. There must have been at least a dozen dissonant noises simultaneously claiming still air. The country sounds of goats, chickens, birds, frogs, dogs, donkeys and surf pounding on the reef seemed to massage his brain. All this was a conduit from dreamtime to waking. The grating of the squealing brakes and annoying honking of a factory bus rousting out a constantly-late female worker at precisely five minutes to six every morning was something you could set your watch to. Culturally there was absolutely no inhibition. To consider or respect anyone else's sleep was not part of the fabric here. Cane cutters were already yelling for their friends from the street, never mind who might have had a long night. Behind the cane, out of sight, he could hear the miniature orange train that carried sugar stalks to the factory on the other end of the island on the outskirts of Basseterre. It was all a go, day and night during crop.

As he self-adjusted into daily illusion, his focus was on the sound of the ocean. His morning ritual was to walk past Foster's house up to the promontory just past the old mill. You could tell the French had been there by peering over the edge of the bluff to spot the remains of two cannons that were submerged in shallow water. One evening, needing something to quench his thirst, he walked into the village center to a shop that sold cold drinks and a few groceries and confections. He walked past rudely colored huts and a rum shop to get the beverages. It was actually someone's home that sold goods out of an open French door, bodega style. They had a working TV high on the counter next to the door that attracted bystanders who weren't necessarily customers. As Juri walked up, there was some commotion. A young local man in his mid-twenties was shouting, then yelling, at a female maybe a couple of years younger than he was. The disagreement got louder then quickly became ugly. The young man was getting physical and started hitting her. Juri stepped between the two as things got out of control. The heat was turned up as different factions weighed in. Luckily, with the sheer numbers of people in the fray, there was a lot of talking but little more to back it up. Dewayne, the bus driver he had grown to know, pulled him aside after things settled down and told him, in a sincere but serious manner, to never do that again. Juri was the visitor and their problems were to be handled their way. Dewayne was looking out for him and didn't necessarily see it the same way as the young man, but that it had to be settled by the people involved. Juri told him that he couldn't look the other way and was told it might not end up well if it were to happen again. Juri was between a rock and a hard place and struggling over both sides of the issue, although he felt violence should never supersede in any resolution. When he got back to the house with his drinks, he realized that the only non-West Indian in the village tried to control the situation, so much for his cultural sensitivity training.

The Organization of Eastern Caribbean States was the larger governing body overseeing the region. It regulated trade and was responsible for the health of the Eastern Caribbean dollar, the currency of the islands. In the domain of sport, O.E.C.S. presided over all athletic endeavors that related to the Lesser Antilles. The St Kitts National Volleyball Team fell under that umbrella. Andrew, who was on St Kitts when Juri arrived, was assigned as a sports specialist working with the island's youth. He specialized in youth volleyball development, his field of expertise, and he was the National Team coach. Originally from Cleveland he did his college studies in Sweden. Juri was completely in awe of the skills Andrew displayed with conflict resolution. He was always adept at problem solving in situations that seemingly were at an impasse. His acuity was recognizing the specific issues that needed attention for people to come to the table and negotiate. Juri confronted Andrew about his uncanny ability to diffuse situations without any of the parties in question feeling they gave up too much or that they were unheard. Andrew attributed it to his Scandinavian education, having done graduate work in Sweden. As students, they were grouped into units of four individuals, but after on, their outcome and their evaluations depended on the performance of the weakest individual in the group. They learned to work as a team and pick up the least capable. That required identifying everyone's personal strengths and matching them to the group's needs.

The National Team was a natty group of West Indians with Juri as the token European. The local players were long on athletic prowess, but except for a few, short on volleyball experience. One of those few was Glenn Quinlan. Educated at the University of the Virgin Islands, he was Mr. Volleyball on St Kitts. He was the head of SKAVA and a representative in NORSECA and other international volleyball bodies. When Juri first arrived on St Kitts his two-week homestay was two doors up from where Glenn lived. During games they ran complicated stacks, one's and X's. When Juri was setting the ball, he would be looking up at the bottom of his teammate's sneakers. The hitters' jumping ability was top-shelf. Andrew shaped the team into a competitive unit. There were no gymnasiums on island so the only options were asphalt or concrete courts. Matches against other islands were played at the hard-court stadium at Warner Park where the cricket pitch was located. They practiced at multiple venues, both in Basseterre and other island communities. Since a number of players were from Molineux, on the quieter less-populated side of the island where there was a large Rasta contingent, practice was often held on their courts. Iwah, Imba and Ghana were Molineux regulars. One night after a long, extended practice on a new moon night, Juri rode his Honda 125 home in the dark on the remotest stretch of road on the island. Tired and in a rush to get home, he played the throttle a bit more than he should. Somewhere between Mansion and Tabernacle, he experienced a sudden light-headed jolt of adrenaline after he realized he had narrowly missed a large black pig in the middle of the dark road by inches. It wasn't until he was by the sow that it dawned on him what had just happened. On another night returning to Dieppe Bay in almost the same spot, he saw a blue triangular light low to the horizon on the Atlantic side traversing from southeast to northwest at an inexplicable rapid rate of speed and running absolutely silent. He thought to himself this was a stretch of road he should avoid on the upcoming holiday of All Hallows Eve.

St Lucia was in town and an opponent St Kitts had never defeated. St Lucia as a more developed island had four times the population and certainly more resources. Clearly the home contingent was a definite underdog. With a healthy crowd in the stands, St Kitts dominated the first game of the match as a result of a well-coached and efficiently executed effort. Their practices were paying dividends. In the end they lost a close match when St Lucia realized they had to pick up their game. It was a competition they could feel good about and the program could build on.

Many of the players would continue with their sand game at Turtle beach on off days. And then in a match against Anguilla, in the upcoming month, they defeated the neighboring island's squad. Juri sat down with one of the Anguilla players after the competition and they exchanged phone numbers and stories. Winston related a riveting episode of when he was an evening attendant at Anguilla's Clayton J Lloyd Airport a couple of years before. The airstrip was rated only for smaller aircraft. St Martin oft-traveled tourist mecca to the west of Anguilla received much more traffic than its much smaller sister island. The two airports were barely 10 miles apart. Winston retold the story he probably shared a hundred times of a Pan Am 747 flight that mistook the airstrip at Anguilla for the one at St Martin. Winston, on duty in the waning dusk hours with poor visibility, noticed the jetliner with its running lights on and it landing gear down, drifting in for a touchdown. He scrambled the pickup and raced to the edge of the runway halfway to the end of the strip with lights flashing. He jumped out with his batons lit up and began waving off the aircraft. He confided he was about to bail out when the plane did a severe up on its descent. He said the plane was within a 100ft of the ground. Juri mulled over the idea of what a 747 landing on a strip meant for much smaller aircraft, and even if it landed without running out of runway, how in the world could the Boeing ever get off the ground again. Juri thought his friend had earned a generous bonus. Winston never heard from Pan Am. They probably didn't want the publicity. He was full of stories. On another occasion he was swimming in a remote cove on Anguilla where a large blue yacht anchored in the bay. He stroked over to welcome the boat to his island when the bushy haired sailor turned out to be Bob Dylan.

Peace Corps volunteers on St Kitts, who were issued motorcycles, were called *"yellow heads"* by Kittitians. They were all assigned bright yellow, open, crash helmets that required goggles. Outside of Keys Village in a hairpin turn, Tom had a wasp fly into the opening of his helmet and by the time he negotiated the road and pulled to the side to attend to the crazed attacker, his head had swollen to the point he couldn't take off his helmet. He was ambulanced to the hospital where they had to saw off the headgear.

Juri visited him in the hospital where his head looked like a giant pumpkin. Juri had his own close call one day going into the office to pick up his mail. An ambulance with its siren and lights was coming up behind him on Cayon St. When he inched over his back tire hit a mossy patch on a u-shaped drain channel and he lost control and laid the bike down. Prone on the street he remembered the tires of the ambulance narrowly missing his helmet by centimeters. It was the only time in two years he hit the ground with his motorcycle, not to say there weren't other close calls.

Juri was given directions to an event at the cane factory on Taylor Range Road. The woman told him to turn right at the stop sign, then go as far as the sleeping policeman and turn left into the circular drive. Easy enough, he thought. Keeping an eye out for a Kittitian traffic cop *'liming'* on the side of the road he thought had pulled pretty good duty. Turned out a *'sleeping policeman'* was simply a big yellow speed bump. There were a few things you didn't see much on the roads of St Kitts. There were next-to-no traffic signals and semi-trucks and even fewer freeway overpasses. One day at the other major hairpin turn on the island, wearing his yellow helmet, Juri turned the corner around the hill at Challengers and there, taking up both lanes of the road, was a red semi-truck with a large trailer jackknifing into the turn. Without time to think it through, he rode right up the hill to avoid the big rig. Good thing it was a dirt bike. There was something about yellow helmets and hairpin turns.

A bat in the house must have been an omen. The windows were habitually left cracked open to allow cooling trade winds to breeze through the house and one of the screens fell off. Juri was a novice at trying to catch a bat in the family room with a bucket. It reminded him of an old vaudeville routine on black-and-white TV. With a little bit of training, he thought they would make excellent drones. The Navy tried it with dolphins.

Things were going south again with the relationship. Juri's work was fruitful. Edie's wasn't. She had resentment about the freedom that his motorcycle afforded him. He tried to include her. He had a special seat welded on the back for tandem use. She wanted her own motorcycle and her job description at the school didn't qualify her. But it was more than that. It was baggage that they had brought with them. He had offered her work with the book project through the education ministry. Juri gave her the photographic responsibility for the publication. None of it worked. They were at an impasse and constantly butting heads. He was spending more and more time in his head about what the options were. He had visited this hypothetical place too many times before.

Fateful words, he simply came out and told her he couldn't do this anymore.

Things were said and once the genie was out, there was no going back. It got ugly. They went too far, a regrettable distasteful ingress. Not his proudest moment. It was an emotional ambush.

He noticed smoke drifting from the backyard. In a burning pile of leaves, under the breadfruit tree, was a bonfire. Edie was barbequing his surfboard. His instinct was to rescue the board. Mistakenly he grabbed the board by the rails and then immediately dropped it from the heat of the burning paraffin wax. He scalded his palms and fingers but managed to yank on the leash and jerk the board out of the fire. The melted, disfigured board represented what had just happened to the relationship.

As they went to their corners, there was the silence of a shrill moment. He could feel the confinement in his head. More words for justification needed to be shouted out at the top of his voice that he kept trapped in. The quietness needed to be muzzled. But she had retribution in mind. Genesis was being aborted again. Now she was threatening to withhold the photographs for the social science book project he had been working on for over a year. A line was finally crossed that couldn't be repaired. He had to look at the end as a new beginning.

Edie moved in with Carolyn in Basseterre. Juri found a place next to the ghut in Sandy Point. Their time at Dieppe Bay was over. Truth be told, it was time for new friends and new neighbors. He rode his dirt bike up into the rain forest and brought back exotics. He strapped lobster-claw heliconia, small starter palms and delicate tree ferns to the frame of the custom back seat on his bike. They added a nice touch of color to his landing. Sitting on the porch, passers-by gave him the thumbs up.

Additional trips up the mountain, the anonymous gifts spruced up the neighborhood. In an act of gratitude, the lady next door put a mason jar of tamarind jam on his landing. Running a nursery on wheels made for new present-day friends. Cuttings from his new backyard made for his preferred morning brew of lemon grass tea.

There was a group of four young ladies that sat on the roadside next to his gate. They constantly platted and cornrowed each other's hair. Anytime he returned from town and parked his motorbike inside the gate, they demurred. The *youths* spoke in heavy pidgin when they didn't want him to understand. He wasn't sure if they were *studying* him, but he would *go up so* to find *she sister.* There was a construct that was foreign to his ear when he first arrived on St Kitts but now he was getting the gist of things. They even beaded two small braids on the left side of the back of his head.

His new location cut the drive time to the surf spot in half. A 20-minute ride was now five or ten. Over the course of the next month, he knew every bump and puddle in the road by heart. Road perfect. Buzz came out for a surf visit from Hatteras, bringing with him a patch kit. They spent a day filling cavities and grinding down the freshly set resin. As luck would have it there were no waves his entire stay. Not that they didn't try. One day they had a tiny two-foot swell and Buzz courteously said he could see the potential in the place. Juri was disappointed he couldn't showcase the perfect wave. Surfing alone after Buzz left made for ample introspection. Resolution of rationale and emotions didn't operate on the same schedule. He came to terms with the logical side of it sooner than he did with the emotional aspects. So in other words, he was so-so. He knew time would heal. But how he was seen by other volunteers, especially the women who lived in town in proximity to Edie, took a toll. He would hop on his motorcycle and take the road on the backside past Molineux and Cayon then dodge fallen mangoes on the dirt track over Monkey Hill to Andrew's house. That's what good friends were for.

Romney Manor was built on a finger of the rain forest that encroached down the mountain close to the Caribbean Sea. It was a renovated old plantation converted into a batik factory that entertained tourists with its premiere botanical gardens highlighted by a 400-year-old Saman tree with Carib and African memories. Its branches had a footprint of about half an acre. Bromeliads and a variety of air ferns carpeted its elevated limbs. Majestically this tree was truly a centerpiece. People felt the history underneath it. The most noted tourist site on St Kitts was just up the road. Sightseers bused and taxied in from Brimstone Hill, a massive British fort on a singular conical hill with its cannons overlooking the Caribbean side of the island. Historically, Brimstone Hill was shared with the French for a short period when they co-administered the island with the British. A battery of bronze cannons stood visible on the ramparts. The documented presentation inside the garrison spoke to the days when some of America's leading revolutionaries walked its grounds and sailed its waters. John Paul Jones had a brief hand in Kittitian archives. Alexander Hamilton was born on the sister island of Nevis and surely was familiar with the layout of the fortress. The first British settlers on the island in 1623 led by Sir Thomas Warner cohabited peacefully for about three years with the native inhabitants. The land was brutally confiscated from Carib Chief Ouboutou Tegremante at the Battle of Bloody Point near Challengers village in 1626. It was then granted to the great-great-great grandfather of Thomas Jefferson who subsequently sold 10 acres of what became known as the Wingfield Estate to the Earl of Romney. The Romney Manor estate, after a short period of farming tobacco, shifted to more lucrative cane sugar and byproducts of molasses and rum.

Morris, the current owner of Romney Manor and the one responsible for reclaiming the estate from the jungle, commissioned Juri to paint an original mural sign to go out on the main island road. He and Morris built a strong enough working relationship that Morris asked him to do a long-term project photographing the island and the relics of its history for the posterity of St Kitts and Romney Manor. Morris chartered a helicopter and a pilot to get the dramatic aerial perspectives. Juri sat on the ledge of the open side door with his feet on the skids, hooked in only by a flat strap and an oversized carabiner. He had his Canon at the ready, a 35 mm SLR. The drama came when the pilot started doing cartwheels and 360's deep down and into the volcanic crater on Mt Liamuiga and then a fly over of Brimstone Hill. To build on the daredevil aspect of the project, he rented a jeep to off road to more inaccessible views. He found a steep track up a vertical grade with a panorama of the southeast peninsula and the entire island of Nevis in the backdrop. The jeep was now on two narrow parallel strips of concrete reaching its steep terminus end. Just as it was about to crest the top of the hill, it drifted slightly to the right and lost its upward momentum. Compounding the problems were bald tires, loose gravel and a precipitous drop-off over the left edge. The almost-vertical jeep started to slip backwards slowly down the incline. Juri applied the brakes to stop the slide. The vehicle continued on its unintentional descent backwards down the hill with his foot implanting the brake to the floorboard. He would soon be in free fall if he didn't do something quickly. He caught a glimpse of a small boulder in the left side mirror. He attempted to steer backwards in its direction. What if he missed his target? It worked. The jeep hit the boulder before it had picked up too much speed. It impeded any further slide down the slope. He sat there stone quiet for a moment, playing out different scenarios in his head. How the hell was he going to turn the vehicle around and get back down to sea level? A tow truck was out of the question. There was no way it could negotiate up the steep grade. He walked down the hill to the main road. At just that moment a beer truck came over the rise. He flagged it down and explained his conundrum. *"No problem."* Are you kidding me? What do you mean no problem? A little experience and a lot of island ingenuity. Two of them, the truck driver and Juri stood on the front bumper and with their full weight rocked the jeep up and down while the larger assistant grabbed the back bumper from underneath and with each upswing inched the vehicle farther and farther to the right until it had come full circle and was pointing in the desirable down-hill direction. It was like they had done this before. Juri was more than happy to buy them lunch and a couple of the Caribs they had delivered at the Monkey Bar.

He self-started a project when he discovered shards of broken chinaware in the cane fields. St Kitts had a gradual slope from the sea to the rainforest and the volcanic peaks. The cane fields were planted on the fertile alluvial fans. After tropical rains, the runoff would expose these shards that locals called *"chaney"*. They were remnants of broken china that cane cutters and plantation workers ate their meals from. When the imported plates, which came from the big estate houses, broke in the fields they were discarded, only to resurface on the cane roads after years of exposure to weather. With each individual shard there was a specific story, rich in history, invoking mystery. At first, he walked the cane roads, much like beachcombing, looking for these unique shards. He then employed school kids to go out and find them. They were paid five dollars for each plastic gallon full, a fair exchange for everyone. Soon he had enough inventory to start inlaying them into the concave recesses carved out of wooden frames he had custom built at the Craft House on Bay Road. The outside part of the frames would be brightly painted like Caribbean houses and patterns and the inlaid shards, colorful on their own, would be supplemented by assorted other objects he found on his field excursions. There were broken parts of clay smoking pipes and stems, old glass and bone, remnants of porcelain figurines, boar tusks and doll parts. This would all be an assemblage in a mosaic style that would then work as a picture frame or a fixture for an interior designer's custom mirror. These frames were entirely created and produced by local Kittitians. No two were alike and the components dated back, in some cases, as far as 300 years. They begged the stories of those that used the china in the fields all so long ago.

Juri planned a hike to the crater. The Mt Misery climb had a meaningful effect on him. Tony, a British VSO, was one of Andrew's best friends and suggested the trek in honor of Andrew's return stateside. Everyone missed him, evident by all the genuine goodbyes from volunteers, but mostly by local West Indians he befriended over the course of two years. Besides Tony, Dave and Paul from Nevis joining Juri, were two Kittitian buddies of Andrew. Bridges and Troy worked with him at the Sports Ministry and were far more familiar with the strenuous ascent. Fortunately, the entire four-hour summit offered up a beautiful day and clear cloudless sailing to the top. The view from the highest point on St

Kitts confirmed the exceptional place they lived and a special feeling for their departed friend.

A closure of service conference for EC-47 was scheduled for Barbados. The same group of volunteers he trained with in Miami and Barbados on his way into the Peace Corps before they were all assigned to various Eastern Caribbean Islands was going to gather one last time in Bridgetown. Steve and Juri hatched up a plan to piggyback a journey through the Leeward and Windward Islands in conjunction with the final conference that already guaranteed passage to Barbados. It was taking advantage of an opportunity to reconnect with like-minded adventurers they met two years ago and also include an exploration of most the islands of the Caribbean. Juri also was looking forward to spending time with Senator John Wickham and his wife Esme on Barbados again, especially the walk done so many times from Oistins to Ferney that left nothing but good feelings and longing.

At the COS, it was heartening to see familiar faces with two years' worth of Caribbean experience affixed to their resumes. They all had lots to talk about and much to compare. As with most of the related experiences, it was fascinating to parse similarities and differences. The homecoming kindled a sense of quiet accomplishment and the closing of another chapter. The conference itself was administered by government contractors who seemed empty and out of touch. They were mostly bureaucrats who didn't have a practical knowledge of the trials and accomplishments of what the individuals in front of them had gone through. They were hired to help with a transition, but for the most part, they were just earning a buck. The real closure happened when the conference was over and the volunteers got together afterwards to break bread and toast a few. Juri's insights came with Linda, Marian and Barb.

After a perfect meal of shredded salad, steamed carrots and christophine, mashed potatoes and conch complimented with tea and ice cream, a star quietly shot a line mimicking the contour between a dark sky and a darker jungle ridgeline. After he returned to his room, Edie called. She braved enough strength and risk to initiate speaking without anger for the first time in four months. Talking and knowing it was over and without any recrimination allowed his soul to breathe again.

A praying mantis devoured its victim on the white handle of a porcelain toilet. Feeling pain was erased and all that remained of it was a slight chalky residue.

The next morning was April Fool's Day. He woke at 4:50 to meet Steve for their early flight to St Vincent. LIAT stands for Leeward Islands Air Transport or as West Indians call it 'Luggage In Another Town'. After checking in and depositing their carry-ons in their room, they walked the waterfront along the harbor district. The large open-air market was alive with the bartering of early morning activity. About a half-mile up the road were the celebrated Botanical Gardens that were established in the mid 1700's. Much of the flora was well entrenched. Steve had a wonderful long conversation with an St Vincent parrot, a delightful colorful individual, large as far as parrots go, with an absolutely white head. At a quick glance it could easily be mistaken for a bald eagle at almost the same size. It was the national bird of St Vincent and the only place on the planet it could be found, unless a category four or five blew it off course. Waiting for the boat to Bequea, they sampled the goods at a bakery near the dock as the ship was pushing off right on time, unusual for anything in the Caribbean except sea going vessels. It was eat and run on the gangway. St Vincent and the Grenadines were a charming string of isles, each with their own distinct character running southward to Grenada, the same island that was once in the cross hairs of the Regan administration.

Bequia was off the beaten path as far as Caribbean travel went. It catered to vacationers who were willing to go the extra mile. On a secluded stretch of sand, they saw a row of very small well-crafted sailing skiffs that were part of the only formal whaling fleet in the Caribbean sanctioned by the International Whaling Commission. The tiny colorful dinghies were more like model boats but were especially seaworthy. The Commission allowed a quota of four whales during the season. Many offered the greener option of whale watching as an alternative for their livelihood. Mid-day, Steve and Juri boarded the Snapper, a mail boat from Bequia. It was more of a cargo boat, with people, chickens and all sorts of palettes of precious commodities piled in every empty corner of the ship. They chose the top deck in the light of the sun, took off their shirts and fell asleep in the warmth of the day with a first-class view of deep blue waters. The four-and-a-half-hour sail was interrupted by a marlin doing aerial acrobatics off the starboard side. Small launches carried cargo and passengers from the middle of the bay on Mayreau. There was no wharf for the Snapper. Loading and unloading was old-school style. Everything was taken on and off board by the small launches in numerous back and forth trips to shore. After making their way through the narrow village, they climbed the pinnacle and from its' summit counted over twenty *"eillons"* as the rasta man called them. They asked him what he was doing on top and he sang back…*"pickling' de erb…me brudder he sick…gotta brew de bush tea"*. Juri picked his brain about his knowledge of folk medicine and imagined he was somewhere no one had heard about. Steve suggested they hike the northeast coast of Union Island all the way to Bloody Head. All they found were some boats shaded under some large trees and after a swim they picked some mangoes and bananas in the wild.

The flight out of Union Island was visually stunning. A very primitive airstrip on the smaller island over the most turquoise of waters brought Juri back to his memories of the South Pacific. As soon as the aircraft cleared the tops of the coconut palms, everything turned to a kaleidoscope of blue.

The character of Carriacou had a different flavor and a larger scale than Union. There were banks and buses. Juri used his Visa Card for the first time in almost 2 years. They caught the "Lady in Red", a commuter van, to the other side of the island and were deposited in a sleepy little bay at an outdoor beach bar under a large extended palapa. Down the beach there were a couple of larger wooden fishing vessels, one blue and one red, moored at the end of a rickety old wharf. After a couple of nights on Carriacou, they showed their loyalty and hired the "Lady in Red" again to drop them at the airport. The main road crossed the runway. They had to check there were no approaching aircraft. At the terminal they confirmed their booking to Grenada.

On the flight, the cockpit door was left open and it was strange to watch the approach into the airstrip that the Cubans had built. It was the supposed reason for the American invasion in 1983. St Georges was quaint and displayed an engaging colonial architecture. It was the old established Caribbean. Carol, the Associate Peace Corps Director, was at the airport to assist a couple from St Lucia who were on our flight and were being terminated for early separation. Juri could sense their difficulties. Peace Corps experiences didn't always turn out heroic. Two of the volunteers on Grenada hosted Steve and Juri, so lodging was on the house. Steve stayed at Dodie's and Sandy had room for Juri. Volunteer encounters on Grenada were markedly distinct from those on St Kitts. While all PC volunteers were required to refrain from local politics, just the nature of discourse on the island brought civil exchange to the forefront. In the days prior to the U.S. intrusion, the New Jewel Movement wanted their say in the government.

Sandy, on island for only two months, still had that early beginning enthusiasm. They discussed art and travel over dinner of rice, beans and chicken. Allen who was from Ohio joined them. He was originally assigned in Honduras for three months and then transferred to Grenada. Before their buoyant morning survey of the island, Steve and Juri went to the Venezuelan embassy right across from Grand Anse Beach to apply for visas and then schedule flights for Caracas. From there they walked the oceanfront to the museum and Fort George. From up on the bluff above the entrance to the harbor, St Georges looked like a Mediterranean town. It was one of the best natural harbors in the Caribbean. From the promontory, the natural horseshoe shape of the harbor was laid out for all to view. The road looped past the yacht club and the port authority adjacent to a row of upscale shops. As the story goes, long before his presidency, Donald Trump cruised the Trump Princess II, a 500-foot-long power yacht into St Georges harbor a little hot and flooded the exclusive high-end shops at the "u" shaped termination of the bay with the ship's wake. All the accounts suggested the ugly American made for a "not-so-grand" entrance.

They walked up to Dodie's place for conversation and banana bread. She had that gracious Texan hospitality as lead volunteer on Grenada. Juri and Steve went to pick up the Venezuelan visas and then caught a bus from the market in St Georges to Sauteurs on the north coast. They spent the rest of the day on an empty isolated beach at La Vallera. The esthetic satisfaction of the setting left a quiet rich feeling of luxury. He made a note to return to Grenada someday.

They stepped off the LIAT flight in Trinidad, then onto a British West Indies Airways flight to Crown Point. From the airport in Tabago they grabbed lunch at the market in Scarborough and took a nap in the shade of a silk cotton tree at the botanical gardens. Juri remembered fading in and out, dozing from the sounds of a large family playing cricket against the buttress roots of a banyan tree. It took US40¢ to ride the one-hour-and-twenty minutes to the lush steep hills of the northeast coast. As they rounded the point to catch their first view of Speyside, they were more than pleased with what was presented. There were two islands smack dab in the middle of the bay. They couldn't find any guesthouses so they talked to a shop owner whose name was recommended. They needed anything to get a roof over their heads. They ended up renting a house for $20 a night, 15 minutes up the hill to a breathtaking view overlooking the bay and what amounted to a three-bedroom villa. Where were all his friends, Juri thought, to share in this stroke of good fortune? They stopped by Allison Johns' shop and their landlady fixed them up with huge fish sandwiches. After bagging some supplies to fill the fridge, they convinced Johnson, a local fisherman, to take them over to Little Tabago in the morning. The island was one of the few places outside of Papua New Guinea that had a resident population of transplanted Birds of Paradise, not the flora but the fauna. Tabago was for the birds. At daybreak there were bird sounds and colors everywhere. Strange, exotic vocalizations emanated from overhead. There were an estimated 500 species of birds on Trinidad and Tabago. A flock of Black-Necked Grebes with their piercing red eyes flew over the canyon. Steve and Juri managed themselves down to the village only to discover Johnson had to help someone build a house. So, Howard took them in a better-looking launch with two long-bowed bamboo-fishing poles attached like the antennae of a large blue butterfly.

As Howard headed the boat back, they shouted for him to pick them up at three o'clock. All that was on the beach was a wooden palapa shade and a path leading into the jungle. Large branches of hanging orchids, tree ferns and some things looking like giant green tongues dangled towards the forest floor. On the ground were numerous skeletons of the decayed flat forms. All that remained were moire patterns resembling huge transparent dragonfly wings. The delicate lacework was all that was left of a fragile magnificent network of veins, which were the circulatory system of the oversized broadleaf ferns that grew in the crook of tropical trees. Jungle noises mimicked a natural soundtrack you might hear on an ambient recording. They spotted a large white Tropic Bird with its especially long single trailing tail feather. It seemed to belong with the unicorns and elves of fairy tales as it glided trailing a wisp high above the bay. Steve was startled by the appearance of a fast-flying black bird with iridescent yellow tail feathers and a golden yellow beak as it darted across the treetops. As they rounded a bend in the trail past a couple of switchbacks, they were swarmed by dozens of fleeting Blue Jeans more commonly known as Blue Grey Tanagers fluttering waist high around them. It took on the semblance of light rays beaming on settling dust. Little Tabago was as wild as it got. The trail became thicker and more overgrown. Juri almost tripped over another large grounded Tropic Bird that seemed to be nesting in the middle of the path. Startled, the bird tried to escape but the canopy was so thick it could only fly down the trail of the narrow green hallway. Juri was surprised by how large it actually was up close and by the checkerboard of grey markings on its back. Seen from the sky looking at it from underneath it was a pure white bird with a long trailing white streamer much like the tail of a magic kite. They returned to the beach five minutes to 3:00 pm and spotted Howard motoring to shore. He turned out to be the most punctual West Indian in two years. Everyone in Speyside was extremely friendly. It's as if there was a secret joke going around and he and Steve weren't in on it. They ran into some old-timers who coaxed them into a few rums and shooting some Eight Ball on a badly dinged billiard table. Everything broke toward the ocean, much as on a seaside putt. It was good camaraderie and Archie, Melvin and Chunkie all proclaimed life-long bonding and continued to repeat the oft asked question... *"how you like it here?"* They liked it just fine.

The journey to South America was definitely not in a straight line. The connection went from Tabago to Trinidad, then to Grenada and on to St Vincent. From there the flight took them to Grantly Adams International in Barbados and they spent the night at the Shonlon Guest House, walking distance from the airport. In the morning it was finally on to Venezuela and the South American continent. What was baffling was that in Trinidad they were only seven miles from Venezuela. Go figure. For reasons too complicated to mention, this was the one route available to them. On the first leg in Tabago they caught the early blue bus from Scarborough to Crown Point for the morning flight. They were on standby and missed confirmation. The two people directly in front of them were the last ones on the flight. They had a five-hour wait for the next scheduled flight but they were first in the standby queue.

Steve and Juri searched out a fine white-sand beach. They hiked up a ravine over an eroded bridge and stumbled onto some ruins and the remains of an old iron waterwheel. Up the creek bed there were more ruins of what were, at some point in time, elegant houses. They found a courtyard with wonderfully crafted red Spanish tile and a blooming lilac bush. The arching path took them past the local pitch next to the sea where an all-white clad cricket match was in progress. They sat in the shade of a cluster of large trees on the embankment and enjoyed a few overs, the equivalent of baseball's innings. The walk back to the terminal was ultra-slow in the warmth of the noonday sun. The hours of extended trekking had put them at about the speed of a glacier moving up hill.

Venezuela

Back in Barbados, Juri realized the next flight would, for the first time in two years, put him in some culture other than West Indian. The Latin

American version of vacation was going to begin. Walking the streets of Caracas, there was one obvious thing that stood out. Couples strolled arm-in-arm. Public affection was commonplace on the sidewalks and in the parks. Men and women showing intimacy was something foreign in West Indian culture, at least in public. Young and old alike, couples occupying benches in plazas and at sidewalk cafes were blissfully ignorant of anyone around them south of the Caribbean. At a Chinese restaurant they ordered from Asian waiters struggling with their English in a Spanish accent. He settled on 'camarones al ajo'. Juri realized many Venezuelan words were quite different from the Mexican Spanish he was familiar with.

Disappointment took form in the fact that the Canima Airstrip was closed. One of the foremost landmarks he wanted to visit was the world's tallest waterfall. Angel Falls, a designated UNESCO World Heritage site, had a height of 3,212 feet. It literally fell out of the clouds. It was a cascade on Juri's bucket list. That the tarmac was being repaved was truly bad news because the only other way in was by motorized canoe. That route amounted to an expedition, time which they didn't have. But it was time to explore options. Luck recommended Miguel to them. He was well educated, in his twenties and spoke fluent English, Spanish, French and Italian. Miguel was remarkably well traveled, had lived in California, went to school in Iowa and resided in both Paris and Rome. His moneymaker was a brand new 4-wheel drive Toyota Land Cruiser, which they hired to take them anywhere they wanted to go. But first they needed to pick his brain for where that would be. Miguel turned out to be a fortuitous choice as a guide. He suggested a double-pronged excursion. Two treks rolled into one. A nature tour to the Llano, a Serengeti-like grassy savannah area of immense size in north-central part of the country, similar to the plains of Africa with at least as many species of animals and birds in the wild. And as a bonus they could traverse the Sierra Madre, a lush coastal mountain range, between the llano and the sea.

The three of them headed out for a little more than a week, feeling confident of adventure and a real slice of Venezuela not seen on Fox or CNN. Miguel talked of taking them to areas and small towns tourists never see. Miguel was perfecto. They set their sights on San Carlos. It would be their base camp between the llano and the mountains. The two of them rented a room in the only available place in the town where Miguel was born. His grandfather used to be governor of the area and he was well known. Being with him, they were accepted immediately. He was the prodigal son. Everyone welcomed him with open arms. The next day they rose early to set out for the sanctuary of Hato Pinero. It was a long drive in the heat of the llano to a large rancho comprised of an enormous amount of hectare acres. It was so big you couldn't see its boundaries from one point to the other. In Venezuela a rancho of this size was called a hato and this particular one was an environmental conservatory not open to the public. Hunting, fishing and logging were all prohibited. The main concern for locals was cattle ranching of Brahmans, but it was also a biological observation station where top biologists came to study the wildlife. They allowed reservations by a very few British and Canadian bird watching groups on the hato to view in limited areas. They paid hundreds of dollars a day for this privilege. The money went to run the scientific station. This ideal was set on miles and miles of desolation. A long dirt road wound off the paved surface, hours from San Carlos which itself was so far removed from Caracas, it seemed no one could ever find them. More miles down the dirt road, they came across an adobe house of a family with obvious features of indigenous people, who knew Miguel. They unlocked the gate and let the Toyota pass past a very official looking sign in Spanish forbidding entry under any circumstances. Juri tossed the little boy some bananas. He smiled from ear to ear as the vehicle's tires crunched the gravel.

Miguel was joking about how serious the scientists were and how they boasted about the range of hills the three of them had just traversed being 500 million years old. He liked throwing barbs at them. The hato had four major rivers running through it and beyond the hills, it looked much like the African plains with solitary standing trees dispersed far apart from each other on a vast grassy expanse. It was the dry season and except for the green of a few large mature trees, the predominant color was the flaxen-beige of changing grass. They passed an area so full of raptors it was hard to imagine that they could all share the same territory. Steve, an avid birder, counted 4 falcons, 11 hawks, 9 kites, an eagle, 4 vultures, 5 buteos, an osprey and a kestrel all in the span of a quarter mile. Miguel pointed out exotic birds Juri had never heard about. For nature lovers, this was paradise found. Besides the birds there were over 300 species of various animals associated with all sorts of different environments. During that particular day they saw and heard howler monkeys, parrots, vampire bats, anteaters, otters, foxes, deer, armadillos, iguanas, turtles, toads and tree frogs. Miguel vouched for pumas, jaguars, ocelots, tapirs, boa constrictors, anacondas, caimans, crocodiles, manatees and river dolphins. Noah would have had a full house. At a bend in the road under the shade of three mature mango trees was a pure white reclining Brahma bull. Miguel stopped the jeep and told them in a hushed tone to listen. Suddenly there were loud squawking screeches coming from the flaxen meadow as two pair of scarlet macaws with their trailing tail feathers contrasted against the dry, tan colored grasslands painted their way to the horizon. The color distinction from the field made them stand out like flying rainbows, the ultimate opposite of camouflage. They almost bobbled in flight, hooting until they were out of range. The three amigos drove where others weren't permitted. Miguel was a free spirit with connections. Juri jumped out to swing open a gate and they parked under a tree with a broad marshy lagoon in full view. One hundred meters away on the edge of the bank were a flock of scarlet ibis that stood out like lit-up casinos in the desert. Mixed among them were a few glossy ibis and roseate spoonbills. Visually the whole landscape took on the feel of confetti sprinkles on an after-dinner dessert. They walked on foot to get within 25 meters of the fluorescent birds and decided not to get closer with the chance of disturbing them. Juri collected some red coral feathers by the edge of the water. Miguel motioned to try the other side of the lagoon where there was a small island immediately off shore. At the southern end of the marsh, as they got closer, they noticed almost imperceptibly slow-plodding forms among reeds. In a bizarre display, a group of about two dozen capybara, never panicking, got up and lazily ambled off into the water like lemmings. Capybaras were the world's largest rodents approximately the size of small ponies. As they swam off across the lagoon, there was a single file of bobbing heads on the surface of the wind-blown water. It was quite a lot to take in one day. They thanked the people at the rancho and headed for a small village by the name of El Baul. It was tiny even though it had a small cathedral and a central plaza. Miguel took them to another homestead for a home-cooked meal of chicken, beans and rice and guava juice. A family consisting of a mother and two daughters served the meal in a structure with nothing more than an oven, four adobe walls and a table. He had a comfort level with Miguel making it seem they had known each other for years. For some reason, Steve tended to be more formal with him, maybe out of respect. After the meal they made plans for renting a launch 25 miles up the river but the locals were so removed that even Miguel was out of his area. The villagers said the river was too low. Juri's feeling was that the tenants saw them as strangers. It was all right. It was time to head back to San Carlos anyway.

They loaded up with supplies, fixed yesterday's flat tire and set off for the Sierra Madre. Winding up the foothills into the mountains, they rode into the village where Miguel's mother was born. He notified them once past Manrique it was all new territory for him. *"Es la primera vez para mi"* became their new redundant Spanish battle cry in the stupor and heat of a bumpy ride like the echoing of a meaningless repeated jingle. It was only something bonded males could find humorous. They were now constantly in 4-wheel drive passing over the highest ridge and down into a ravine. They arced around a dramatic eroded pinnacle about 100 meters high that the dirt road had to bend around. Juri sprung out of the slow-moving vehicle almost as if he were a magnet attracted to the spire in the road. He started scaling the vertical finger as Miguel begged the loco gringo to stop. Miguel started throwing stones and swearing at Juri as he scampered up out of Miguel's range. Not speaking *"Venezuelanese"* Juri kept climbing. As he got nearer the summit of the rock it turned to shale and became brittle and granular. He didn't let on that the loose rock was getting scary. Going up was one thing but coming down was another. Juri then realized the climb up was aided by his weight on the rock, but coming down gravity was not the ally it was going up. The tiny ledges were littered with sand and loose stone and each measured step down took minutes. There was one place near the top where he had a difficult time deciding what line to take. All of a sudden, it started to look like 1,000 meters instead of the approximate 100 it actually was.

As they wound down between the two steep ridges that dictated the flow of the San Carlos River, they calculated their tack in the direction of an old iron and wooden bridge. At this point they were making their own road between the exposed rocks and sand islands of the riverbed. There were three abandoned palm-thatched shelters, two on one bank and one on the other. Juri walked ahead of the Jeep through the shallow water as Miguel parked the jeep on a stone island formed by the branching of the river. Steve climbed out and waded to shore to snap the obligatory adventure photo.

Outside of Tintero, they stopped at a roadside stand for traditional Indian comida of chachapa and queso de mano. A big friendly heavy-set man prepared the meal on top of a primitive *horno*. Miguel said this was the real deal, impossible to match anywhere in Caracas. Creamed corn pancakes and homemade mozzarella cheese on tortillas from scratch danced on his tongue from the heat of the grill and the spice of the picante sauce. It was the first town of any size in a while. They booked a room at the Savoy Hotel and ventured out in the afternoon. They walked through a convention for the deaf signing each other. They were spread out in smaller groups in an arcade of a fashionable mall in front of a Burger King. It could have been a backdrop to a Fellini movie. Saturday was their last full day in Venezuela.

Just north of Caracas was Avila National Park, an extension of the coastal mountains. It was their last opportunity to hike and explore with Miguel. They exchanged addresses and goodbyes. They made connections and good friends. It was seemingly a memorable month packed into a week.

For one last outing they took the metro to Belles Artes and the art museums. Good fortune, again smiled on the artist-traveler. There was a very special exhibition of Fernando Botero's work at the National Art Gallery. Born in Medellin, Colombia he was one of the preeminent Latin painters and a severe political satirist who depicted form in large exaggerated volumes. It was one of the finest retrospectives Juri had seen in a long time and offered a thoughtful insight into the South American esthetic. One last evening on the Sabana Grande, he ordered chicken empanadas, atun vinagarit and fresa, melon and patilla batidos.

LIAT was its old rare self again on Sunday morning with a three-hour delay from Caracas and a two-hour hold-up in Barbados. After a long, drawn-out layover in St Lucia, they arrived in Martinique at 10:30 in the evening and were pushing midnight when they got out of the airport. As always in any French territory, he was at the mercy of the language. Sunday night, almost Monday morning, Martinique had a reputation of being expensive. It was late and he and Steve didn't have reservations. Jean Luc turned up like a parking space at the beach on a busy summer weekend. He worked for the French Embassy in Trinidad and recommended the place he was staying at in Fort de France and offered to share a cab. It was a pure stroke of luck that put a roof over their head and tucked them in for the night. In the morning light, the room was on the top floor of a stately two-story colonial next to a grand park that took up the four large city blocks adjacent to the cultural center and was walking distance to the harbor district. Steve and Juri spent their last day on Martinique touring the island, never tiring of white coral sand beaches and 80° teal blue water. They bought a brick of cheese, a fresh baguette and a bottle of Pinot and savored the rest of the day. Around sunset they walked the city center and invited themselves to a gallery opening on Place du 22 Mai. By the looks of the audience, it was a well-received exhibition. They jumped at the chance to blend in with the crowd, striking up a conversation with Blaise, a young Parisian, and Everest, a Haitian painter who did images in a primitive style reminiscent of Balinese landscapes. They spoke of art and travel; something all among them had silently earned the right to talk about. Everest was forced to leave his family in Haiti when he did a political painting of his friend, a student who was killed in the streets by the Tonton Macoute. Expatriation was something Juri shared with his new acquaintance. Everest was exhibiting in good graces in Martinique and trying to get shows in Paris. He shared the madness of trying to sneak back into Haiti.

The three final legs of Tuesday's flight went through Guadalupe and Antigua, then a content feeling of familiarity with a touch down at Golden Rock International. St Kitts had become an intimate friend. For a second time now, he was caught off guard at the fondness of returning. For two years he worked on building a home. It was community. He learned more than the people he taught. Juri was more than someone just passing through. People around the ghaut were genuinely welcoming on his return. He had become part of the fabric. His fortune was, he knew he was living in a movie. Jurij was conscious when he recited the script. He was certain that he would miss St Kitts. Time was short.

Home Front

CHAPTER 21

Juri came of age in a period where surfboards were getting shorter. Guys swim trunks were getting longer. It was all too confusing because women's swim ware was becoming more revealing. Short boards were performing better. Longer board shorts now guarded against rashes and accumulated board wax. Thongs made women confident and self-assured. They could be on view if they wanted. The boardwalk became a runway, a catwalk sandbox. Beach fashion put everyone on display. It was window-shopping and window-dressing. The beach, in a way, exposed people for who they were and beachwear wasn't hiding a thing. Surfing became more co-ed. On the volleyball sand courts, women were now the televised attraction. Titillation was on the menu across beaches everywhere. Hedonism was on the rise.

Main Beach became the office and Juri put in a lot of overtime. Laguna Beach being an artist community made for a circle of artist friends. Then there were the surfers, a group completely distinct from the volleyball crowd. Together they comprised the beach circle. And then there was academia, the third spoke in the wheel. It was the holy trinity from which he drew his spiritual sustenance. The cadre of artists, the brood of beach people and the body politic of professors and students from a collection of Southern California educational institutions became the thread that knit his community together. The circles tended to embrace a number of accomplished people from each of those worlds. He was quiet and proud to be part of that larger family.

When Michael Jordan temporarily retired from basketball and stepped up to the plate to play baseball, fans everywhere paused for a moment. Juri was winding down after some volleyball at Main Beach when his attention focused over to the basketball court between the boardwalk and Coast Highway. Sitting in the sand below the raised wooden walkway, his line of sight was towards the back of the backboard and rim. He noticed a large hand well above, not the rim but the backboard! From his angle the measured estimate to the top of the hand had to be at least 14 feet above the ground. That player had to be somebody. Juri noticed other people running to the court from all directions. It was an ant swarm overtaking Main Beach Park. The crowd rushed in to watch MJ in a pick-up basketball game. The next day the paper reported that Mr. Jordan was in negotiations on a new contract at the Ritz Carlton down the road a way. Juri imagined Michael decided to let his lawyers earn their money and took a break to bicycle to an informal playground game.

The movies came to Laguna. Juri was waiting for his order at the Stand, a health-food take out, when a car pulled up with the fifth incarnation of James Bond sitting shotgun in the passenger seat. Pierce Brosnan was in town.

Oliver Stone shot portions of his crime thriller *Savages* all over Laguna and Main Beach Park. Juri was making his way to the south courts on the boardwalk when he noticed Benicio del Toro filming a scene next to the benches across from the landmark Laguna South Coast Movie Theater on Pacific Coast Highway.

Greg MacGilivary the preeminent IMAX filmmaker was a personal friend and invited him to special screenings of his new films in the works for peer review. Greg, a leading proponent of the environment, directed and produced numerous award-winning films on the extra-large film format that were screened around the world.

Juri knew a bit of geographic trivia that John Steinbeck, the esteemed author, wrote his first novel *Tortilla Flat* in Laguna Beach on Park Avenue right around the corner from where he currently lived.

Juri had known Zach from the volleyball courts since Zach's early days at Laguna Beach High School. It wasn't until many years later into their friendship that he learned by chance that Henry Miller, the vaunted and celebrated novelist was his grandfather.

There were also the notorious episodes in the mid-sixties of LSD guru and Harvard professor Dr. Timothy Leary and the Brotherhood out in the canyon. Myth was carved out in the hills of the Orange County seaside community.

Laguna Beach was a drawing card. It always had a special resonance. The early indigenous inhabitants had a creation narrative that the navel of the world was Bird Rock. Mankind and all cultures were spawned right at the coastal end of Laguna Canyon in 25 feet of water at Bird Rock.

By now Juri had settled down into his teaching. It was a bridge between his art and his students. He wondered when they openly discussed artwork during critiques in the classroom where the words came from. He could remove himself from his voice and hear his words and imagine he was just a conduit for some other muse or personified inspiration. Sometimes what came out of his mouth was metaphorically astute yet he had no clue to its origins. He didn't prepare his lectures beforehand. An impromptu style allowed for these unfettered discriminations to simply surface. The acumen of his unbridled intuitions was an avenue for his images or his writings. The notion he was not the solitary author became more common and acceptable. Alchemy was possible in the classroom, at the drawing table or behind the excerpts.

Visual ambush, whether with paint or with words, was always the petri dish of surprise. The conceptually unexpected was creatively preferable to the predictable. Genesis of ideas has always been, for most cultures, universal food for thought. Juri didn't think much of teachers whose student work looked similar to the instructor's work. He believed the individual student must choose his or her own path. The teacher didn't dictate that path but only opened possible doors to it. Surprise and risk were a valued currency. They led to uncharted territory. Artists were explorers.

As an artist it was almost as if the state of flux was the universal medium. If he reflected on the effect of travel and culture on his work, he could see obvious parallels. As long as he could remember, he looked at maps and imagined that the lines he traced on them signifying his travels and connecting the places he had been were actually drawings. Early on his parents and the war imposed those journeys on him. Coming to

America from Slovenia as a child via a route through Austria, Germany and England seeded his desire to travel. He realized he had not stopped transporting himself to remote places up to the present day. It might be said that his "drawings" were getting more exotic. Travel required ingenuity, improvisation and the willingness to risk, all of which were advantageous traits in making art. Because he grew up with one foot in eastern European culture and one in the American dream, he could never put himself entirely in one basket. He gravitated to expression from many differing points of view. This allowed him to work comfortably as a painter, a designer, a photographer and even as a poet and an athlete. The drive to create kept him grounded in making images. This was more than an outcome and natural conclusion of his formal education. It was part of an urge for expression. His inclination to teach was a balance of giving back what he had been fortunate to receive. The depth of growth and evolution as an educator was so ingrained with being an artist that it became a necessary symbiosis.

He could not say for sure whether it was the art that drove the teaching or the teaching that drove the art. For him they affected each other. To verbalize the subtleties of the creative impulse required pedagogical judgment that was nuanced, transcendent and ultimately a creative act in itself. Teaching brought with it a deeper understanding of the process of making art. What was more profoundly understood could then be shared with students and applied to his art.

His students were making names for themselves. They were transitioning from the classroom as recognized professionals. Sean, while enrolled in the senior portfolio class exhibited at a satellite gallery of the Whitney Museum in New York. Sean, Kevin and Jason were all featured in an article published in *Juxtapose Magazine*. Brett's work was part of the *Traditional Ink* show in Los Angeles and Sara won the Red Cygnet Press Publishing Award for her children's book *Scared Silly*. Robert won a Plug Award in New York for music related artwork with Capitol Records and was selected for inclusion in the *Graphic Noise Traveling Show* curated by the Museum of Design in Atlanta. Adonna exhibited in the *"Surrealism Today"* show at the Nassau County Museum of Art, Long Island, New York and Rick had a solo show at Art Whino in Alexandria, Va. Casey was awarded a visiting artist position with Carib Graphics in St Kitts, West Indies.

A significant number of Juri's former students went on to teach at numerous colleges and universities. The accomplishment of his students was the singular merit that mattered. It was a gauge of his commitment to his teaching that enabled him to make a difference.

It was time to kick back and pay attention to less-weighty matters. Marty and Juri teamed up again and entered the Mother Lode Masters in Aspen, Colorado. The annual beach volleyball tournament was held in the summer at the world-class ski resort. Ski bums and beach rats mixed it up. All of Aspen turned out to welcome players from both coasts and in between. The hospitality was gracious and raucous, the energy spirited and the altitude severe. Many of the athletes hit the wall. Elevation and endurance didn't blend well together. Marty and Juri made it to the finals of the tournament. The following year Juri played in the senior's division with Jon Lee from Santa Barbara. Jon's brother Greg was a legend of the beach sport and also played basketball at UCLA for John Wooden. Jon and Juri meshed well together and won the tournament. The booty was sweet for an amateur tournament. They won all sorts of gift certificates from the fine establishments in the village, restaurants and retail shops. The cherry on top was a full year's ski-pass on Aspen Mountain. Juri tended to head south in the winter. The fewer clothes he wore the happier he was. Although his parents actually met skiing in the old country, he had only been skiing a couple of times. On the last occasion in Brianhead, Utah had a recorded high temperature of -22°. Needless to say, it was miserable. That week permanently etched his status as a life-long beach person. He found a young boy who watched some of his matches at the tournament venue and gifted him with the ski pass for the upcoming season. Juri made his day.

Leif and "Freddie", two of the players from Laguna who participated in the open classification, took Juri out to dinner at the Mother Lode restaurant, the tournament's sponsor, to celebrate his victory. Their waitress was in her early thirties, dark-haired and attractive. She happened to wear her smile well. As far as the ladies go, Leif was a hound dog and Freddie a heat-seeking missile. Juri kept apologizing for his friends. The competition was still on at the dinner table. Kathy, a good sport countered advances with nimble humor. Juri was impressed by her quick wit and dexterity, which was peppered by a slight accent. As the evening wore on, they invited her to join them when her shift was over. They bantered until last call. When it was time to go, she handed Juri a slip of paper with her phone number on it. It was warped fortune this happenstance occurred on his very last day there. He had an early morning flight back to Orange County, but he kept the note.

The subsequent two years, Jon and Juri teamed up again. The day before the tournament started, first thing after dropping off his bag in the room, he took the lift up to the top of the mountain. He proceeded to exert himself by running the trails at a very intense pace for about two hours. He subscribed to the idea that this allowed his blood to become oxygenated when he returned to the lower elevations of the village. Whether it did or not didn't matter. All he knew, coming from sea level was he didn't have the same difficulty with altitude that he had the previous year. With Jon as his partner, he became champion over three consecutive years. The Mother Lode tournament was on his list of favorite escapes from beach life to revel in the Rocky Mountains.

St Kitts v.2
CHAPTER 22

He promised Glenn that he and Andrew would come back. This time it was with an entourage of AVP volleyball players on what was billed as a Caribbean Goodwill Tour. This was top drawer. Andrew negotiated with SportCourt, the sports flooring manufacturer, his new employer, to donate a professional transportable game court surface that could be laid over concrete, asphalt or just about any hard surface to the country of St Kitts. Juri enlisted a roster of some of the better players on the tour that included Randy Stoklas, Brian Lewis, Mark Eller, Scott Frederichsen, Rudy Dvorack, Marty Gregory, and Tim Brown. The team was sponsored by Massimo Beachwear and housed in a five-bedroom at Bird Rock. They had two Suzuki Sidekicks at their disposal. They also brought their surfboards, which were anxiously delayed by American Airlines in Puerto Rico, to occupy them during down time.

They spent the first full day exploring the island and its beaches with Juri as the unofficial guide/baby sitter. Randy and Brian commandeered one of the Jeeps to go check out the early surf and coming back broke down in the cane field. They just left the stalled vehicle where it died and flagged down a ride after walking up to the main road. When they returned to the team house, the only thing they talked about was the surf. After their surfboards caught up with them as late baggage from Puerto Rico, they had a lot of catching up to do. A good swell was running and plans to get in the water pronto were the point of order, so they grabbed the keys to the second Jeep. Not a word was mentioned about the disabled one. Juri self-nominated himself for clean-up duty and tow service. He had an obligation to Glenn who had arranged for the two vehicles. Juri picked up a mechanic from the car rental place and went to remedy the situation. A bad coil wire was replaced and he drove the Suzuki back to pick up the stragglers and catch up with the prima donnas. He assumed that someone had taken his board when he didn't spot it at the house.

At the reef break, it was 6-8 feet with good shape and the point just up the beach was about 4-6 feet peeling off the rocks next to the bend in the bay. The first carload were scattered out in the water between the two spots paddling back and forth to get a taste of both. There was quite a lot of playful hooting and trash talking that you could hear from shore. Juri scanned the area to see if he could identify his surfboard, but it wasn't there. He asked around and Tim said he saw it lying on the floor in his room back at the house. So Juri was stranded on shore without a board until someone had their fill and paddled in. He was totally frustrated riding someone else's board that was way too small for his preference.

The six-man contest that counted a number of Olympians on the U.S. side was scheduled against the St Kitts National Team on the first weekend at the outdoor stadium in Warner Park. The un-veiling of the new SportCourt was inaugurated by the Prime Minister with much of the island's sports fans in attendance. Pregame decorum exposed the vestiges of bygone British pomp and ceremony. The new playing surface gave Kittitians something to be proud of and more importantly, something to talk about. The heavily-underdog St Kitts team fared well and put up a spirited effort. The flip side of the coin would be a two-man beach tournament with steel bands and BBQ the following weekend at Frigate Beach. The draw for partners would be one Kittitian paired with one U.S. player drawn randomly at a scheduled party for the selections and then of course the real party would start the Saturday of the tournament. After names were placed into two hats and selected, it was reason enough for celebration. The fete lasted all night only because on St Kitts nothing started before midnight. When someone said 10 p.m. that meant you started getting ready at 10. The gentry were fashionably late. The culture was one for creatures of the night. For people like Juri who were used to packing it in at 11 or 12, this required a mid-day nap. On this evening, the women wore their finest dresses and the men obliged with silver-tongued conversation. Juri remembered Mark sweet-talking one of the society belles from St Peter's Parrish. They were both literally in each other's ear and later in the a.m., carried on the tete-a-tete at the house at Bird Rock.

In the morning, happy to be reunited with their surfboards, most of the volleyballers planned to go surfing on the other side of the island again. Two white Jeeps loaded to the gills with nine eager dudes and their boards, plus one island beauty in a black evening dress, took the short cut out of the cane fields and up the circular drive to the plantation house. Unceremoniously still in her formal attire, she plodded up the stairs of the front porch balcony where her parents were being served breakfast. The nine gentlemen in board shorts stuffed into matching jeeps trailing dust drove off and disappeared back into the cane fields. The second surf session was as satisfying as the previous one. The cane field road skirted the ruins of a working plantation with the remains of a tall chimney and windmill. The way through the tall cane was a maze of dirt tracks with no distinction other than the experience of previous treks to lead the way. After the lone tree, they took the second right. They saw the white feathering lip of spray over the top of the sugar cane and surmised the drive would be worth it. There in front of them was a reef break about 100 yards offshore. The wave peeled perfectly in both directions so you could go either front or backside. Whether you stood up on the board with your left foot or your right foot forward it didn't matter, regular or goofy foot. Juri had surfed it as big as 15 feet. Up the beach, just to the right, was the point break slightly smaller but a longer ride. The choice was theirs. There were plenty of waves to accommodate the crew. On the beach the sentiment of the Stones *"can't get no satisfaction"* playing on the Jeep radio in the background was inappropriate.

Someone with SportCourt arranged for a large catamaran to sail over to the Dutch island of St Eustatius. Whenever Juri surfed the secret spot, he always used the peak of the dormant volcano on "Statia" as a marker for gauging his takeoff in the lineup. Mt Quill was less than 10 miles directly across the channel from the west side of St Kitts. Most of the group boarded the "Fortunate Sun" for the full day sail to Oranjestad. The swell had subsided and the seas were calm for the crossing. The crew consisted of the captain, one deck hand and three female hostesses attending to all their needs. The boat was *now* and St Eustatius was *then*. It turned out to run at a much slower pace than St Kitts, assuredly far off the beaten path. One of the highlights of the day was a needlepoint demonstration by a woman in a white bonnet. When they drove around to the east side to get a view of St Kitts it was eerie and hauntingly quiet. It was through the looking glass at what he spied, focusing back on the peak most those days surfing in the water. He didn't know places like this still existed except in works of fiction. Saba, the next Dutch island, was literally a spike that rose out of the ocean so sharply you almost expected the run off to still be flowing on the surface. The Dutch Island was so steep it had a town called The Bottom at the lowest point and Hell's Gate, another at the top of a diabolical climb. Saba had to be the scariest airport in the entire Caribbean. The landmass looked like "Kong Island" reaching for the sky. Passengers would fly directly at the mountain and at the last-minute bank sharply to the left onto a small alluvial fan at Core Gut Bay the only possible site for a landing strip. If you sat on the right side of the aircraft, you got pretty intimate with the rugged escarpment during the approach. Saba, a celebrated marine reserve, was a world-class dive destination and entertained divers from various countries.

On the late afternoon return, they pointed out three other islands visible from the catamaran. Two of them were high volcanic islands and the third was a low-profile atoll tucked in behind Saint Martin, or if you prefer, Sint Maarten, depending on whether you were on French or Dutch territory. France administered over the northern sector of the island and the Netherlands over the southern portion. It was easily the strongest economy of the outlying region between the Virgin Islands and Antigua. With its many resort beaches and reputation for nightlife, it attracted over a dozen major airlines to ferry beachgoers and sun worshipers alike. Anguilla, the low-lying island, was flat and had more than its fair share of white sandy beaches with its complement of turquoise water. Rather than scores of high-rise resorts, it showcased more casual beach amenities, but still had a reputation of catering to elite travelers such as the British royal family. For the discerning beach vacationer, Anguilla checked all the boxes.

One of slavery's least-vile effects was the derivation of language. On the plantation the shortening of names was commonplace for those speaking Pidgin or Creole. Shackled visitors to the Caribbean two or three centuries ago had to make sense of their newly acquired forms of speech. There was regular structure to the recently generated speech patterns of the enslaved that was concluded to be poor grammar by their masters. St Christopher became St Kitts and St Bartholomew was now St Barts. The third island in the sight line, St Barts was just northwest of St Kitts. For Juri it was untouchable. As far as reputations went, it catered to the rich and famous and on a Peace Corps volunteer's salary he wasn't going to vacation there any time soon. Spotting St Barts from the promontory at Dieppe Bay was probably some 35 or so miles away on the horizon but it might as well have been a thousand. It turned out to be one of the very few islands in the Caribbean that he never set foot on.

Back at the house at Bird Rock, episodes of the cruise were divulged to those that chose to stay behind, nothing noteworthy, only diversions from the regular topics of surf, volleyball and women. For Juri a household of nine unrelated young men wasn't too far from the familiarity of a military barracks. The present entourage of housed testosterone was kicking back with the mundane. They were hanging out watching TV, brushing their teeth out of unzipped shaving kits and raiding the fridge for meaningless snacks. He had to get out of the house for his sanity so he took one of the Jeeps to Friars Bay. Worn out from his catering and baby-sitting duties, he fell asleep on the relatively empty beach in the mid-day sun. He woke to a sound not too different from a babbling brook. It was the soft rolling giggles of three young ladies who had approached him carrying a small compact Polaroid camera. "Could you please take our picture"? In today's world it would have been an iPhone and they wouldn't have left any evidence. He managed to get up to his feet and stand tall, "...for sure". As the three New York City professionals gathered shoulder to shoulder with their backs to the Caribbean Sea donning big fashionable smiles and Juri adjusting the picture plane, they dropped their bikini tops. Wearing a little less made the smiles look considerably bigger. After successive photographs they bashfully readjusted their bathing suits and Juri asked for a favor. "…My friends will never believe this. Can I take one of these shots with me?" They turned out to be very generous.

Back at the house, the first person he showed the photograph to had to be "Freddie". Scott had missed out on two occasions. The day of the catamaran cruise, he chose not to go because of a cold and wasn't there to be waited on by the three fine young hostesses. And, he of all people would have wanted to be present for the photo shoot. It would have been a photo op he would have opted for.

A tune-up was in order. Marty, Scott, Andrew and Juri went to the court at Frigate Beach to get in a game or two in preparation for Saturday's beach tournament. Working up an appetite, Juri suggested dinner at the Sprat Net restaurant in Old Road Town. It was owned and operated by a family he knew very well back from his Peace Corps days. They had to push tables together in the beachfront open-air diner to accommodate everyone. Glenn and the Kittitian players joined them for surf and turf. The lobster was outstanding and the tropical ocean breezes performed admirably. Tacky fishing nets and shark jaw decor were perfect and the Caribs flowed freely.

The kitchen and the fridge were in need of resupply, so they went to town to the open-air market on Bay Road. They bartered for breadfruit, christophine, peanuts, melons, mangos and papayas. For packaged goods like raisins and laundry soap, they went up the road to Rams run by a middle-eastern family. Families were big on St Kitts. Historically the establishment knew each other well. The Horsfords owned the gas station and the hardware store, the Amorys the bakery and the Skeritts the drugstore. Richardsons were in education and politics. The Spencers were restaurateurs and acknowledged fishermen. Simmonds, Douglas and Harris were all prime ministers from opposing political parties. The longer your tenure on St Kitts the more you knew who was who on the island.

On Saturday the swing of things started early by island standards. The competitors were out warming up on the two courts tidied up for the tournament. Courtside, the music stands for the steel drum bands were being erected. As spectators and players alike started infiltrating the beach, there was a pronounced festive quality in the air. Randy's partner in the draw was Imba and Brian teamed up with Iwah. Those two teams would eventually make it to the finals with Iwah and Brian the eventual winners. Juri was matched up with Glenn. It was a tournament full of play by any stretch of the imagination.

Upon reflection, the tour brought a connection to the island nation because of two volunteers' fondness for the time they had previously spent on St Kitts. And a group of athletes from California got the opportunity to exchange common ground with their counterparts from St Kitts. The community at large came together for a short time to enjoy the festivities and gifting of a professional playing surface for the national stadium was a significant benefit, all in all, a good day's work.

On the plane home, Randy and Juri were in aisle seats across from each other. The volleyball legend and the volunteer simply smiled contentedly at one another in knowing it was fun. He was amazed at how large Randy was. He hadn't noticed before, and it wasn't a man crush, but his athletically proportioned body hid the fact that he was a huge man. His barrel chest blocked the view of the rest of the passengers in his row. Juri thought he would have been a vaunted linebacker or tight end. He asked him why he didn't play football at UCLA. As a member of the Bruin volleyball team, he had the finesse of a setter's hands and the arm swing of a fierce hitter. He shared that his mother wouldn't agree to let him play football.

The Cofan of Zabalo
CHAPTER 23

The Laguna College of Art and Design campus was set in the canyon a little more than a mile from the Pacific Ocean. His job title was professor and department chair. He truly was a teacher who loved his work. The fact that he contributed in the same town in which he lived was job satisfaction. He always felt part of Laguna. It was something deep seated. He was part of the community. He had exhibited in some of the city's galleries and at the summer festivals but working at the art institute was substantial.

The new hire in the administrative offices caught his attention. She caught everyone's attention. Gertie was hard to miss. Elegant, stately, blond, she was a Danish emigree pushing six feet tall. They both showed an interest and the connection was easy. They started to see each other and shared a passion for travel.

Juri had read a remarkable account about the Cofan, an indigenous tribe in the remote Cuyabeno Reserve in the Ecuadorian Amazon. An American missionary couple settled with the tribe. They had a son who was born and grew up in the village. When he became of age his parents sent him back to the states for his high school and college education. Upon graduation Randy Borman made a decision to live with the people he grew up with. He ended up relocating back to Dureno and marrying into the tribe. Because of the encroachment of oil exploration, he led the tribal Cofan to relocate their village deeper into the Cuyabeno Wildlife Reserve, an area of 603,000 hectares of primary rainforest in the northeastern corner of Ecuador. This was real life out of a fiction novel. When the oil companies came into the area of the newer more recent settlement for a second time, the Cofan took a strident, aggressive stand against oil drilling by occupying the illegal well. The reserve was designated only for indigenous settlement. The current state of affairs found the Cofan in a long protracted litigious battle against oil concerns and forced to fight for their land in an arena outside of their tradition, knowledge and heritage. While they were more than capable with a consortium of international support, the question posed was who spoke for them. The land and the ecosystem they knew so well had been handed down for generations.

Juri inquired without politics about the possibilities of spending some time with the Cofan. There were permits from the military that needed to be acquired, but because he was a professor with access to many individuals and organizations in the educational system, he was granted permission. He was connected to an Ecuadorian outfitter who would handle the arrangements. It turned out he was allotted a total of up to six permits, so he asked Peter, the "snake man" in the canyon who was a naturalist, and his wife Libby and Andrew's brother Roger, who worked at the Cleveland Arboretum, along with his wife, Dawn to join them. Gertie was enthusiastic about pairing up for the expedition.

With everything in order, the trip started out of Quito with a flight to the frontier town of Lago Agrio, the last leg of civilization on a trek that was just starting. Chirtza was barely a clearing of vegetation on the river with a couple of palapas where they exchanged off-road vehicles for watercraft. The shore was scattered with five beached canoes, two of which had outboard engines. A grass hut assumed the identity of a café on stilts. Their twenty-four-foot motorized dugout, so nervously narrow it seemed longer than it was and more stable than it seemed. It was reservedly painted in ox-blood red and periwinkle blue. It was loaded with gear, gas and supplies, Franklin, the poignant and reflective Ecuadorian pilot of the boat, bled complete command of his mastery on the water. Juohn, the deck hand, a twenty something, last in a line of a depleted tribe, looked more Asian than indigenous. His way back and forth on the tipsy moving canoe balancing the narrow side beam at our eye level, going from bow to stern, was especially acrobatic. Juri imagined him on a fiberglass plank at Pipeline or Teahupoo. Under different circumstances he would have been a remarkable surfer. Sanni, a soft-spoken but spirited woman who left Columbia because of the violence, was in charge of the kitchen and the preparation of food. She was an unexpected gem. In spite of the sparse isolated conditions, they couldn't explain how she did what she did. There wasn't one meal where they ate the same thing more than once in almost two weeks. But what was wonderful about the food was how healthy and truly good tasting it was. The wild somehow flavored sustenance. Meals like these were a blessing in the bush. Alfredo, the low kid on the totem pole, was usually sprawled out on the blue tarp blanketing the gear up in the bow of the canoe. Alf, not as agile as Juohn, managed a few gangling missteps resulting in unwanted splashes in the drink. Everyone chuckled. The boat would circle around to pick up the fully clothed, sopping-wet teenager. Ramiro, our guide whose knowledge and experience made the visual theater fuller with a wealth of rich information and always with a sense of not having to play the part of the expert, as some gringos were apt to do. Juri visualized previous boatloads of *norteamericano* adventurers in their uniforms from REI to LL Bean and Eddie Bauer, in contrast to our crew who looked like they were outfitted at a Salvation Army second-hand store. In a quick downpour, the only other boat they saw on the first segment of the river was a large canoe cruising in the opposite direction with a troop that broke out unvarying blue ponchos pretending to be a carton of ultramarine colored Easter eggs tucked low into the hull. As the first day progressed, and they put miles between them and Chirtza, a wonderful sense of solitude began to pervade the riverscape. Nature was never dominantly quiet. It was always a backdrop for the howler monkeys, the squawking parrots and a host of other species. The minimal water traffic in the first stretches of the broad white Aguarico River, now nonexistent, left them at the mercy of the rainforest. They were, for all practical purposes, alone with nature. Smaller black-water rivers like the Imuya flowed into the wider main channel that was transporting them into the heart of the jungle. The white river was actually the color of tepid coffee with too much cream in it with grand volumes of runoff and silt. It was enormous, flat, wide and the singular relief from the overgrowth. Unlike in the jungle, on the river you could see the sky. It was the only possible access to the rainforest. The canopy reached over two hundred feet in places. Mind-boggling trees were everywhere. The surface of the channel was relatively smooth and constantly moving at a much faster pace than Juri expected. Thick vegetation forked around islands, sometimes so big, you assumed one of the courses was another river. Their exit was on the left to the Imuya, a dark river that was narrower, more serpentine and slower flowing. It was absolutely black and, at times, smooth as a mirror. Its mystic qualities were due to the reflected upside-down image of everything in your field of vision. It was on the border between Ecuador and Peru where Colombia came for an adjacent look-see. Brazil was closing in, threatening to make it the South American version of Four Corners. They beached the canoe at a stockade right out of the black and white movies. They were required to check in with the military at the confluence of three rivers. There was a spot right outside the gate where soldiers stood and relieved themselves that drew scores of butterflies attracted to the salt in the urine. The collective blanket choreography on the wing hovered in unison. On one of the other embankments, maybe a hundred yards away, was the Peruvian military outpost. Located within sight on the third side was the Colombian compound. Everything seemed secure where the three rivers came together. There was a distinct, crisp, visible graphic line in the water, as if drawn with a straight edge, where the black and brown waters merged.

The Aguarico had a powerful disposition. The Imuya had a fairytale feel and was home to river dolphins. On both rivers, the wildlife was overwhelming and a testament to how zoos are feeble attempts at studying nature. The rule of thumb was that you heard it before you saw it. Squawking, chirping, hooting, howling, crackling, rustling and other foreign sounds echoed through the forest. Exotic birds, even fair to say quixotic, were everywhere too numerous to note. For a novice birder like Juri, it was akin to being dropped into a cathedral of nature. Butterflies, bats, monkeys, dragonflies, toucans, anacondas, tree frogs, tamarins, jaguars, tapirs; all were on the list and it was endless. On the second day they were at their deepest reach into the rainforest at a seemingly point of no return.

The Imuya's river dolphins were the major highlight. Shyer than their salt-water cousins, they were virtually blind. Eyesight was mostly useless in the opaque tannin-stained black waters. The humpback-shaped cetaceans used sonar to navigate through dense mangrove roots in the water. Ramiro encouraged the group to be proactive and swim with the dolphins, knowing that piranha and caiman populated the river. The feeling of going into the ocean after seeing *Jaws* was resurrected. Apprehension turned to playful abandon after a little time. Hopefully, it wasn't recklessness. The area was a flooded forest with little high ground. The river in places simply flowed over its banks into the whole forest with its channel described only by water lacking trees. Childhood fantasies were realized when they plowed through beds of reeds and hacked their way through the few openings of branches with machetes. Standing on the bow of the longboat, they struggled to get to larger pockets of the lake only meters on the other side of where they were. They found what seemed to be the only patch of dry earth anywhere. On a hillock of dry ground, they pitched camp for three days of what they came for. Swimming with curious but elusive shy gray-pink dolphins. The water was jet black with zero visibility when they swam except for the top four to six-inches, which was semi-translucent red amber just beneath the surface. The coloring took on the vague, indistinct shape of your submersed body in an unearthly appearance. In the late afternoon after a long session of adventure, they boated back to the camp for piping hot popcorn and ice-cold beer. Some simple pleasures, and then the rainforest lived up to its name. They grabbed everything and dashed for the tents. Big mistake. After snacking, he woke from a short nap by an unceasing line of greedy little fire ants that stung like hell. He stripped down to his shorts and made a beeline for the water.

The next morning, they did a lazy slalom down the Imuya, and then west, upstream against the Aguarico's Atlantic intentions towards the village of Zabalo. The curious expectations of what the locals would look like were quickly dispelled with greetings from Cofan in Chicago Bulls baseball hats and Microsoft t-shirts. An especially tall native in his twenties in surf shorts and knee-high rubber boots greeted the entourage. The village itself was right out of the pages of National Geographic, huts on stilts, palm thatched roofs and monster trees. Overgrown and green with designs on reclaiming the clearing that exposed the simple structures. The quarters were simple, clean and idyllic with polished hardwood floors. After tents, real beds with mosquito netting seemed decadent. They were across the clearing removed from the main portion of the village. They only went into the living area with Maricio, their Cofan guide. At 5' 6" he had more of the stocky body of a Samoan than that of an Amazonian. You could tell he had spent a lifetime on his legs. His next noticeable features were his gracious smile and singular calmness. He was the master of the forest. He knew all, what trees to score open with his thumbnail for ants whose taste seasoned like nutmeg, or garlic or vinegar. He pointed out what trees or leaves or vines were used to cure toothaches or infections or what plant combinations conjure up poison potions for hunting darts or what blend of herbs were used for birth control. At a turn in the trail, they came to a massive mossy log strewn across a wide span of a raging tributary. They were encouraged to go first and cross to the other side. Planted about three feet apart alongside the fallen tree in the water were a series of willowy bamboo shoots approximately the thickness of his little finger, waving flimsily in the current. No one volunteered until Maricio explained a simple principle. The point was not to use the thin wavering antennae for support but rather for balance. The theory was not to grab the poles but to deftly touch them with the end of your finger for stability and footing. It was a resourceful insight that worked remarkably well. After an hour-and-a-half of "classroom hiking on the hoof", Peter noticed his $250 prescription sunglasses were no longer in his shirt pocket. Sacrifices had to be made. Maricio asked them to wait at that precise spot, and he disappeared, backtracking into the larger green "haystack". No longer than 15 minutes later, he returned and they continued to walk. Nothing said, with the perfect timing of a stand-up comic, he magically produced the sunglasses. Mind you, if you dropped a quarter where you were standing, it was so overgrown you probably wouldn't find it. Juri asked Maricio in Spanish, primarily not his native tongue, how in the world did he do it? He replied... "busque algo diferente". He looked for something different. The glasses could have been lost anywhere over the last few hours and this native Merlin found them.

On the third day he indulged the troop for the first time with full ceremonial dress, a purple camise with embroidered trim and ringed headdress with green and red parrot feathers. He had the traditional wooden pique through his nose with red facial paint across his brow and cheeks. They were taken across the river to the long house, the meeting place for tribal matters. Inside were skulls of every imaginable animal including larger caiman, jaguars and tapirs. To one side in the middle of the lengthy hall were a kitchen hearth with oversized carved wooden tools and an enormous iron kettle. A very large clay platter used for baking flat bread was demonstrated for their tasting. A tiny ceramic urn containing a heated colorless liquid was strung over the fire. The response to the question was…"the poison for the hunting darts had to be kept warm or it would lose its potency". There it was, strung directly over the fire where they cooked their meals. A variety of decorative weapons were displayed on the wall, including a clutch of some fierce-looking spears and a four-foot-long black tube. Maricio proceeded to demonstrate the art of the blowgun. He handed Libby the tube along with a couple of darts. They were at one end of the large hall and he packed the darts with the white fibrous filaments of a Kapok tree into the tube. From about 30 yards she aimed at a carved wooden parrot Marico had hung on the wall. Her first projectile stuck in the wall about 18 inches from the bird decoy. Not bad for the first attempt. The rest of the crew took their turns, not fairing much better with some of the darts bouncing off the wall. It was not too distant from ping-pong diplomacy. Juri was taken by surprise at how little mouth pressure was required to send the slender little feathered dart on its way. Maricio then repositioned the wooden target as far across the enormous room as was possible, easily three times the distance they had aimed from. Taking a page out of Robin Hood, who he surely never met, Maricio struck the carved parrot dead in the heart on three consecutive attempts.

At the end of the week on the path they mimicked leaf cutter ants trailing through the forest with their packs and gear on their backs. They were loading up the canoe for the journey back to the land of electronic messaging and plush jungle lodges, ones with hot showers. During their classroom in the jungle, they came across huge anthills that were every bit as large as some of the great termite mounds, they spotted previously. One of the most unexpected sights in the darker reaches of the trail was a mammoth ten-inch pure snow-white caterpillar that seemed to be cloaked in soft luxurious cashmere. On the river, the first signs were scarce, dotted small private clearings and modest single hut farms. Then further up the river were remote communities of two or three dwellings. Up ahead on the right bank, Juri spotted a volleyball arcing across a primitive net braided out of nylon rope. Actually, volleyball was ever present in Ecuador. Even Zabalo had a court and a soccer field. The makeshift net doubled as their clothesline.

They retraced their steps back to Quito through Lago Agrio and then on to the Andes. Once at their hotel, they bid Dawn and Roger good-bye. The other four stayed for another week to decompress the transition from the rainforest to the suave and civil density of urbanity. Libby and Peter opted for an alternative compass heading and Gertie and Juri headed off in the other direction more out of separate interests than the proximity of 12 days of close quarters in the jungle. The road went north through the narrow openings of dramatic gorges and extinct snowcapped volcanoes to San Rafael, nestled by Laguna San Pablo. At the foot of a major mountain, it smacked a bit of Switzerland. The llamas and alpacas brought them back to Ecuador. Octavalo was world-renowned for its weavers. The plaza had one of the best reputations as an indigenous artisan marketplace. In the evening they walked the narrowing and tapered uneven cobblestone streets with the typical thick South American adobe structures. Brightly painted buildings sharing massive sidewalls as if they were some type of architectural Siamese quintuplets. Gertie dragged him into a place called *"The Pie Shop"* with a sign over the door in English trying to be cosmopolitan. Inside there were young Octavalanoes with long thick black wrapped ponytails and their girlfriends with cool Al Capone fedoras. They ordered raspberry pie-a-la mode and Juri was a little confused as to where he was.

In the morning they set out to the plaza again to pick out blankets, ponchos and gifts to bring back. They hopped a crowded bus for the three-and-a-half-hour trek south to Quito and then hailing a cab back to the hotel to drop off the goods. Further south at the first few stops around Latacunga, hawkers and snake charmers boarded the bus to make their pitch to a captive audience. Giving out free samples of wholesome edibles and then taking them back if no purchase was made. At one point, two young boys dressed as clowns climbed onboard and did a skit totally in rapid fire Spanish, got a few laughs and a few coins then simply jumped off the moving bus. Latacunga was not a particularly esthetic place but a venue where you could find a nourishing meal of wonderful corbina hundreds of miles from the coast.

They were up at 5:30 to catch a bus to Saquisili, the most famous Indian market in Ecuador and possibly all of South America. It was not intended for the tourists, a series of eight plazas each containing different goods. One was an unbelievable animal market where the sound of squealing pigs and clacking chickens punctuated the auctioning of uncooperative sheep, cattle, horses and llamas made for something reminiscent of a John Cage opus. They watched where they stepped. The other plazas offered produce, plastic ware, clothes and furniture. In between, the streets were lined with vendors. The penultimate flea market with throngs of villagers from all over the Andes that came to this weekly Thursday event was an ideal place to photograph people. After market, it was the 90-kilometer Quito express back for the last supper. Logrito, a potato and avocado soup, corvina plancha, camarones con arroz y chorizo and flan was complemented by mammoth bottles of pilsner and a piña colada. At the airport the journey was over at the 5 am check-in back to California. The ticket counter always marked either the beginning or the end of a trip.

Enemy Territory
CHAPTER 24

It was time to turn the page to the next chapter. Paul and Richard put an idea into his head. How would he like to go back to Vietnam? Why not? So they packed their bags, stowed their gear and headed behind enemy lines to Hanoi. It had been 35 years for Juri so he had to prepare for changes. Paul had not experienced wartime Vietnam but Richard actually went to high school in Saigon in the very early 60's when his father was with the State Department. They debated that it might have actually been with the CIA. Richard never knew for sure. He always spoke fondly of his high school experience. It might have explained his inclination towards Asian women.

Paul had heavy doses of Asia on his resume. He had covered most the continent with his studies and teaching in India and Sri Lanka. His recreational travel encompassed most of Southeast Asia. The three of them certainly weren't rank strangers to the orient.

He rarely thought about the war and talked about it even less over the many odd years. He wasn't sure what the duress was that kept him from sharing his experience of Vietnam. Was it some unconscious protective barrier or perhaps a deep-seated concern to put it all behind him? He didn't think of himself as damaged goods like some he knew. He was lucky. He didn't have physical or psychological scars that he was aware of. Whatever it was, the only time he managed conversation about Vietnam was with those who knew the experience, veterans of a combat zone, surprisingly even occasionally, with those younger than him who served tours in the Middle East. It wasn't exclusionary. He didn't make those who weren't there out to be less. In fact, he envied them. It was that he could look into the eyes of a vet and know that they understood. It was an unspoken brotherhood. The spoils of war were left on America's shores. Why did it happen? Were we sold a bill of goods? Merchants of conflict were the only ones who made out. And for guys like him, what did they get for their effort? Images of helicopters pushed off the decks of US ships during the evacuation of Saigon. They came home to disgust and even hatred. They were despised for what they were asked to do. They were impotent and forever at the mercy of history. The mood of the country didn't see them as heroes like the soldiers returning from Iraq and Afghanistan. He had evolved into an ex-soldier who was staunchly anti-war. He put in his time plus the two years in the Peace Corps. Unlike Vietnam, he considered the latter in service of his country. Those four years earned him the right to dissent and speak his mind. He looked up to his friend Lou, a journalist whose stories ran in Stars and Stripes and who was also an editor for the army's First Division newspaper. They were both in country at the same time. When Lou returned to Cleveland he put on his uniform and went to major events with his American flag that had a peace symbol in the blue field instead of the stars. Lou was an enigma for mid-America and would constantly share some of his strange confrontations through frequent emails.

During the war the DMZ was a buffer but now he was in Hanoi behind enemy lines. Touching down was the familiarity of landing at an airport of a developing country. Busing into the city proper, the roads were simple and the structures even more austere. Juri couldn't help going back in time and imagined how those very streets were during the bombing of Hanoi and the north. He noticed the unmistakable vegetation of the sub-tropics with stands of brick pagoda houses in the middle of green vacant rice paddies. First glimpses of the past triggered sensations of water buffaloes and figures in black pajamas with conical straw hats. The farmers stooped in wet green rice paddies told him it was Asia and smiling young Asian women on the back of motor bikes conveyed it was friendly. As they got into the city, even though none of them had been north of the 17th parallel, they knew they were in Vietnam by the narrowness of the storefronts along the avenues of Hanoi. Vietnamese tax codes calculated by the horizontal foot. All the commercial properties had that distinctive ultra-narrow look with the square footage made up mostly of floor plans that extended deeply to the back of the building. It made for a feeling that one was walking through a tapered model train landscape. Almost as if the whole block hit the brakes really hard and the buildings piled up on one another. The policy dictated an architectural stylistic distinction. You could say Vietnamese cut corners when it came to their taxes.

The human flow of bicycles and motor scooters somehow managed to merge without catastrophe. Simply crossing the street as a pedestrian was taking your life in your own hands. Vehicle traffic on the arteries of Hanoi was like watching blood flow under a microscope. They asked a taxi driver if he knew where the Rose Hotel was. After the affirmative nod they drove in circles jacking up the rate while the guy behind the wheel insisted the other establishments were better. Better because he got a kickback. Juri's necessary cynicism suggested that everyone was a con artist. It was all a working system of negotiation. They settled for a green hotel, very clean, a bit on the narrow side with antique furnishings. Two computer stations in the lobby were the barebones making of an Internet café. The daily rate of $9 included breakfast. For lunch he had Tiger Beer and sweet-and-sour fish at an open-air restaurant on the lake.

On the streets, Juri kept getting pulled into shops with ethnic crafts. It was an affliction he had and it was starting to annoy Paul and Richard. Food was a highlight all three looked forward to. He woke out of a deep sleep for the evening venture to go look for dinner.

He was getting to the point where the only way he could tell what country he was in was by the label of the beer he was drinking. The doldrums of travel were a fond affliction on memory. The burden of the first day was to acclimate. The sounds of the waking streets urged the call to breakfast. The hotel's second story balcony brandished tattered flags of the countries that exported the tourists. Somehow the stars and stripes flying over Hanoi seemed out of place.

Ho Chi Minh's memory had the complete esteem of the country. In the afternoon they went to visit the "Ho Daddy" or more respectfully put,

"Uncle Ho's" mausoleum. He was their Washington and Lincoln all rolled into one. It was a somber viewing. Richard, Paul and Juri were reprimanded for talking. Another foreigner was asked to take his hands out of his pockets because it was a sign of disrespect. They weren't sure if the resemblance of the whole area to Tiananmen Square was a show of gratitude to China. Ho Chi Minh himself did not stay in the presidential palace but in a more modest house intended for servants. The mausoleum fundamentally was a stark minimally designed building, not at all Asian in character. Ho's museum on the other hand, was a true highlight and not expected. One of the bravest, esthetically surrealistic exhibition spaces anywhere in the world, the stunning nature of the exhibits was a breathtaking work of installation art. It was a total surprise. In the afternoon he saw the first indications of any emotional memory connected to the conflict. The War Museum was the only place that housed any recognition of the hostilities. Enough said, Juri didn't utter a word.

There was mayhem walking the streets of Hanoi. Oceans of two-wheel traffic cricketed a falsetto of horns. The cooperative merging and absolute lack of road rage was striking. The constant stream and flow of Vespas, motorcycles and bicycles were indeed deliberate and the idea of making short bursts and sudden dashes when crossing the street was a really bad idea. Pedestrians required a very slow and measured pace so that oncoming vehicular traffic could anticipate and gauge, barely missing the foot traffic. He found out that if he fine-tuned his walking speed across the road in sublimely subtle increments, depending on the speed of constant oncoming objects that it all tended to work surprisingly well.

They went to plan out the next week. Reservations were in order for next day's bus to Haiphong, then on water to Cat Ba Island. Yesterday he felt a little more seasoned, as though he melded into the street. He didn't stand out as much, although he knew he would never be completely anonymous to the Vietnamese. Maybe because of stature, it was what a pro basketball player probably felt when mingling with mere physically average-sized people. Juri at 6' 2" on crowded avenues seemed to stand above most and thought it ironic that a nation of more-humble diminutive people brought us to our knees those countless years ago. When he saw amputees about his age ambling on crutches around town, he had inklings of responsibility. He had pangs of pain and hurt. There weren't enough answers to visit the past. Was it more than cynicism? Was that the hard truth?

A two-hour bus ride went through villages and towns to the seaport city of Haiphong. His only previous knowledge was of a harbor that was mined because it was the port for Hanoi. Off the bus they were still a distance from the docks to catch the 9 a.m., which was rescheduled for 8:30. None of the taxi drivers spoke English and they couldn't find anyone in the vicinity who did. So they put Richard on the cab's radio to negotiate where they were going to go and to haggle the price over the intercom, *"over and out"*. After weaving through a maze of streets and alleys with a couple of helping locals leading the way on a motorcycle, their taxi made it to the dock just as the boat was leaving. One of the guys on the bike rushed us on board as they were pulling up the gangplank. Juri thought because there was only one sailing, they were cutting it a little close. The vessel was a sleek Russian-made tube that turned out to be a jet hydrofoil. That mode of sleek unexpected transport cut the crossing time from four hours by junk to 45 minutes. Cat Ba was the one major island in an archipelago of myriad green spired limestone pinnacles that dotted the waterscape in about a 50-square-mile area, some of which was identified a UNESCO Biosphere Reserve. Turning the corner of the headland into Cat Ba Bay was a water world of peculiarities and juxtapositions. Idiosyncratic, bizarre rock formations directed attention to constantly be looking upward. Surrounded by water in a natural tropical marine setting, there was an intentional sprinkling of islands just so they couldn't keep to a straight course. Coming into the town of Cat Ba, the familiar tall narrow tightly packed structures drew a skyline contrasting the more dominant outline of startling and jutting peaks of the ridgeline and surrounding islands that literally towered over and butted up to the back of the buildings. Hotels fronted a tree-lined promenade on the shoreline that looked out over the oddest eclectic assortment of sailing vessels, fishing boats, junks, barcs and floating restaurants. The flotilla was a visual quilt of what was aquatically possible on the byways of far-flung backwater refuges. Sunflower #1 was the full name of their hotel. On the sixth floor, which was actually eight flights of stairs up, afforded them a spectacular view of the bay. It was 90° and humid. Running out of bottled water was something to prepare for.

The three of them headed out for the harbor to inquire about hiring a boat for the next day. Diyzuen, a 14-year-old pixie, who understood the way things worked, captivated them. Charming to the end, she was one of those youngsters who had the confidence to succeed at anything she put her mind to. She was actually procuring business for her family by convincing them her father's boat was the best one to hire. Tomorrow was to be a long day, starting at six in the morning. They would spend the next wonderful day on a rickety old diesel junker with a blue tarp sunshade jerry-rigged with bamboo and wire puttering across the waterways and passages of Cat Ba National Park. Diyzuen's command of English as well as mathematics made her the consummate concierge. She was worldly beyond her insulated experience. A 14-year-old girl hustled them and they were relatively naïve about it. They were in truth, fortunate to be taken in by the sprite. They finalized an all-day trip past Monkey Island, deep into the park. The plan to meet by the boat at 7:00 in the morning included an onboard mid-day meal and then returning after four p.m. The deal was sealed with a handshake and refreshing ice-cold coconuts with straws.

Juri flagged down a motorbike and asked the driver to take him to the nearest beach. The bike struggled up the hill and near the top, a bamboo pole painted red and white with a large block of concrete strapped to one end spanned across the path posing as a roadblock. His driver gestured he must proceed the rest of the way on foot. They wouldn't let the bike pass. Walking over the steep crest of the first bay there was a view of many overlapping islands just offshore. Down the stairs, he crossed the sand up to a railed boardwalk welded into the side of the cliff face. The second beach around the cove turned out to be his choice for the afternoon. He claimed a plot of sand with his towel and headed for submersion in the 82° water. He was in his element. The simple pleasure of knowing he was at home in the ocean. It just happened to be the Gulf of Tonkin.

The early morning rendezvous was at the harbor docks. They met up with Diyzuen. Her father was prepping the boat and her aunt, Hieu, joined the crew. When they got to the bottom of the ramp it was low tide so they had to hop over exposed rocks to get onto the boat. They climbed onto a brightly lacquered green deck, noticing the wicker woven shell sitting in the water in the shape of a bulbous antique bathtub. On the surface of the hull was some sort of tar or rubberized pitch that waterproofed the weathered old vessel. Under removable planks on the foredeck was an ancient hand crank diesel engine that raised a question about its dependability that was loudly disquieted once it started up. The sailing junk shoved off at a slow skim. Harbor speed took them inching by rows of a rogue's gallery of unimaginable watercraft. They were the vestiges of form follows function and then some. The scattered unconventional fleet was the largest neighborhood on Cat Ba. People were doing laundry, sweeping floors, cooking breakfast, everything they did in the streets of Hanoi they did out on the harbor of Cat Ba. After turning south and east they left the commotion of the anchorage behind in exchange for a proportion of serenity. Every twist in their charted route was worthy of picture postcard status. If beauty was what they sought they were certainly in an attained form of paradise. Around every tall enigmatic limestone formation rising out of the sea was another virgin beach whispering to be explored. Every turn, every rise and fall of the junk was a new adventure. The maze of sentinel rocks slowly became a labyrinth they welcomed getting lost in. It wasn't an exaggeration to say they were devoured by nature. Every square inch of their field of vision was daunting tranquility. There were places on this planet that demanded and reserved the highest order of esthetic respect and this was one of those. The enormity of scale dawned on them. The meandering was limitless, endless really. All day they went deeper into beauty.

Captain Willard had a mission. They didn't. They were in nature's belly. They gave into natural grace. The watered limestone hallways turned into an aquatic cirque and they were surrounded. They couldn't take it anymore and jackknifed into the water. It became their lover. It was perfect.

The temperature of the air, water and their bodies all merged at the point of submersion.

They sputtered across the surface of the water towards a crested beach that doubled as a boat ramp. With landfall they had terra firma underfoot again. The inclination to explore immediately set in. Beachcombing in a northerly direction Juri was dumbstruck by his luck. He stumbled onto a freshly washed-up specimen of Cypraea Mappa a lustrous brown enameled cowry shell with cryptographic markings and an unusual pale blue cast to it. It was a stunning three-and-a half to four inch offering from the sea.

The entire crew set off for Monkey Island their next destination. The caretaker told them the red-bottomed gibbons hadn't made their appearance for a few days. The three trekked across the beach onto a path in the overgrowth, tunneling their way until the only direction was up. Wearing sandals on rocks meaner than lava, each step was excruciatingly slow and measured. They wound up on top of the ridge for an aerial view of the island-studded waters for a 360° panorama. A treacherous down climb required double the time, triple the concentration and the weight of their t-shirts was quadrupled by perspiration. When they hit the sand, they sprinted for the refreshment of the water. Glancing back at the jungle, the shaking and swaying of the treetops, in the absence of any breeze, signaled the arrival of the monkeys.

The return to Hanoi marked a change in plans. Richard and Paul were immersed in a conceptual art project they conjured up back home, so Juri used the opportunity to go solo and hire a driver and set off for hill tribe country.

A hellacious downpour interrupted the agenda for the day. White surging sheets of water brought on a new drama demanding his attention. It was relentless for about half-an-hour. And like the tropic deluge she was, she quickly changed her mind, which was her prerogative. The smells borne on the winds of aftermath were negatively charged. The hair on his arms stood straight up. The clarity of light mirrored a small Dutch masterpiece. It was not any port in a storm.

Juri decided to travel light and left most his belongings and his bags in the storage room at the same Rose Hotel they finally found and checked into coming back from Cat Ba. His hired car showed up in the form of an air-conditioned Mitsubishi van that he had all to himself with legroom to spare.

The itinerary included some 200 kilometers to the northernmost edge of Vietnam near the Chinese border. It got pretty rural really quickly out of Hanoi. What was it that was usually more magnetic the further you got out of a big city? The character of the villages changed radically in proportion to the number of kilometers they distanced themselves from the capital. As the road started to gain altitude the winding ascent seemed to take them back in time. The Mitsubishi traversed around oxen and golden Brahmas pulling wooden carts. He waved to boys with switches herding a procession of water buffalo. A gaggle of about 200 light beige geese in perfect cadence came toward them on the right margin of the road. The one-lane highway became a narrow metal ramp as it hugged the steepening mountain gorges. Limestone peaks moved inland as if Cat Ba was somehow misplaced. Guilin had been carbon copied. Breathtaking was an often-overused cliché. This place looked as if you heard the word for the first time. They came to an absolutely flat lime green, river valley rich with rice paddies. Looking up, there were tall, jagged overlapping peaks in parallax all around them. There were certain locations that reduced human beings to a mere point on the landscape. Ahn, the driver took the road into the village of Mai Chau where people displayed rounder more ethnic features. Juri's eyes scanned both sides of the road through the village to spot any signs of multi-colored weaving. That kind of evidence would lead him directly to his quest, a hill tribe marketplace. The town diminished quickly as they turned down a dirt road toward a lone 300-meter-high rock surrounded by gigantic hardwood trees and stands of bamboo. Their destination was a lush island in a sea of green rice. The impression Juri got from the vague negotiations in Hanoi was that his driver would take him to a place of accommodation called the Stilt House. He based his conclusion on photographs he was shown. As they drove closer to the structures, he saw all 20 of them were indeed on stilts and were the homes of Montagnard tribal people. Ahn gestured in a query as to which one he would choose. Juri was a little slow at realizing he would be staying with a family and not at a hotel. Inching back by each stilted bamboo structure they all, every last one, displayed the tell-tale signs of indigenous art of all kinds hanging from every possible vantage point in the open-air space beneath the living quarters of each home. To whet his appetite even further, he came to terms with the fact good fortune was staring him down. Montagnards aligned themselves with U.S. forces during the war so English was commonly spoken in the community. He would have an opportunity to converse with families over many topics of their choosing, past and present.

Steep pitched thatched roofs and sanguine colored teaks with ornamental carved rails decorated the elevated homes. Under the houses, large box-frame looms occupied the breezeways. He chose one away from the dirt road out of habit to avoid traffic. It was a kneejerk reaction. Mai spoke broken English with a thick accent but that was reason enough to select this particular homestead. She was an attractive 25-year-old woman with a five-year-old son, wearing the black attire common to the culture with a typical straw conical hat, a small hand scythe and stalks of un-gleaned rice under the crook of her arm. Obviously, she was a working mother. He made the appropriate arrangements for food and lodging with her. Mai walked him up the stairs. Juri left his Nike flops at the entryway to see a stark but beautiful long room with a floor of especially smooth slatted parquet bamboo. It was divided in rectangular sections and partially covered with grass mats. There was a slight spring to each step over the floor. The subtle bounce was like trying to negotiate an oversized trampoline. In the absence of any furniture, Mai took a brightly colored narrow bed mat from a tall stack in the corner, unfolded it in the middle of the room, with the head facing the open windowed wall. She accessorized it with two hand-woven straw pillows and one sheet under a generous ceiling fan.

His only agenda was to walk the village and get the lay of the land, to get a feel for where he was. Each village home specialized in some form of craft or art. The goods were authentic and of high craftsmanship. He couldn't say how much he loved the hunt. The joy of haggling and negotiating price was an art form in those remote and faraway destinations. The late afternoon light called for a walk in the steep, cragged valley. He stopped to take it all in every hundred meters or so. He found himself on a rope bridge crossing a surging river into another village that was, in itself, another world. The sky unleashed thunder and lightning. Silver pellets strong enough to beat a drum exploded diagonally across his face and shoulders. He dashed for the cover of an overhang of the first available structure in the company of three other villagers. After 20 minutes of pressing their flesh against a bamboo wall, there was a form of communication without the use of verbal skills. Back at the homestead and drenched to the bone, his second showering was courtesy of a grey PVC pipe and a red plastic spigot. Upstairs, over his sleeping mat, a grandfatherly figure chewing betel nut was attending to the mosquito net. So far, Southeast Asia had been devoid of insects compared to previous visits. Juri just thought of the white mesh as preventive medicine. Maybe the elder of the family knew that the rains would summon the plague. The little boy was curled up on the floor, catatonic from either his day at school or the eternal heat or probably both. Juri was offered the honor and the opportunity to eat dinner with the family in the main room adjacent to where he slept. His previous meals were served downstairs in the open on the familiar blue plastic tables and chairs. Having passed some sort of scrutiny, he was graced to dine with the entire family in their living quarters in a much larger room decorated with vintage photographs of a family's history. One particular snapshot taken in a cave during a military siege of a much younger grandfather elicited inquiries. It was an unrecognizable Dien Bien Phu and the major battle of the French Indochina War. Further photographs, medals and framed certificates indicated a war hero who fought side by side with Ho Chi Minh during the French campaign. It hit Juri hard that most the faces his age that he saw in this country were on the other side of a rifle from him some 35 years before. The most poignant photos on that wall were of women from three generations of this family, especially images from a time gone by. The conversations, over the course of four days, revealed the universality of hope that adversaries can find common ground and share kindness and friendship.

He didn't know if he found what he was looking for with his return to Vietnam. He didn't know if it existed there anymore. Too much time had passed. It may be that it was more alive in people's psyche back in the US than it was here. The Vietnamese had moved on. It was street fashion to wear stars and stripes scarfs or sit on red, white and blue seat covers. American brand names endorsed t-shirts and baseball caps. The culture had become entrepreneurial and it could be a blessing to observe and let go. What he found in Vietnam were people who could be accepting of former antagonists, despite a history that was forced on them. It was a country of sheer physical beauty and serenity.

Ava

CHAPTER 25

There were always those few who had to immediately swoop when any pretty lady laid her towel down at the beach. Jeff was one, or in the early days, crazy Billy and maybe Lynn were usually first in line. On that day Juri did something out of character. He noticed someone taking in the sun and reading a book that caught his eye. She was a solitarily stunning enigma lying there alone a few yards south of the main sand court. He didn't know why he did it, but he kicked a random volleyball in her direction and then went over to retrieve it. *"What are you reading?"* in a soft measured tone was literally his opening line. She would reveal to him years later that in those first days she would eagerly look for his yellow board shorts to see if he was at the beach on any particular day. At first, they were just friends. He was casually seeing other people and she was in a relationship that turned out to be headed in the wrong direction.

He was going through women like he was going through countries. It might have been he was on a quest to find a woman like his mother whom everyone said must be one of the kindest and most giving human beings they ever met. The problem was, he thought, all he had to do was find someone attractive enough and the rest would take care of itself. He was satisfied enough, being independent and single. Being wary about past alliances was tiresome. The ultimate optimist had become a cynic about relationships.

About two months before he met Ava, he was at an art opening and ran into Sanja, who on the surface had it all. She had a prosperous art gallery in Laguna Beach and knew her trade well. She, coincidentally, also emigrated from the Balkans. As a Serb, she spoke a language understandable to Juri.

She was tall and originally in the states on an athletic scholarship. Confidently outgoing, she dressed provocatively. Juri intuited it wouldn't go anywhere in the long run. She was a player. They were just friends enjoying each other's company. That was how it was when he met Ava. If it was possible for such a thing, he now had an overload of genuine female friends. He sensed it would be regrettable if he tried to orchestrate the situation so he just let it be. The dynamics would be telling about everyone's personality.

As he assumed, Sanja bored easily, constantly needing new stimulus and attention. For a while, all three hung out at the beach together with an affinity for easygoing company. Gradually it became more of a twosome. Ava turned out to be more accepting and delightfully playful. She chose to be more present. In the end they all remained friends but now after a few months Ava and Juri were a couple.

The annual Aquathon, a cherished local tradition, was their first date. People gathered early on the Memorial Day weekend at the north end of town at Emerald Bay. Participants, at their own pace, walked and swam the entire length of beaches and coves of Laguna Beach ending up at the closing party at the Ritz Carlton south of town. Unseasonably cold water for the summer made the impassable headlands a bitter swim. They both had swim shirts, advantageous for the wind but not so much for the chilly water. Ava had a slender lithe body with absolutely no natural insulation, zero body fat. She began to shiver violently. After two or three hours, hypothermia was setting in. Here they were on their very first outing, chilled to the bone, and she was going to die on him. They swam to the closest beach with a large stairway leading up the steep bluff at Monarch Beach, a private community. At the top of the walkway, among the upscale beachside residences, he had her lie down on the heat of the black asphalt in the middle of the road. He was selecting which doorbell he would ring for help when a young teenage boy appeared. After a short explanation, Juri pleaded with him to ask his mother if they could use the shower to raise her body temperature to a safer level. His mother was gracious, caring and concerned. Ava spent 20 minutes with only the hot water running.

Mom offered to drive them to South Coast Hospital, but at that point Ava seemed out of the woods and he suggested the Jacuzzi at the Ritz Carlton, where he had previously parked his car earlier in the morning. After a long session in the hot tub at the hotel pool area, Aquathoners gathered for margaritas to celebrate the completion of the shoreline trek. Revelers all bonded through the shared endeavor. Ava and Juri got a lift for the last mile from a Good Samaritan.

He walked her to the Nigel Library parking lot across Coast Highway where she left her Prius. The library was situated in a park with a large grassy knolled area spotted with trees. They found a secluded sunny patch to sit and warm up a bit and to reflect on what happened during the course of the day. She started to shake again so he wrapped her in a towel he retrieved from her car. He curled his arm and brought his body closer to warm her. She laid her head on his shoulder, tired from exhaustion. After months, it was their first kiss. Not out of a sense of some conservative standard, but because it took them that long to realize they were more than just friends. It was an unexpected surprise, maybe brought on by the trauma they shared.

They settled in after a few months. She put her past relationship behind her and moved in with a friend who had an extra room. Juri was happy she had a new place even though she was staying with him most the time. It was an unexpected surprise to have her there on a full-time basis. She was candid, street smart and naïve all at the same time. Ava had a generous heart. Things were good. It was sage to now say she was different. In other relationships it was that unannounced sucker punch from left field. In this relationship it never came. Recriminations and hostility were rare and not experienced like before.

Juri was renting the lower floor of Marty's three-story hillside with an ocean view of Laguna. The location was perfect. He shared part of the second level as his art studio. Everything was centrally close. The village center and Main Beach were visible from the balcony. He could actually see if anyone was playing volleyball on the courts and he could check the surf out at Rock Pile from the house. The Art Institute where he taught was a ten-minute drive. Everything he needed was right there for him. She was a diamond in the rough. His life had become more than just convenient and it took some getting used to.

When they first met he could make her laugh. He was funny in the morning.

Being independent and alone was always easy for him, but he knew that relationships were where the real work was done. Being solo, decisions were selfish by nature. They depended on just one person. Being in any kind of relationship required consideration, compromise and conciliation. And, boy did he learn that the hard way with previous women. There were givers and takers. He felt outcomes weren't good when you had one giver and one taker in a relationship. Obviously two takers would both grab at the bigger share of the pie. In his opinion the only relationships that worked were the ones that had two givers. The unanswered question remained…"could a single person be both a giver and a taker?"

Marty took a trip to Thailand and in subsequent years the two weeks became four, then the stay extended to two months, then three. The writing was on the wall. Juri and Ava talked about buying their own place. He had been a renter forever and it was time for a change of lifestyle. They couldn't afford real estate prices in the beachside community so they got a place one zip code inland in Laguna Hills, a fifteen-minute drive to the ocean. Marty was talking about cashing out and making Thailand his permanent residence. Juri had been living at assorted different locations in Laguna Beach for twenty some years. He was still part of the community but the drive home was just a bit longer. Marty was fortunate and sold his house just before the bottom of the market dropped out. He was now a permanent resident of Phuket, Thailand and preferred the anonymity of being out of the scope of a watchful eye. Juri had always been the world traveler but now his friend was overseas and he was the homebody.

In a kind of perverse irony, he enjoyed making a home with Ava. They rescued two kittens, *This* and *That* from the animal shelter and settled down next to the warmth of a fireplace. The new property became a constant project requiring attention, like a dependent friend, until they molded it to their liking. As the fix-it-up phase exhausted itself, they had more and more time to themselves for the beach and bike riding and for travel. They started out planning small. A birthday camping excursion to Catalina Island where they watched an unannounced missile launch from a naval vessel whose trajectory went directly overhead crossing the channel towards Los Angeles then veered sharply north following the California coastline leaving in its wake a transparent green magnetic aurora. Then they set out on a couple of trips to Joshua Tree National Monument and Lake Powell, just to get the adventure juices flowing again. She was more than suited as a travel partner and didn't rattle under stressful situations. When a coyote raided their campsite and ran off with a gallon container of ice cream in its mouth, Ava didn't panic. Her only wish was that she had thought about videoing the intruder's audacity.

Ava had a son, Leroy, who sometimes lived with them and sometimes not depending on what job he was holding at the time. And it was the one difficult thing for Ava when he was not. It was hard for her to live with him and, on the other hand hard, to live without him. Juri chose to tell Ava about a daughter whose mother had put her up for adoption. He had written down the name of the lawyer who handled the case in the year after he returned from Vietnam. The attorney said he remembered because it was his very first adoption. He still knew the legal parents and said that if Juri wanted, he would pass on a letter to them. He would be the go-between but he didn't think they would be accepting of Juri. That was his intuition. Juri told Ava that he recalled taking pains to write the letter and forwarded it to the lawyer whose instincts turned out to be correct. Juri never heard a thing for all those years.

Ava and Juri were eating dinner at home a few weeks before Christmas when he got the phone call and he instantly knew what it was about. He could just tell by the voice that it was the call he had long expected. She was being encouraged by two other female voices in the background. His first and last names were echoed a couple of times and he acknowledged it was truly him that was on the line. They agreed to meet and she suggested Starbucks right around the corner from his home. The next day he went early and intentionally chose an outside table on the patio. He spotted her walking from her car. She didn't look as he imagined. The resemblance was nothing like her mother or her father. He thought she was shaped more by nurture than she was by nature. He very much enjoyed the conversation, filling in spaces he had missed out on. She lived in Irvine and he imagined that in the past they had crossed paths on occasion. Cathy confirmed that she had played volleyball at Main Beach numerous times. That left him lightheaded. She had graduated from Arizona State University and played the sport there. That was too much of a coincidence. Maybe it was nature versus nurture after all. She had a son named Jackson who played point guard on the Woodbridge High School basketball team. Cathy was separated from her husband but they both attended Jackson's games. While Juri was eager to hear about the empty gaps both with Cathy and Jax it was a lot of new input for him to process. He was still using a large sampling of his empathy for Leroy, Ava's son. He had gone from a solitary daily life to one that included his siblings and their immediate fluctuating families to Ava and Leroy and now to the inclusion of Cathy and Jax. That was a lot of intricate family dynamics without any prerequisite experienced history. Ava and Cathy got along well, which was important for Juri. In fact, they were so comfortable with each other that sometimes he was left out of the conversation. For the holidays, Cathy and Jax became part of the extended family. Juri's questions were about her childhood and her adoptive parents. The real surprise came when he asked about her biological mother and if Cathy had contacted her. There was a hesitancy to be direct as to why she felt she didn't want to connect with her. Her response was she only felt compulsion to learn about her biological father. What was it with her birth mother? That would be a conversation for another time.

He was readjusting and consolidating his professional life. He accepted a full professorship in the Art Department at California State University Long Beach where he had taught on a part-time basis while focusing on being a full-time artist. The artist-teacher was now a full-fledged educator. The classroom had always been a natural fit with him but now he also had administrative responsibilities of committee work, faculty senate and student counseling at a major university. He relocated his faculty office from Laguna Beach to Long Beach. It was a significant upward move. Laguna College of Art and Design was a celebrated but small art institution and CSULB was the second largest university in California with a recognized academic standing especially in art. He was now full-time on the other side of the desk from where he initiated his college studies as a freshman.

South Pacific

CHAPTER 26

Bora Bora

Treading water in that iconic lagoon on Bora Bora was like swimming in brilliant transparent paint, more aqua and bluer than one might find in an ultramarine mosaic. In the South Pacific, turquoise was nature's opus. It was a wet color done well. There were places where the cobalt blue-purple of deeper water looked like it was drawn exactingly with a ruler next to the shallower lighter blue hues of the lagoon. Snorkeling below the surface, what they found were colorful curtains of fish superimposed over mechanically perfect ledges dropping into the abyss.

At the Sofitel, he was not in a rush to survey the island that morning. Travel could pile up sometimes and it was good to just unwind. His attention was on the motu out in the lagoon from their thatched garden villa. The hotel had a few newly constructed over-the-water bungalows they wanted to check out. Anyway, he felt he deserved an especially slow paddle out. Juri took the rest of the day off and Ava took off her top, Tahitian style. They rented an aluminum boat with a single outboard to explore the lagoon. The freedom to go where and when they wanted was liberating. It was not an amusement park ride on a dictating rail but a prerogative to drift where they wanted. They were turned loose in paradise without having to answer to any tour guide. In complete privacy of the uninhabited motu they took full advantage of Bora Bora. When they got to the wharf at Bloody Mary's, they realized there was no line to tie up the boat so they had to tether two beach towels together to secure the skiff to the small pier. They ignored the sign and ordered two Hinanos.

The next day was reserved for a bicycle venture of the island. The island road skirted in and out of the bays and the lagoon. The island was basically a flat 19-mile trek of spectacular Polynesian shoreline overwhelmed by the one unmistakable landmark. Mt Otemanu always seemed to keep an eye on visitors regardless of what they were up to. Tahiti had the reputation in Polynesia. The French seemed to procure the best of the South Pacific and Bora Bora was the epitome of the Tahitian Isles. Juri always preferred this part of the world, with due respect, always feeling it was Hawaii to the power of ten. They were caught in a downpour. The deluge was so heavy it hurt when the rain beat down on them. They ducked under the roofline of a local church for salvation. The thing about the tropics was that the weather was mercurial. It could change on a whim. You expected it to contradict itself.

When they first landed on Bora Bora and boarded the boat from the airport to the hotel, Juri took immense pleasure in watching the joy and awe on Ava's face as she reacted to the natural beauty of her first visit to Tahiti. It confirmed for him why he repeatedly chose French Polynesia as a favored destination. He was a color maven and the light played tricks on him. Saturation was unaccountably amplified. It was obvious why the French Impressionist painters had come to this place. Their palettes were bathed in an extraordinary light. For an artist, this was Eden.

He found himself below the equator in the aquamarine waters of the lagoon and all he could hear in his head was his repeated challenge to his students of the importance of risk. Was he just paying lip service to going out on a limb, or could he brave the mile out to the reef and swim with the black tips? It was one thing to say you were going to swim with sharks but a completely different thing to do it. Could he put the shoe on the other foot and actually back up what he asked of his class? The motorized outrigger piloted by Manoa, a strapping sun colored Polynesian who couldn't stop chuckling under his breath, navigated them out to the rim of coral heads that ringed the green volcanic island. The depth and saturation of color that you took in from the water, land and sky confirmed that Gauguin was not a hyper-colorist but simply painted what he saw. Their watercraft was the typical South Seas canoe with a parallel pontoon. What brought it out of a Michner novel and into current time was the 125-horse Evinrude attached to the transom. As it glided effortlessly over shoals of multicolored fishes that became liquid rainbows in a wet blue sky, the sheer transparency of the lagoon was clearly apparent. They could see forever. Manoa killed the engine and they drifted to a stop. Juri realized the jolt of adrenaline, just under his flushed skin, signaled that it was time to enter the water. The safety of the shore might as well have been ten times the mile it actually was. Although he had an unobstructed view, he stood on the plank that was his seat out on the passage to get a better view of the approaching fins. Within three minutes there were dozens of six-to-eight-foot sharks patrolling the waters between the boat and the reef. Were they there because they acquired a taste for tourists or did, they know that the chum in the water was an easy meal? The all too familiar tune of *"dum..dum...dum..dum"* played in his head and he asked if he was really going to jump into the water.?!!! Swimming with alpha predators, the linchpins of the food chain, had a way of taking you out of theoretical discourse and putting you face up with the visceral. That was not probability. It was the real deal. Their only instructions were at all times, keep one hand on the anchor rope that was stretched out diagonally about 25-30 meters. This supposedly made the swimmers look larger as a group rather than random floating tidbits that might have been easier pickings. He couldn't get over how he looked submerged like a hors d'oeuvre dangling in his mask and snorkel from the bowline. What was unexpected was how his fear was displaced by sheer awe at the grace of those creatures. Their ability to dart and change direction on a dime was startling but obsessively fascinating. As the sharks cruised the area checking out potential prey, eye contact was not something he even imagined. To look an eight-foot shark directly in the eye from about a foot or two away was primordial. To stare down the barrel of a set of jaws bearing down on you certainly stirred all sorts of genetic and ancestral memories. Ava was actually brushed by one of the sharks and Juri thought he heard a muffled scream underwater.

After a warm shower, the raw coconut chunks by the hotel pool held their appetite at bay until dinner was served. The Sofitel grounds were delicately manicured for the tropics but what impressed was the surrounding natural serenity of one of the jewels of the South Pacific. Matira Point exhibited nature's defiance when it came to creative expression better than any film or novel or travel collateral. The recorded image immortalizes the experience and makes it immutable, but nothing could substitute for the actual embedded encounter. A photomural on their dining room wall honors their horseback ride on Piti A'au, one of the larger motus on the island. It depicts them mounted in the lagoon in shallow water with the backdrop of the unmistakable limestone formations of Bora Bora. Being there eclipsed any proxy image or residue of memory. All travelers seek the experience, many with an insatiable hunger.

Society Islands

They were married at the courthouse in Santa Ana, the same historic stone building where his parents became United States citizens. Ava and Juri wanted to have a ceremony in Tahiti so they took the plunge by boarding the *Paul Gauguin* in Pape'ete on the main island of Tahiti and cruised much of French Polynesia. Across from the ship's berth was a park where they chose to sit under the shade of a banyan and watch enthusiastic passengers boarding onto their dream. For that moment, they exhaled. Moorea, immediately across the channel, became the starting point and home base for not only that trip but also many future visits to Tahiti. They crossed unlimited color in the passage through the reef. The thick dense jungle was breathing over the topography of disfigured volcanic peaks. Coming in to the landing, they scrambled to get the best possible view on the top deck. The one island road scattered with manicured South Seas homes led first around Cook's Bay, a tourist enclave, and then Opunohu Bay where more locals lived and Captain Cook actually anchored. From the deck of the modest cruise ship, they charted the same course plotted by the captain through both bays. Most history buffs would have stirrings of those Eighteenth Century sailors at the very same anchorages where Juri was witnessing native Tahitians approaching the boat, paddling their outriggers wreathed in the traditional garlands of flowers around their heads and necks. He was transfixed on the shape of Mt Mouaputa, resembling the distinct upward looking head of a warrior with a clear hole through the limestone just below where the nose was. As the myth went, Pai aimed his spear from the big island of Tahiti, directly across from Moorea, to prevent Rotui from being captured and taken to Raiatea by Hiro, the god of thieves. The legend seemed to fit, as the "eye of the needle" on the pinnacle was visible for miles. Expert mountaineers rated the peaks of Moorea among the most rugged in the world. Many of the mountains, unlike the Himalayas, were considered impossible to climb with many still waiting on their first ascent.

The Paul Gauguin sailed on to Raiatea and Taha'a, two sister islands so close to each other that they seemed to take on the shape of an hourglass. The ship dropped anchor in the slim watery neck area between the two islands. The Gauguin's tenders dropped picnickers off on empty beaches between the two islands and supplied the food, beverages and music. After getting a feel for the lay of the land around the adjacent primal tropic forest, Ava and Juri decided to slip on their reef shoes and set out. They walked the beach for hours, uncovering the upside of Taha'a before re-boarding.

They kicked back for a reunion with Bora Bora, the second time for both of them, to one of the favorite destinations of visitors to French Polynesia. He could see the muted familiar peak on the horizon hours away from entering the lagoon. The closer they got, the more anticipation there was. It was like reconciling with an old friend. The passage over the break in the coral reef that protected the island from storms was kind when they crossed over to their anchorage. The boat's mooring was on the opposite side of the island from where they stayed the previous year. They tried to get their bearings but everything was reversed. Instead of the main mountain form being on the right it was on the left and the other side of the landmark was subtly dissimilar. The symmetry was off. It was nuanced, like the difference between identical twins. It went to show how the effects of first impressions were so important in creating one's world and one's loyalty. Bora Bora was forever imprinted on their experience. While the people were different on this journey, in the short time Ava and Juri were there, they did many of the same things and weren't let down. They were just as affected and it was as imposing as the first time.

Tuamotu Archipelago

The next sailing to the Tuamotus spanned two full days and a good swab of Open Ocean. The remote South Pacific Island chain east and slightly north of Tahiti were all flat low-lying coral atolls unlike the volcanic islands they just visited. Rangiroa had one of the largest lagoons in the world with a high elevation of only 12 meters. The 50 miles across the inside length of the lagoon to the other side was below the horizon and the land was not visible. These islands were renowned for their virgin reefs and attracted divers from around the world. There was some slight drama when a group from the boat came back from a dive and one of the assistant crew had a mangled bloodied hand and wrist from feeding the sharks, injuries that required stitches. Juri felt Tuamotuans were left hanging in the wind and vulnerable to major storms, despite the infrequency of recorded tropical cyclones. The entire archipelago of almost 80 islands was quiet, agreeable and easy on the senses. For discerning travelers who craved distance from the madding crowd, atolls like Rangiroa, Tikehau and Mataiva were a chance off the beaten path. The soft trade winds fanned the tropic heat to very comfortable levels. With a year-round temperature that varied only about eight or nine degrees between high and low it was very easy to adjust. The island's main town, Avatoru, was really only a village with a couple of shops. A number of young islanders were busy peddling their bikes somewhere but Juri could never quite figure out where that was. All the streets were crushed coral. The only pavement was the local boat ramp. There were no traffic signals but there was a bench by the wharf under the shade of a huge tree that had fishing floats strung from its branches. The locals took pride in trimming and landscaping their homes. A lush green lawn seemed to be a badge of honor. Houses were decorated with mother of pearl on the half-shell, nailed in repeated patterns onto the eaves. Islanders lived the luxury of simple lives. They were stress free and they knew it. Islanders lived in a warm climate with 80° crystal clear turquoise water and all the fruit and vegetables you could grow and all the fish you could catch. The idea you could live your life wearing a t-shirt and flip-flops everyday didn't present much of a problem.

The Marquesas

The Paul Gauguin was underway again while they slept in their cabin. It was the longest haul of the journey and would take two full days to reach. The Marquesas were the most remote and distant of all the islands on the cruise. Because they were cast away somewhere in the vast ocean between Tahiti and South America in anonymity, they were out of sight and out of mind. Few people visited them as a destination. They were out of the main shipping lanes and airline routes and tended to be more self-reliant and less dependent on tourism than most other island countries. The landmass of the islands themselves was dark and rugged and projected an air of mystery. Their physical distance from other populations was always there just out of awareness. The isolation was a mental condition. On the morning they first sighted landfall in the Marquesas at Hiva Oa, the seas were rough. Rough enough for the captain to make a decision not to brave anchor but instead to move on to Nuka Hiva, which had a much more sheltered harbor. A sense of disappointment washed over passengers. To endure the long ardent passage and then not disembark with the island well within sight seemed futile and frustrating. Juri's philosophical rationalization had to be that of those who tended to overload their itineraries…"you can't see it all in one journey…you have to save something for the next time".

As the undersized white ship inched its way slowly into port sheltering from the swells of the current sea, he imagined they were sailing into some outlying whaling station in search of the great colorless whale and into the heart of darkness. Unlike the atolls they had recently experienced with their ever-present coral sand beaches, the outcroppings that marked the approach of the Marquesas were towering vertical fingers of pitted rust brown stone. In the absence of fine white powdered sand, the beaches were generally darker and more volcanic in composition. Nuka Hiva was mountainous enough to restrict the expected circumscribed road around the island. The one tedious strip of pavement that traversed the island in a southeast to northwest direction over the top of the island's spine was a hardy venture and required 4-wheel drive with any kind of weather. Streams and creeks passed over the pavement rather than under it. This oceanic region with its isolation and unique biodiversity had some of the more rare species of shells in the world. Intrepid divers and serious shell collectors had the Marquesas on their bucket lists. Juri came home with a number of glorious specimens he picked up on tucked away shores. The town was laid out like a blanket over the steep topography of the harbor. Hiking the paths that led to some of the elevated homes offered up views that lifted the spirit. Horses were grazing in generous backyards; sisters were giving haircuts to brothers on lawn chairs and dogs were wandering the neighborhoods. Taioha'e was Polynesia as far removed as one could find. The customs were familiar. Individual and bravely carved tikis of all sizes and startling shapes stood guard over the shoreline. Young children in the water were learning to surf. Farmers were cultivating mango, papaya and taro. Fishing, farming and ocean life were all at the center of it. There was a young woman lounging in the crook of a gnarled tree reading a book and slow, drifting smoke from a fire of dried palm fronds was doing its job abetting the mosquitos, affectionately called the vampires of the Marquesas. The island's rugged, unimaginable beauty was mostly inaccessible except from a distance. Wanting to get knee-deep into it in the short time they had, Ava and Juri conceded to spend more than they allotted for Nuka Hiva and hired a lone out-of-context helicopter. They met the pilot in a treeless plot of the jungle that had a cache of orange 50-gallon drums tidily lined up together to fuel the big white bird. In a prelude, a veil of black and blue-purple butterflies lifted off the patch of grass that was the landing field. The next hour became a condensed aerial perspective well worth the effort. While flying up the coastal valley, a long white ribbon of water defiantly rose up on a vertical directly at them. The glass bubble offered up the sight of a significant tropical waterfall. In a formidable vertical downward panorama, they witnessed the foreshortened rush of water cascading obediently to gravity on its slide to the rocks below. Further up on the mountain there were five side-by-side pinnacles resembling a green-fingered hand jutting up out of the ridgeline. Slowly, more topographical drama of outcroppings appeared underneath them. From the air it was nature's amusement park. As they hovered forward above the coastline, they were surprised to see more than a few private sailing yachts sprinkled in the bays and coves. He assumed serious long-distance sailors moored for supplies and sanctuary. That evening it was dinner on board and preparation for the long return voyage back to Papaeete.

Tahitian Wedding

On the island of Tahiti, it was off one boat and on to another. The Aremeti ferry took 45 minutes to transport them to Moorea, considerably shorter than the last sailing. The now-familiar road around the north shoreline to Les Tipaniers, their home away from home, was where the local native marriage ceremony was organized. The drive from the ferry dock was awesome. A thatched room affair right across from three small motus assured a qualified view of paradise. He found the odd sensation of air, water and body temperature all to be about the same. Snorkeling in the lagoon was like swimming in a Gauguin impression. They didn't want a tourist wedding so they entrusted the owner of the simple enclave to arrange for something authentic. Juri had become a regular patron at the hotel and had confidence in the arrangements. Sonja, Juri's sister and her friend MJ from Hawaii, flew in and Christy, Ava's childhood friend and Tom, her husband, would be the mainland contingent at the ceremony.

They all had some laughs at Sonja and MJ's perturbed concern with their booking agent who lodged them in the red light district of Papaeete. Two single women in the hotbed of island social life posed an odd juxtaposition. The wedding preparations included the island ritual to be ministered over by a local tribal chief on one of the three uninhabited motus directly across from Les Tipaniers and then back on Moorea for the evening luau and fire dances.

In the middle of the day, the six-person entourage waited on the Les Tipanier dock to be shuttled to Motu Fareone. Ava wore a smile worth writing home about and a bright white pareo with the customary garland of Tahitian flowers adorned around her forehead. The launch carried them to the shore of the motu where a large troupe of traditionally attired Tahitians waited for them swaying in song and dance. Tapa-clothed figures strumming ukuleles sang Polynesian songs lined up along the beach. They were traditionally welcomed to the sandy isle. The women surrounded Ava and took her in one direction and the men circled Juri and escorted him in the other. They were both transfixed and wrapped in Tahitian print and feathered headdress for the ceremony. Sonja, MJ, Christy and Tom all wore tasteful sarongs and all six visitors were far outnumbered by the participating Tahitians. A motorboat cruised by with a curious local family aboard adding to the celebrants. The attire was predominately red and black with highlights of yellow and green. The young thin angular chieftain wore a pure white-feathered miter and stark white pareo marking his status. The small sub-group that included the chief, his female second and the wedding couple were marched out into knee-deep water. Ava was handed two long flat ginger leaves and Juri held a large husked coconut. He then gave the new coconut to the chief and his attendant took one of the broad leaves from Ava and placed it in Juri's hand. Both their hands were palms up holding the foliage in the form of an "X". The chief took a machete and struck the coconut and poured the coconut water and then scooped seawater over their clasped hands holding the crossed leaves. The pouring of water over outstretched arms and green leaves finalized their wedding in the blue lagoon.

Back at Les Tipanier they were bused from their bungalow to a night of festivities. In the village, preparations were in play with a large pit lined with huge banana leaves and a variety of ample-sized fish along with clutches of vegetables. A pig had been roasting all day and it was all covered with more banana leaves, burlap and large stones. The whole trove was left to simmer for hours. There was more than enough food to go around, a true Polynesian wedding feast. After the meal, more locals joined the festivities, making Ava and Juri the guests of honor during the Tahitian drumming and fire dancing. The beats of wood on wood were the familiar clacks of drum crescendos. The percussion worked up a slow building swell much like a faster South Seas version of Bolero. The torches were lit at both ends in complete darkness and the fire performed by dancers scripted a calligraphy that mimicked a bolder form of children playing with sparklers on the Fourth of July.

They were on Moorea for another week. Their private bungalow with its honeymoon setting of lush palm-treed motus and lagoon painted a consummate backdrop for their wedding. The next morning, they decided to paddle an outrigger back to the scene of the crime. Looking back, they spotted Christy and Tom pointlessly paddling in circles in their version of an outrigger. Ava and Juri went into the protected channel between two of the motus when they stumbled onto Kevin a transplant from SoCal. Quick with his wit and sharply good-natured, he soon became a friend that they would call on in subsequent visits to Moorea. He was an architect who had lived aboard a boat in Fiji for a couple of years, then gravitated to French Polynesia with permanent-resident status. He rented the perfect little place from a local family right up the beach from the hotel that was absolutely a slice of paradise. It was one of those chance coincidences that he happened to go to high school in Santa Monica with Jim Menges, a volleyball friend of Juri's. Kevin paddled his kayak with them to a shallow part of the lagoon where they all got out into the water. Kevin unzipped a baggie of shrimp and held out a sample just above the surface. A number of large smooth silky grey rays swam up for a free lunch. They crowded around Ava who now had the bag of prawns in her possession. Three different rays were actually swimming up her body to compete for the food. She was wearing that smile again.

On the last full remaining day on Moorea for Sonja, MJ, Christy and Tom, they decided to do a trek to the waterfall on the east side of the island. The trail was thick and lush and full of the sounds of birdlife. Apparently, there had been some rain in the mountains and the falls were raging, cascading down the black lava face with a steady attack of whitewater. They laid out a picnic on a sunny patch and savored the rest of the afternoon. On the way back to the hotel, they stopped at the lookout on the road with a vista of the blue reef below and the big island of Tahiti across the channel. It was a fitting way for friends and family to wind up their trip and bid bon voyage.

With company in the air flying back to the states, it left Ava and Juri lapping up every drop of nectar from their honeymoon by themselves. They lounged on the beach, swam in warm water and took another paddle. They ran into Kevin again and couldn't resist feeding the rays. The three of them hopped onto their bikes and peddled to a favorite lunch hangout on the beach. Snack Mahana was a popular outdoor eatery on the water that was a favorite of many of the locals. Kevin planned his own version of a farewell meal for Ava and George in front of his place. He took a plastic table and chairs and literally sat them in the shallow water of the lagoon and brought out the pizza and Hinanos. It was a heartwarming sunset and they toasted to friendship and Polynesia. On their departure from the hotel, they were handed a tapa cloth with crossed brown ginger leaves inscribed in Tahitian. It was their wedding certificate. They could never get enough of Polynesia.

The Ties That Bond
CHAPTER 27

Ava's mom Renata had a somewhat parallel life to Lija, Juri's mother. They had both endured Europe's second world war. The conflict displaced them from their respective countries and along with their families expatriated them to the U.S. via different routes. Lija and her family arrived from Slovenia through Austria and Renata from Germany through Canada where Ava was born. The first order of business on their return from Tahiti was to edit and arrange a slide show of the wedding for Ava's mother who was now in her mid-eighties. The priority was to share pictures of her daughter's tropical wedding her mother was unable to attend. It was confirmation of the joy she had for her daughter until the day she died.

He always loved being on the run. Travel recharged his batteries. While it was good to be home with the added new episodes and experiences, Ava had something he didn't. The nesting gene was evolution's elaborate plan for home décor. With apologies to women, he thought it mostly a female trait to obsess about interior design. The new house became a black hole. It sucked up everything within its unquenchable appetite, time, money, energy, effort and accessories. While he preferred the journey of the road to the tedious role of caretaker and househusband, travel would be on the back burner for a while.

Ava was a breath of fresh air. She gave him space for his idiosyncrasies, taking them on herself sometimes. They shared so much more together as best of friends. He knew from the beginning she was unconditionally different from all the other relationships he had struggled through. She had empathy for the downhearted; giving care to anyone she felt needed compassion. Whether it was a homeless single mother or a stray kitten she had room for it all. Juri knew he was difficult when he felt passionate about something. Instead of feeling left out she joined him in pursuit of whatever it was. She always let it be and never demanded that he change. Ava accepted him for who he was. It was a completely novel concept. His contribution turned out to be returning the favor.

The Victoria 4-man annual volleyball tournament was simply a case of adults behaving as children and children behaving as adults. The elders got a chance to *play* and the kids got a chance to *compete*. 'Vic' was a family-oriented beach, and Main Beach usually was not. There was something about Chase, who grew up on Victoria Beach that seemed familiar. Juri thought he knew something about him that Chase didn't know, but Juri wasn't sure what it was. He had that unnamable something. Juri was someone with a history, just an old school relic, who might be able to help Chase with coaching his youth volleyball classes. For the time being, that would be where it stood. Juri watched Chase's tournaments and it reminded him of something not from Juri's past performances but of an air of the game when it was played how it should be, as a purely creative art form.

Back in his 20's and 30's it was easy to cast fate to the wind. He still believed there was no reason why he couldn't drop out later in life. Was it peer pressure and family life that tried to sway him from his natural tendencies? Luckily, Ava had a touch of the wanderlust too even though she was tethered to her maternal instincts and her son's passage to full-fledged adulthood. California was where they put their roots. Laguna was as close to an ideal place to call home. But it all was changing through the accumulating years. More people were relocating to the milder climate. It seemed everyone wanted to come to Southern California. The orange groves were long gone. The roads were clogged every day after 3 o'clock. Some days the air was unfit to breathe from all the traffic. The window for getting around L.A. became smaller and smaller. Freeways turned into gridlock. Fantasies of island living on a permanent basis were more frequent. While he was named most likely to live on a tropical island by his high school class, he already had a number of friends who purchased one-way tickets closer to the equator. In his heart, he didn't understand why he hadn't yet pulled the trigger. In the absence of travel, they consoled the void by watching reruns and slide shows of their journeys.

Maupiti

It took a while, but they were starting to entertain the idea about permanent overseas residence. Polynesia was low hanging fruit. It was tried and true. They both loved the notion of warm water tropical beaches. Just the thought of getting on a jetliner and flying to some far-off place, where the trade winds blew, stirred their imaginations. Itineraries would have ulterior motives. Travel would become an audition for where their future home might be. Moorea was certainly in the running, but they also wanted to venture out into lesser-known backwaters. Maupiti was somewhat remote by most standards. It was the westernmost volcanic island in the archipelago and had only one weekly flight in on Tahiti Air. You needed French translation to get lodging. If you tried going by boat it was iffy crossing the pass into the lagoon during any kind of heavy seas. Supplies could sometimes be scarce when boats were stranded from reaching their destination due to high surf.

The approach to the airstrip at Maupiti made one feel like an Olympic gymnast trying to stick the most pressured landing of their life. Not much room for a misstep. Circling the island by air, one could see there was a large volcanic peak in the center of the lagoon ringed by a myriad of smaller, flatter barrier islands or motus. A single Polynesian hut, posing as the airport terminal, narrowly fit on one of those motus. Hardly a finger of land, the shallow lagoon lay on one side with the deep ocean outside the reef on the windward. More than half the landing strip extended out into the water of the lagoon on top of a rock jetty. It was urgently strange to look down from the air and imagine putting a plane full of passengers down on that tarmac. After the tires signaled the touchdown, the plane continued to rifle down the runway with nothing visible but ocean water out both sides of the aircraft.

Passengers gathered under the shade of the lone thatched palapa roof supported by slightly irregular varnished poles. They watched a farm tractor pull the trailer with their luggage from the Twin Otter DHC6 and young Tahitians unload it on the ground by their feet. Ava and Juri grabbed their bags and hustled over to the concrete dock on the lagoon side of the terminal. A few Polynesian Francs got them to the village center on the main island where most local people lived. They then boarded another boat to Pension Papahani on Motu Tiapaa for two nights before they took their quarters in their preferred lodging at the Maupiti Residence on larger Maupiti Island. The two other families that shared the boat to Pension Papahani would become close acquaintances by proximity. The brief sailing included a French couple with two young children and a Tahitian woman about Ava's age and her young son who were visiting her father, the Methodist pastor on the island. They all became friends as travelers do, especially those confined to a small motu that you could walk completely around in 45 minutes. Lucy, the French couple's young daughter, and Ava became best of buddies. Lucy was practical and wanted any help she could get learning to speak English. Juri and Ava took regular walks around the motu, sometimes taking the short cut through the pension's property to the Pacific side of the small island. His favorite hike was out to the point where he could see the pass into the lagoon up close and the motus scattered on either side. He could tell with all the coral heads and the little swell there was that passage could be tricky during any storm surge. From that point, he saw the volcanic peaks of the main island in the middle of the lagoon from ground level and made a note to climb the summit. On Easter Sunday they were invited by the Tahitian family to join the services at the church on the main island. It was good timing because it was their first day to change over to Maupiti Residence. They could take the boat over to the church and then check in to their accommodations after the invocation. They felt honored to be asked by the family and sat in the front row with them as her father recited the sermon. Tahitians in their finest white, adorned with leis and broad-brimmed hats, sang their hearts out. It was a glimpse of missionary tradition. Juri recalled his very first trip to Tahiti and watching a larger choir of all white-clad singers seated on the floor, swaying to the rhythm of song, looking very much like the undulating of sea grass in a gentle ocean swell.

248

The Maupiti residence was one of two side-by-side bungalows in a setting impossible to improve on. It was a choice locale, something he would use in designing a travel poster. They had it to themselves. The other bungalow was unoccupied. They were literally the only two foreigners on the east side of the island. This kind of low-density population was certainly hard to find in paradise. The residence property had fruit trees ripe for the picking and a shed full of water toys, snorkeling gear, bicycles, a dune buggy, two kayaks and a Hobie Cat catamaran. The front porch faced a perfectly empty qualified five-star beach and you could walk waist deep in the lagoon all the way across to a deserted palm fronded motu in search of shells or adventure. Ava helped two locals unload watermelon from a brightly colored scow down at the end of the beach. They gave her one they grew on the motu for her troubles. When she cut it open for her enjoyment on the landing, Ava was stunned to find it yellow, and not red, with a few black seeds on the inside. She had never seen that before. It was the color of a mango but cold and crisp. From the same front porch, Juri pointed out two familiar Terei'a Beach dogs chasing fish in the shallows of the lagoon. They were hilariously mimicking the arctic fox that sprung up and pounced on the white hare in the snow. The same pattern of stealth was repeated persistently, after a short sprint, chasing trails on the surface of the water.

The next morning the landlord arranged for a boat to take them on a picnic to one of the motus. They grilled local fish on an iron plate and ate fruit and coconut until they were full. Ava took a paper plate teeming with freshly seared mahi and sat in the water. A couple of large rays, easily four feet across, swam over to inspect the commotion of all the smaller fish. She ended up feeding them by hand accompanied with a generous smile. Ava was always happy when the rays showed up. After lunch the boat cruised out to a specific spot around some boulders submerged in about 20 feet of water. They put on their masks, fins and snorkels and fell backwards into the lagoon. It was a location frequented by giant manta rays that would habitually clean off parasites by scraping against the rocks. They were fortunate this time. They spotted two large individuals shepherding a younger adolescent. The mantas never exhibited a sense of urgency or panic in the divers' presence. They always maintained a calm, effortless pace, allowing Juri and Ava to glide directly above them keeping up. He spread out his arms to measure the wingspan of the enormous gentle rays. At times he would forget that he needed to take in air to breathe.

Wednesday was as nice as Monday and Tuesday. While deep blue skies with a few inflated white clouds drifted into the mountain peaks, Juri and Ava decided to make the climb. Just past the church on the inland side of the road was a graveyard full of flowers and decorated headstones. The path up the mountain started there. It wound around a stand of trees, then through denser jungle. At one point, there was raw rock face too steep to hold vegetation, with a fixed rope and knots to assist the challenging climb. Surprisingly, closer to the top, the trek got easier. Mt Teurafaatiu, the highest point on Maupiti, offered up staggering elevated views of the reef and the lagoon with its scattered small flat islands ringing the larger mass of the main island.

The routine was riding bicycles around the island's 10 km road, sometimes taking the right fork just beyond their beach giving them the more dramatic view of the mountain. Other times they chose the left fork on the road that went past Marae Vaiahu. It was a sacred outdoor temple constructed of large simple lava slabs traditionally significant not only on Maupiti, but in all of Tahiti. That leg of the road continued its southern approach into the village to Tarona, an outdoor dine-in with the best food on the island. You had to get there early to get a table and chair on the water. The stir-fry was awesome.

On Saturday they decided to scavenge for shells on the deserted far motu. They were old hands at beachcombing. He wanted to kayak and get an upper body workout. She opted to exert her lower body so she used her legs to walk across the lagoon in waist deep water and he paddled alongside her. It was an odd conversation because she had to work harder to keep up. When they reached the shore, he pandered to his stateside conditioning and stashed the 'yak' in the bush. They continued the walk up and around the deserted sandy point. Considerably further out on the reef, the surf was pounding white but inside the coral heads the water was serene and clear. He noticed a long flat coral finger jutting above the water surface, pointing at the beach. It looked like a naturally formed quay or dock. Between the dry crag and the shore was a deeper blue hole that filled up with warm seawater on every sweep of the tide. The pool was a private tropical spa, complete with the most transparent crystalline water. As they lounged in the water, a young Polynesian woman paddled by in her sleek single outrigger and they gave her a Tahitian *"Ia Orana"* and the little finger and thumb hand sign of hang loose. They wound up walking another mile or so on the totally empty beach, scooping up wonderful memories that the ocean left behind. The last sunset on the lanai was fitting. They packed their bags for the airport getaway the following late morning. After one last cup of morning tea, they saw their plane circling the motu for the landing strip and it was time to head out. The incoming flight dropped off newcomers and then prepared for the return to Faa'a that would depart in a little over two hours. Their French landlord and his Tahitian wife dropped them at the dock in town where they bid *au revoir* and crossed over to the terminal by boat.

Mataiva

The mental space at the beginning of a tropical overseas getaway was always sheer delight. They had their sights set on one more remote island. A sign of time really slowing down was evident when it took longer to get to Mataiva through multiple connecting flights from Papaeete than it did from LAX to Faa'a International Airport. It was adaptation by marking time. The pace of California transformed to the slower tempo of faraway Polynesia. It was like turning the clocks back for daylight savings time but without any significant reason. Over-packing, her need to be prepared for anything made for extra kilos. At the check-in counter they had to rearrange items between two pieces of luggage to satisfy the scales. Someone's truck picked Ava and Juri up at the single hut next to the tiny airstrip. On the way along the beach road there was nothing. No development, no structures—just a dirt road with wild natural island oceanfront. When they got to someone's property that had a few extra units on it, they realized how isolated it was. It was so remote they had to call the place they bought groceries from on the landlord's landline so they would open up for shopping. Apparently, it didn't pay for someone to sit at the store. All the things that mattered, like warm blue water and deserted white sand beaches, were plentiful. Sharing the simple establishment were two young couples and all four of them were in the French Air Force stationed on the main island of Tahiti. They were all taking holiday on Mataiva. Juri thought that spoke well to the selection of this island for a short commitment of time. If people who lived in the capital of French Polynesia chose Mataiva for their travel destination, then it had to have something going for it. Or maybe it was that it didn't have anything was why they decided on it. Whatever the reason, time stood still on this strange little island. If the goal was to get away from it all, then you came to the right place. It had all the typical things one would expect from an island paradise except a crowd. It was strange to see motorized vehicles because there were so few of them. For the visitors, bicycles were the basic form of transportation for anything farther than a long walk.

They were walking the beach near a long inlet into the lagoon when they saw something from their perspective that looked like two bicyclers peddling on the water across part of the coral heads. The bicycles actually turned out to be on a low-lying concrete causeway barely above the water surface just wide enough for a pick-up truck that was erected as a shortcut across the inlet part of the lagoon. It was odd to see cars on this series of uneven concrete blocks laid end to end. It seemed a monumental effort to save an extra 15 or 20 minutes of drive time.

They found a natural pool in a coral formation that was so perfectly rectangular that it looked like it was mechanically constructed. Casuarina trees lined the edges of the submersed depression. The water was so clear you couldn't get a good fix on how deep it was. One of the guys in the group shimmied out to a larger branch, maybe some twenty feet up, and performed a well-executed swan dive. The depth turned out to be adequate, so the rest were all obliged to take their turn. From his perch, 20 feet looked like 40. As soon as he released his hand, gravity took over. Luckily, it was a vertical entry not as elegant as the Frenchman's but admirable enough.

Killing Fields
CHAPTER 28

Every time he returned from the tropics, the sky was not quite as blue and the pace of traffic was subtly more inescapable. The world around him seemed a little nuanced, yet separated somehow. Had he grown younger or was the world around him now older? Quietly, he entertained the idea of *where* he should be. His conversations with Ava were about Moorea and Maupiti and not about Orange County or California. His work was here but his mind was there. He had learned artists and teachers could do their thing pretty much anywhere in the world. That wasn't the reason he was still in the frenetic tempo of Southern California instead of the South Pacific.

During a meeting, Carlos, a faculty colleague in the Art Department approached him with a proposition he couldn't refuse. Carlos had been toying around with starting the Art and Social Action program that was scheduled as a three-week winter term course for college students from California State University Long Beach experiencing art for social awareness abroad. The first offering would be between the fall and spring semesters during the January winter term break and then again at the same time the following year. Carlos and Juri, the two faculty assigned the course, would travel to Phnom Penh, Cambodia. Collaboration with their counterparts from Pannasastra University would find them matching up with Cambodian and American students in teams allocated to various NGO's in and around Phnom Penh.

His plane lifted off the runway four minutes into the New Year. Coincidentally, taxiing in the cue directly in front of them was an aircraft with Tahiti Nui markings. His mind was with Ava's warm bon voyage and not with the many kilometers that lie ahead. The rest was easy, with a premium exit aisle seat well worth the early investment at the check-in counter. Fourteen hours of extended comfort legroom on the first portion of the Taiwanese Eva Air flight was tidy, spacious and workman-like. Lots of courtesy to go around, gratefully it was smooth sailing for BR#001 the transpacific leg to Taipei. Ten hours into the flight they still had the equivalent of JFK to LAX left to complete. Then in transit, it was a smaller jet on to Phnom Penh. Down below, the Mekong, a dominant ribbon of water, twisted through the hills carving out ox bows in the rice paddies on its way to the Vietnam delta and the South China Sea. Even though it was the beginning of January, there was that warm floral assault on the senses, shirtsleeves and sweet breezes in the air. Customs were efficient. The uniforms were not as strident as most, more just putting in their nine-to-five than looking for contraband. Smiling faces belied the horror of a not-too-distant past. The late seventies and the Khmer Rouge had their rampage not that long ago.

The following year, Juri would do this all over again, *Ground Hog Day*, same time, same station, only this time as the lone faculty chaperone Juri wheeled his luggage past two huge sliding doors out onto the street where a flimsy wooden latticed barrier pretended to hold back throngs of greeters and well-wishers. A few individuals in the front held up placards in many scripts he couldn't begin to read. After his rolling bag endlessly clacked over cracks in the sidewalk, he spotted a sign in English with his name on it. Did that mean he belonged? His driver was a young Khmer whose lack of English clearly told Juri it was not Mardi whom he just spoke with over the phone. The young man behind the wheel got Mardi on the walkie-talkie and they had an "over and out" conversation in crackling English. Chanta, his driver knew just enough words in the visitor's language to be polite and began making small talk. Juri got the idea the driver wanted to try his hand at English so he began pointing at things on the street then mouthed the phonetics of the object. After the driver echoed the word a couple of times he would answer back with the word in Khmer. Still a neophyte, Juri was already in the classroom. Chanta was a study in contrast compared to Roger and Caroline, the couple he sat next to on the last leg of the flight. Both were strong sturdy Cambodians wearing white straw cowboy hats speaking fluent English. Turned out they had been living in Ohio for the last 38 years. Roger was Cambodian military in the Vietnam era and was sponsored to the States when Pol Pot posed a threat to his family. They had more than one similar thread with Juri running through their lives. They shared more than stories for most of the entire flight.

As they drove deeper into the city, the familiarity of chaos with purpose came back in a flood of bicycles, mopeds, motorcycles, cars, buses, and trucks, all flowing and merging in a mélange that inexplicably worked. It was madness with grace. Traffic flow braided in and out in headlong abandon and poetry. The matrix, as to how and why it all worked, was a reflection on mayhem. Why no one ever got enraged or made overtly selfish and sudden moves remained a mystery. Safety in crossing the street relied on calmness. Sudden bursts of speed were hard to calculate for others and put everyone in jeopardy. Exotic temple tops called "Wats" mimicked tree lines throughout the city, becoming his landmarks finding the way home to the Goldiana Hotel. They hopefully would help steer him through the maze of Asian urbanization. A spaciously marbled crescent driveway with two entry gates welcomed him to his residence for the next three weeks. His room #102 was on the second floor and the biggest surprise was an open arboretum and swimming pool sprawled out on the third floor. Tired beyond tired, but in need of getting to the bank before it closed, the walk to get money uncovered two restaurants worthy of investigation at a later time. One was Indian cuisine and the other offered a vegetarian bill of fare. He was fortunate to find 'Lucky' a supermarket within walking distance. He decided to put off unpacking and took a glorious shower and got some "sweet mother sleep". The Goldiana was selected for him. Amenities were always a luxury at the heart of an issue to consider. Personally, even though he could afford them, he wanted his patterns to reflect the portions that he chose to be more austere. He thought there was something admirable, something more efficient about simple. How much of what was comfortable did we really need? What originated the colonial mind that preceded us? Did it make us happy? His tired musings might have had too much introspection.

Mardi and Juri sat down to lunch. He chose the vegetarian plate at the restaurant Juri spotted the day before. They were seated on the third-floor veranda to wonderful fresh food and even better conversation. It was an exchange of ideas in getting to know each other. Carlos' contact with him was an invaluable asset, especially for the scope and reach of the project. Mardi was one of those people who had the connections and the ability to make things happen. He had the mind and more important, the heart. Juri hopped on the back of Mardi's motorbike and they headed for the university. Shortcuts through narrow streets and alleys brought them out on a major boulevard before turning into a cul-de-sac that led to a large modern structure that looked more like a government building than a private educational institution. They went to his office on the second floor after parking the bike just inside the fortified gate. Administration was spelled out in English across the rippled glass of the door. It struck him that all the signage was in English and then he remembered that so was all the instruction. All the courses at Pannasastra were taught in English, the quasi-universal language of business. All the staff was in professional conservative western dress. Juri quipped that he was "in disguise" to explain away his shorts and t-shirt. After introductions, surprisingly, one of the full-time professors was American, a bona fide maverick who applied and got the position on his own. They continued the tour and made the rounds of the campus. Up the stairs, past the statue of Buddha with a lotus in a fountain, then down the wide hallway to a door labeled *"Mr Sarim"*. Inside Mardi's office, they sat and he brewed some tea and offered Juri a cup. They conversed about some of the projects the student teams would be involved with. It was all about networking. Collaboration with their counterparts from Pannasastra University, they would match up with Cambodian students in teams of four allocated to various NGO's in and around Phnom Penh. The students from California with their Cambodian counterparts would join forces together with the resources of a given NGO, or non-governmental organization, to work with different target groups of the population that were in need. Whenever necessary, the Cambodian students would translate Khmer to English. The task at hand was as vital and basic work as one could do. Each team was assigned to one NGO during the three-week period. Each NGO already had an infrastructure of housing or facilities. Using art as an intermediary form of communication, they worked with groups of HIV-positive orphans and young girls rescued from trafficking. Decades after a decimating war and ensuing genocide the consequences most of these young people found them homeless with either a family that was deceased or had sold them to survive. The NGOs provided a home and the art a way to rebuild a sense of community. It was empathetic and emotional work, about as raw as you could get.

Mardi offered Juri a ride back to the hotel, but he preferred the walk. It was two miles to the Goldiana. Mardi was concerned Juri would get lost in the maze of streets. But his wide grin put Mardi at ease; especially after reciting the landmarks he was going to follow along the route. He'd been in enough jungles to find his way home. Mardi recommended the "Russian Market" as a must-see site. It acquired its name because it was frequented so often by discerning Russian tourists looking for a bargain in one of Asia's better-known indoor flea markets. Juri concurred it was the mother of all local markets, at least measured by his humble travel experiences. The Russian Market covered four full city blocks of Kasbah sellers and stalls that wound into a puzzle-like labyrinth. The deeper one got into the bowels of enclosures the less natural light there was until it was lit only by small flickering bulbs. Each cubicle compacted its ware in over-crowded displays of anything and everything imaginable, sold for the right price. For him it was a new vision in selling and trading the old-fashioned way. It was the analog version of Amazon. Here in this den of marketable iniquity, in the acres of Asian Flea Market gone wild, goods were bartered and trades were plied. Jewelry, shoes, purses, bolts of cloth, handicrafts, metals, wood carvings, fruits, vegetables, fish, and meats were only a small amount of the items sold. Welders with their torches, seamstresses stitching on their sewing machines, Tailors fitting with their tape measures, barbers cutting hair, butchers hacking sides of meat, all in a hive of activity as far as the eye could see. It was Khmer merchandizing made easy, entrepreneurship at the grass roots.

His big decision yesterday was whether to have Tom Yum or Tom Kha soup for dinner. Everything else pretty much fell into place, unfolded like a lotus flower. It all, no matter how exotic, seemed so appropriate yet so different from how it was at home. It was that difference that Juri was addicted to. He stood on the balcony looking down at the activity in the street and recognized this was his fix. Travel spawned life into his blood and the curiosity of youth was satiated.

Three vans, three drivers, four staff plus Mardi and Juri drove a convoy to the airport where China Airlines delivered 20 CSULB students weary from their 18-hours of friendly skies. Mardi held up his little sign clearly marked PANNASASTRA UNIVERSITY. Juri wore his calling card. A black t-shirt with the big yellow block letters spelling out the familiar BEACH representing Long Beach State for the new arrivals.

Everyone gathered outside the terminal and from the mountain of luggage as tall as the vans, it could definitely be concluded that they were Americans. A mixed bag of seasoned travelers and first timers, but all with that glazed look in their eyes. In all fairness, 20 crates of art supplies could fill a room pretty quickly. Since the students spent the next day sorting out and getting their affairs in order, Juri decided on one last solo venture. While everyone back in the states was sleeping, he went to the Killing Fields. Words couldn't begin to describe the feeling in a place like that. There were simply things prose could not do. Walking in the fields and through the open pits that were the sites of mass graves on a scale unimaginable to a civilized mind. Remnants of clothing, still half-protruding from the soil, left intentionally exposed as a monument to the genocide brought back flashes of what it must have been like for Juri's grandfather in Dachau. We were, after all, one family and must not forget. A sign in English was nailed to a tree explaining this was where a loud speaker was hung to drown out the moans of the executed. Cambodia lost well over a million people in a little short of four years. A stark white stupa stood solitarily as a memorial on the grounds. Its glass encased shelves displayed human skulls neatly stacked over ten stories high. Choeung Ek was a reverent place, a place where no one spoke. Introspection commanded the grounds. Visitors walked around in their own heads, silent, not necessarily out of respect but because they were numbed and overwhelmed. A young man in his twenties, wearing a hoodie with contemporary graphics, sat slumped over at a table under an excruciatingly twisted vine with his head in his hands, in all probability mourning an ancestor.

Choeung Ek, a final resting place for victims of the genocide, was 17-kilometers outside of Phenom Penh. Equally brutal was S-21, the former Khmer Rouge internment camp, a former high school on the edges of the city and presently functioning as the Genocide Museum. Implements of torture remained exactly where they were used on mostly higher targeted political adversaries and dissidents. On display were hundreds of black and white glossy portrait photographs of the interned, nothing like putting a face with the tortured. The photo of a young Australian who was in the wrong place at the wrong time affected Juri. The Aussie, like many westerners probably eager to see much of Cambodia, was one of six foreigners out of 2 million Cambodians who were killed at the hands of Pol Pot. It was remarkable the Khmer psyche could heal from something like that, yet there was a consensus they were among the warmest and most welcoming of Asians.

The California entourage had their first group meeting in country in the afternoon on the sixth-floor terrace of the hotel and then a reception in their honor at the Pannasastra campus at 4:30. Banners introducing students and faculty from California State University Long Beach announced their pedestrian arrival from the Goldiana to Pannasastra. All of them did their best impersonation of a Chinese dragon parading through the streets and alleys of South Phnom Penh. A formal reception with protocol and speeches allowed Juri to recognize all those names they discussed in their briefings. The Pannasastra faculty consisted of individuals from Norway, Thailand, India, the Philippines, Hawaii, New Zealand, China, and to no one's surprise, Cambodia. Not to be outdone, the CSULB contingent countered with Brazil, Slovenia and to no one's surprise the United States. Among the students were two Cambodian Americans, one born just across the border in Thailand and the other in Vietnam. There was a Mexican American born in Honduras. So in the name of cultural diversity, the endeavor had it pretty well covered. The buffet spread out on three full portable tables with Khmer finger foods encased in a variety of origami folded broad leaves cooked to a range of various greens. The taste of each was surprisingly unpredictable. It would have been rude of him not to sample his guests' offerings. He shied away from anything that looked like beef but risked everything else. After the meal, they broke down into lines and learned the fluid hand gestures of classical Khmer dance. He left the evening and hopped on the back of a motorbike instructed to drop its passenger at the Goldiana Hotel.

The following day was basically spent breaking open the boxes of art supplies and organizing them in the supply room for easier access during the remainder of the program. The student teams planned their individual projects for the kids and worked out their introductions with the children at the various sites they would visit tomorrow. Juri was assigned to observe two groups in the field. CDCC was an NGO that worked with youth who scavenged the refuse sites. The HOA, Hope Orphanage Association housed kids from six to fourteen years old. Juri's focus was to do oversight of the Cal State students to make sure everything ran smoothly on the first day with the help of a translator.

For the larger group of individuals, the long-awaited visit in two weeks over an extended weekend to Angkor had to be mapped out well ahead of time. Phea, Mardi's assistant, booked the necessary lodging and transportation, and as it worked out, she was able to squeeze in one extra day more than originally planned. The schedule had them in Seam Reap from a Friday through late Monday. He thought the additional time would work out well so they wouldn't have to rush recklessly to see everything. He had been trying to get to Angkor for over twenty years and finally here it was on his doorstep.

Walking back from campus in the afternoon, he took a different route and stumbled on to a simple storefront that sold handicrafts made by people with various disabilities. At Rehab Craft Cambodia, the guys he talked to were proud of their endeavor. Some were in wheelchairs and had lost limbs from the discharge of land mines. The manager had lost an eye to ordnance that exploded when he was walking in a field. He spoke fluent English and he and Juri talked at length about the art and craft they did. Juri purchased a number of small items as gifts to take back with him. After he opened his backpack, they spotted his camera and asked if they could pose for him. Only too happy to oblige, it was heartening to see the joy they got from seeing their likeness in the pictures on the back of the camera taken with a serious lens.

The whole purpose of the project became evident in the morning. He took a motorbike to HOA in a neighborhood on the southwest outskirts of town. As soon as the gates opened up to welcome Amy, Lori and Juri, he had five of the most endearing Cambodian children climbing on him as if he were a tree. They just squeezed him for every ounce of affection they could get out of him. All orphans clung on to the little they had. The only differences between them were the reasons they were orphaned. The organizations that housed them classified according to why they were on their own. Most of their parents were deceased and because they were either HIV positive, victims of traffic accidents, sex trafficking or simply abandonment, they had no family. Taking care of the needs of abandoned children was about as fundamental and peaceful as work can get. The lesson plans by the student teams seemed to be cast aside and the interaction just simply became organic. Emotional attachment was an almost automatic response. There was no resisting the children. They represented the hope and future of all of us.

This was absolute. It was completely arresting. At one point a small thin boy on crutches with a permanently disabled leg slid on the smooth tile floor on his butt to get around. During a game the children were playing, Juri instinctively walked over to where the boy was sitting against the wall and picked him up under the arms and chest from behind and went out with him to where the other kids were dancing in a circle. Holding Phiseth around the torso, Juri could feel quiet squeals of delight and had to hold back his emotions to keep his composure.

That evening, despite the day's long hours, he went to an art opening where most of Phnom Penh's contemporary artists gathered. Besides the locals and the imported California crowd, there were quite a few Europeans in attendance. It turned out the gallery owner was a German ex-pat who was married to a Cambodian. The art was interesting but the scene was even more intriguing because of the cultural mix. Even though he had an urgent need for sleep, he got roped into a Chinese dinner with about 15 of the group in a completely different part of town. They savored the meal with the joy of the day on everyone's face. It was obviously going to be a long night so he gracefully excused himself and left the evening to youth.

On the street he bargained a price back to the Goldiana with a motorbike driver. After about 20 minutes, it became obvious despite the affirmative shake of the head; the driver had no idea of where the hotel was. They ended up in the unlit parts of town. The driver and Juri were not on the same page. What made it even more difficult, other than the language barrier, was the fact that Juri typically used the buildings along the way as landmarks. And now, because of the lateness of the hour, they all had their metal roller security screens pulled down masking all the storefronts, making every city block seem uniform and identical. Unnervingly, they were in the dark caught in the maze of the city when Juri spotted a radio tower he recognized. Somehow, he was just a few blocks from the hotel.

The next morning, he had an extra bounce to his step. His strides through the neighborhood were self-assured. He knew the way. In the neighborhood near the university, he saw a crowd spilling out on the sidewalk from a walled compound. As he approached the entrance, he witnessed in complete disbelief a huge mob surrounding a volleyball court with players who obviously knew the game. He sat down on a bench at the least occupied side of the court to observe. A young athletic looking Khmer in gym clothes walked up to him and asked if he "played". Juri thought carefully before he answered. He had noticed large sums of money were placed on a mat next to one of the net standards with a "bagman" as the designated overseer. After a short conversation and assurance Juri wouldn't have any fiduciary responsibility, he agreed to join the challenging squad against the team that was winning most of the cash. After a vocal and raucous game, Juri was offered a fistful of Cambodian Riel. He held up an open hand saying the pleasure and fun was enough and headed back to the hotel for a shower and a change of clothes.

In the classroom on the fifth floor at Pannasastra, the California students paired up with their Cambodian counterparts to select what individuals would make up the working groups. It was like choosing teams for a pickup game on the playground. It wasn't done alphabetically or by any other rote logical means but simply a negotiation of those who got along with each other or wanted to work together. The Khmer students made up half of each team of four individuals and turned out to be invaluable interpreters with the kids out at the various sites. Juri accompanied Becky, Siem and Marros to the Cambodian Center for Protection of Children's Rights, which was the NGO that worked with girls rescued from sex trafficking. It was further out of town and in a more rural setting. After taking a secondary country road for a few kilometers, they turned off on a dirt track for a couple hundred meters. Our tuk-tuk driver sounded his horn as two large sky-blue gates opened up to a beautifully gardened compound with a number of small wooden structures in front of a large clean, but simple, concrete double-storied house typical of tropical construction with a metal corrugated roof. It stood at the back of the two-acre parcel and was untypically roomy and open, compared to most of Phnom Penh's urban architecture. The first structure, closest to the gate, was the office where the organization was administered and the second was a modest covering of stalls for the animals that was as tidy as everything else. Pigs in noticeably clean pens, ducks, geese and chickens paraded on the right side of the property as they approached the main house. Just outside the entryway, under a rectangular thatched roof, were the outlines of two reclining figures in green hammocks. The foreman of CCPCR was older, well dressed and strong but considerate. The lady in charge, slightly younger, in her fifties was adorned in an elegant red and black Asian-cut silk dress from neck to toe. Both had an air of quiet reserve and intelligence. Three very young girls ran out of the house and wrapped themselves around Becky and Siem in an overtly welcoming gesture making it obvious they had already met. The contingent was escorted into the house and up a flight of stairs to an especially long and wide hallway with additional doors on both sides that served as sleeping quarters and classrooms. Because of Juri's preconceptions, he was stunned at how young and how small these girls were. He was uncertain if it was because of their age or their genetic ethnicity.

When he observed the program with the young women, there was one adolescent girl who wanted to attach to him. She had an obvious traumatic experience that impeded her ability to speak. Juri felt it inappropriate to connect with the girl because of her past encounters with western men and better for her to relate to the female students on the team. It was especially difficult for him to remain emotionally neutral. He chose to remain as a background observer, not sure how she would react to him. The home for the girls was their only community. Becky introduced the game-playing exercises with Marros interpreting. The girls were reserved and introspective, but friendly. The program reinforced their self-esteem by having them create pages of photo collages of what they wanted their new life to be like. Most those images were surprising and atypically candid. Through pictures, the young people were able to express themselves. Juri thought his culture made movies, among other things, to express the destructive bent of war and that these girls were using glossy magazine photos to represent the emotional possibility of a new life. After they set down their art tools, each one individually clasped her hands in an appreciative prayerful manner and bowed in the Khmer custom of thanks. There was a sense of fragility that Juri projected on some of them that required him to check any air of pity he might have. What they needed was compassion and contact that allowed for trust.

The lady in the red dress called on her cell phone for a motorbike so that Juri could make a scheduled meeting at HOA. Speaking Khmer, she gave directions to the driver who had just come up the dirt road. The driver didn't speak English and Juri was once again in Timbuktu. To avoid rush hour traffic and the onrush of careening vehicles, they wove through the backstreets steering clear of the main arteries. It was déjà vu all over again. They stopped nowhere near Pannasastra, but this time Juri was much better at figuring out where he was. He spotted the Independence Monument and in five minutes they were at the university. That particular evening, they had a much bigger contingent than the day before at HOA. Besides Yiel, Michael and himself, there were three students from Pannasastra and Matt and Mathew also joined them. Yiel and Michael rode tandem on back of the students' bikes and the rest of them hailed a tuk-tuk. Juri had been to HOA only once and that was in the dark. He knew it was just a few blocks past the Russian Market. As they arrived in the neighborhood, he started scrambling to locate the second-story blue tiled balcony that was on a corner building. He realized he had no choice but to return to the hotel if he couldn't find it. By sheer luck they found their way. This was the most enthusiastic and appreciative of all the groups of kids and the poorest. The man who ran the home was quiet, understated and street-smart. The story was that he was an orphan himself. He was a former drug addict and street beggar. Atith turned his life around and started the orphanage. A well-meaning organization trapped as a financial underdog. They desperately needed seed money. Juri put him in touch with a Canadian fundraiser he met at CCH, the Children's Center. On the previous day he connected him with Save the Children Foundation. It would be a difficult road.

Friday, Juri was scheduled with Aziza, a school run by Drew, a six-foot, seven-inch tall peak through the clouds from Colorado. Aziza was a school deep in the poorest urban area of Phnom Penh. Drew lived and was taken in by the curtain community where the school was located. When crossing over from one section of town, there was a distinct line of abject poverty. People lived in the shells of abandoned concrete tenements. The political reality was that developers were trying to take over the area for gentrification. Drew took the small group on a short tour of his computer lab, a primitive structure more suited as a chicken coop with a padlock on it. The workstations displayed a medley of desktop and notebook computers of all sorts of varied styles and brands. It was all makeshift but well-functioning. Drew seemed to be tech savvy, a knowledgeable goodhearted geek. He mentioned a need for photographs to create a website and pamphlet to promote the school. Juri pulled out his Canon and started shooting.

In the afternoon he took advantage of the third-floor swimming pool and swam a few laps to exercise all that had transpired on the streets of the day. Pleasantly exhausted, he fell asleep in the inviting warmth of the late afternoon sun. He recalled the small things. Secretly passing his last piece of Bazooka bubble gum to Phiseth from his daypack so the other children wouldn't see. He didn't want to be the ogre for not having enough to go around. Juri remembered going down the stairs feeling like the Pied Piper with a line of children following him out to the street. They chased after the small coach pulled by a motorbike as it rode off into the evening. Being a teacher was rarely rewarded that immediately.

Angkor
CHAPTER 29

One of the world's premier archeological sites covering over 400 square kilometers, Angkor has been a legendary destination of adventure travelers from all over the globe. Juri needed to pack his bags in the evening because he was flying to Siem Reap a day earlier than the others to confirm everything was in order for the excursion. Long distance reservations could be somewhat iffy in this part of Asia and 20 individuals stranded without a place to stay would be a big problem. This was the most anticipated part of the trip. For him, this was one of the most renowned shrines to the past on the planet and he had four glorious days to experience this complex of mystery and contradiction. Consensus had it that the Hindu and Buddhist structures were built across a vast swath of land between the Eighth and Twelfth Centuries. The structures covered sites that were as far away as 35-40 miles and uniquely different so as no two were alike. Juri noted they were a far cry from the construction design principle of suburban America. On future visits there would be growing question as to the origin and function of these structures might be from an alternative history. There were well over 70 major temple complexes, along with many other minor sites, making the entire area overwhelming and mysterious.

During the early morning ride in the dark to Phnom Penh International Airport, the van stopped for a red light while most others didn't. The rules of the road were pretty much up to the individual. Rule number one was *"watch out"*. In the airport lounge his mind mused, not on the destination, but the going that was so rich. A gecko darting across the wall brought him back to the present moment. He was boarding a Thai Airways aircraft, even though his boarding pass said Siem Reap Airlines. The word *"Phuket"* was scripted under the pilot's window. Phuket was where Juri's close friend, Marty, relocated and was now living in Thailand.

The countryside was a fresh change from the streets of the capital. Siem Reap materialized out of the rice paddies and greenery of the Asian jungle. It was a smaller airport, but there again was a tuk-driver with Juri's name on a hand-written sign waiting for him. A smorgasbord of travelers filled the hotel-lined streets into town, all there for the same reason, to come face to face with the remnants of one of the most enigmatic civilizations to build on this planet.

Peace of Angkor was tucked away on the much quieter side of the river. A two-story simple tropical open house with high vaulted ceilings, it had dark hardwood bannister stairs that turned 90° halfway up to his room. Over the bed was a thin-veiled saffron colored silk fabric of elegant gold weaving. A huge bed fit for a king stood alongside a smaller twin that quickly became the resting place for his bags. Outside the window in plain view were a fruiting mango tree and a stately traveler palm that brought back sweet memories of tropic travel.

Juri decided to take the scenic river walk into town and find an ATM. In the park that paralleled the river, a young Asian who was reading a book printed in English greeted him. The man dressed in a simple white shirt with black trousers invited him to sit, probably wanting to practice his elocution of idioms. He explained he was a teacher at an orphan school, so they had something in common. His experience and insight shed light on Juri's current task at hand. The conversation drifted to his knowledge of the area and specifically to the various sites at Angkor. Juri asked about a more-remote ruined temple he had read about that was quite far on the map. Waha informed him that he regularly worked as a driver and guide for visitors at various sites to bring in money for the orphanage. It was a perfect win-win situation. Juri would hire him to tour and the little income would help the school with supplies. He would have ample time in the next few days to visit the better-known sites on the well-traveled road after making sure all the students checked into their hotel in the middle of town. Because Juri was staying on an extra day after the rest of the group planned to return, he agreed with Waha to map out a longer road trip after they left.

The park melded into the hustle of the town center. The path along the river forked into city streets lined with shops and restaurants. In the midday heat, he was feeling the weight of the yellow daypack loaded with his camera and other necessities Cambodians didn't seem to need. He sat down at a table of an outdoor café under a yellow umbrella, not noticing the color coordination, and ordered a banana mango smoothie.

As students are prone to do, the contingent from CSULB went by boat up the Tonle Sap River from Phnom Penh to Siem Reap instead of choosing the higher cost of flying. Their timetable had them docking at 12:30 in the afternoon, so Juri had to scramble about 30 minutes out of town on a bumpy pot-holed dirt road with shanty-shacked houses on especially long stilts lining both sides. It was an indication of the amount of flooding in the area during the monsoons. The river widened into a vast lake but at this time of year looked hardly deep enough to allow a boat holding over a hundred passengers to enter. A circus of assorted watercraft of all kinds was lined up along the muddy shore as far as the eye could see. Rudely colored boats were double-parked without structures, piers or docks. They were simply lashed to the muddy riverbank. Disembarking travelers and cargo used narrow wooden planks with small inadequate horizontal slats nailed for better footing. Depending on the size of the boat, people debarking with their baggage found themselves 10-15 feet above the exposed water and mud braving a high wire act of a 12-inch-wide gangplank without rails. You could tell the locals had done this before. The length of one's stride on the swaying floorboard dictated what country you were from. In Phnom Penh many people spoke English, in Siem Reap a few people spoke English and at the river no one spoke English. As the sleek torpedo boat arrived, Juri's parody of a CSULB placard was a big hit producing audible chuckles from all the other tuk-drivers holding up signs preprinted in Khmer script. Who was this foreigner muscling onto their turf? The tuk-drivers were the equivalent version of assertive taxi gangsters in other developing countries. They were all good-naturedly taking bets on who could make the walk down the plank remaining upright and who would end up in the drink.

Juri arranged for a tour bus to transport the 20 students and luggage to their hotel. He followed in the tuk with his driver. The group was staying at the Green Garden Guesthouse, a low-end lodging in the middle of town. Students tend to vie on the side of their bankroll. It was, foremost, a clean place with a pool. He conveyed the arrangements for a 4 a.m. sunrise walk up the hill overlooking Angkor Wat and headed back to his quarters for a quick shower and a deserved meal. He felt fortunate not to have to chaperone a virile group of twenty or more twenty-something advocates.

Four AM seemed to be the waking hour at Angkor. There was always much to see and fit into the day. They trekked up in the dark to hilltop ruins that served as an observatory for both them and the ancient Khmer. The spots of light from their flashlights twitched progressively up the path, much like the marching trail of army ants. The large quarried blocks of stone that made up the small temple and terrace platform were still warm from the previous day's sun. The massive geometric boulders were just slightly warmer than the morning air. He heard someone in the dark say they wished the temperature would stay like this all day. Everyone knew the relenting heat would be there soon enough. The first inklings of light were imperceptible, making it hard to distinguish the ruins from the treetops rising out of the jungle below. The sun was seemingly late for work that morning, with a low-lying mist settled indiscriminately among the trees. The higher clouds turned blood persimmon, backlighting the iconic triple spires of Angkor Wat.

Immediately below the south side of the ancient observatory at the edge of the jungle, Juri noticed a rustling in the bush that preceded two mammoth elephants with their Khmer handlers perched in box-like carriages draped in green and gold woven silk. This was the first point of encounter where locals and tourists met. The negotiation ritual with tuk drivers for the half-day rate was underway. Four of the group with a taste for getting off the beaten path teamed up as the first temple hoppers puttering down the yellow dirt road. Uncertainty, caution and indecision were left behind for a Pandora's box of archeological ruin. The labyrinth in front of them was an unclear and a present assault on making sense of why they were there in the first place. He was caught off guard by the vastness of the complex at Angkor Wat. The length from east to west was well over a mile long with a staggering array of exotic alien architecture. To understand the importance of Angkor Wat to Cambodian culture was underscored by the emblem on the national flag.

The tuk-tuks took them two-and-a-half kilometers to the gate of the walled city of Angkor Thom, which was easily many times the size of Angkor Wat. A bridged entryway guarded by a phalanx of 27 fierce stone demons and warriors lining each side, crossing the moat that circled the ramparts. The main arched entry was a tall tower with a massive head of a sentinel embedded into the masonry above the gate. Inside the walls were six separate temples, the first of which, unlike Angkor Wat, faced east. He had been waiting to see Bayon since he was a boy. Juri remembered taking wet sand at the beach and dripping conical spires in castle-like shapes. He continued to make them higher by adding more to the structure already there. His imagination saw faces and fanciful forms in the drippings. When he walked up to Bayon for the first time, he immediately knew that he had spent his childhood preparing for this place. The quixotic towers and spires of Bayon were in the form of huge Olmec-looking heads that become part of the architecture. This felt like home. This was his temple. Bayon would always be part of his creative side.

Baphon was two hundred meters north of Bayon. The next three temple sites were within walking distance so their tuk went on ahead where they would reunite after taking in the three sisters. Historical accounts suggested that Baphon would have been one of Angkor's most spectacular had it not been for the saddening destruction by the Khmer Rouge. The approach to the main structure was by an elevated walkway over 200 meters long. The sandstone esplanade held up by a repeating colonnade made up of 10 to15 foot pillars above two expansive ponds that ran under the entire length of the walkway on both sides. It was reserved exclusively for the king and his entourage. Common folk like us took the long way around.

Phimeanakas butted up right next to Baphon. This time it was up a precipitous stairway so steep you wanted to make sure you leaned into the stone. On the way down, cautious climbers treated the decent much like the downward steps on a ladder, only it was the height of a massive three-tiered monolith. It reminded him of a truncated Mayan pyramid with an observation platform on top. The outside layout, unlike most temples, was not in a formal geometric pattern but was scattered out more organically. The grounds were a graveyard of headstones with blocks laid out systematically by the restoration team.

Completing that particular triad of temples was the Terrace of the Leper King, a small but marvelously carved stairway platform structure. Excruciatingly magnificent bas-reliefs decorated the walled sides. History had it that two of the Angkor kings had leprosy. The terrace was topped by a statue of Yama, the god of death, and housed the Royal Crematorium.

The tuk-tuk drivers standardized customer options into two circuits. The small loop was 17 km and a lengthier 26 km version. Wanting to be discerning shoppers, his small group customized their ride by selecting individual specific sites instead of agreeing on either of the package tours.

Preah Khan, one of the more popular ancient sites seen in more than one Hollywood film, had huge vaulted halls and open doorways leading out in all directions. Just inside the courtyard of the east gate were two gigantic banyan trees with monstrous aerial roots that were embedded into the displaced stonework. The jungle was reclaiming the structure. The power of nature was taking back what was rightfully hers. On the north side of one alcove, Matt spotted a white tipped green pit viper, the deadliest snake in Cambodia. It was a serpent to be avoided at all cost.

The main avenue down the middle of the complex was lengthy on its exit route to the east gate. A small musical group playing traditional Khmer instruments sang folk songs in unfamiliar resonances. One of the four musicians, playing a stringed Tro, was blind and had a prosthetic arm. It was a delightful performance on the exit from the temple grounds down the shaded lane. Yiel supported her local artists by purchasing one of their CDs. Our driver suggested a late lunch at one of the many tarp-covered stalls with plastic tables and chairs. Orange coolers filled with cold drinks provided relief. In the cooking area, a middle-aged woman stooped over a flat grill preparing Khmer cuisine. A group of tuk drivers in the corner were playing cards. Juri ordered a soursop juice and then another. Still unquenched, he asked for a large green coconut. The proprietor hacked open the top and popped in a straw which seemed to do the trick. The young father of a 2-year-old infant daughter proudly showed off her balancing skills. With alarming dexterity, he held her up with only the palm of his hand under her feet, as she stood perched like a carnie act. It was as if he was holding her out, offering her up to a captivated crowd. To everyone's amazement she somehow remained upright and rigid as he danced gracefully around to the music.

After 12 hours of ruins and escorting the past, Juri was dropped off next to the small white bridge three blocks from Peace of Angkor and his touring mates headed for Green Gardens on the other side of town. It was without question a glorious day. The next morning, before the students' late afternoon bus ride back to Phnom Penh, most of them did a little more temple scrutinizing. Juri chose to slow down and take Sunday off from temple hopping. He wandered around the town center and checked out the central market. While lazily walking back on the other side of the river, the unmistakable guttural drone of Buddhist monks chanting filled the air. He honed in, trying to get a fix on the reverberating sound. Behind a crème-colored monastery wall was a house-sized open platform with a roof and assorted oriental rugs scattered on the floor. A simple set of wooden stairs led to the platform about six feet off the ground. Veiled smoke from burning incense hung in mid-air as 30 chanting orange robed monks, all with shaved heads, sat cross-legged in the lotus position. Their pulsing mantras resounded in Juri's ears down through his feet. He sat, quieted his mind and took it all in. After an uncalculated amount of time, he made an offering, lit some incense and then drifted back out to the street.

The premature knock on the door came at 5 am. In the early light of the morning, Waha was explaining they would go tandem by motorbike because the tuk-tuk would be too slow to cover the distance to what they

273

wanted to explore. Two specific destinations on a road with many other sites to take in lay ahead of them. Banteay Srei was 32 km to the east from Siem Reap and Beng Mealea a hefty 50 km beyond that. That was a lot of open road to traverse. Juri was thankful it was a relatively new bike with a soft ride. His chin was tucked over the back of Waha's helmet and his feet just fit the back pegs. He donned his blue lenses for bug protection and looked good doing it. The motorbike left the congestion of city streets and then bounced a bit on the rural roads. The further they ventured out, the more space there was between stilt houses and huts until only stretches of rice paddies and jungle thicket painted their landscape. You could count more water buffalo and Brahma cattle than people. The locals in the countryside north and east of Siem Reap, regardless of their economic standing, took pride in the visual appearance of their homes. The region was clean, tidy and photogenic. Some of the villages were simply three or four small farm huts facing the main road while others had a sparse patchwork of dirt roads on both sides of the highway and some even sported a wat poking its spire above the trees. The ratio of bicycles to motor scooters as the chief mode of transportation was higher out here.

One of many lesser temple ruins along the way to our first destination warranted a stop. It was situated immediately on the road heading due east where the pavement made an abrupt 90° right angle to the north. Waha estimated it was erected somewhere between the Twelfth and Thirteenth Centuries because it was constructed out of fired bricks instead of quarried stone blocks. Earlier dynasties used the more weather-resistant stone, explaining why the older structures were usually in a better state of repair. This particular site had significant signs of erosion. While it wasn't listed in the Lonely Planet Guide, if it had been in any other part of the world, it might have been counted as a major monument. Khnar Sanday's footprint was rectangular with a high wall around it and four towers at the corners. The central complex was typical of Khmer architecture, with four spired towers at the outside points of a cross and the main structure itself at its center.

A few more forks in the road and they reached Banteay Srei, the queen's temple. It was the most refined sampling of Angkorian art

Cambodia had to offer. Cut out of pinkish sandstone, it had a richly deserved reputation of some of the most exquisite stone carving and ornamentation on the planet. The friezes and reliefs created pictorial narratives and historical accounts of Shiva, the Hindu deity. The delicate stone cutting created a remarkable and extraordinary work of art that transcended architecture. A heightened sense of grace dictated an air of standing in the midst of a very rare and uncommon place.

While walking back to the motorbike there was the usual procession of blue tarp stalls and thatched hootches. Vending food, drinks and handicrafts were available for the convenience of visitors at most significant sites. Waha offered a choice. A 7-km shortcut over a series of makeshift paths, trails and dirt roads, or the longer cushioned ride over the smooth pavement of an official highway. They opted not in favor of comfort, but elected instead on behalf of precious time as they went the more venturous route towards Beng Mealea. A reputation preceded it as a temple gone wild, literally reclaimed and overgrown by the jungle. And Juri heard it was in some state of repair after the horrific damage exacted by the Khmer Rouge. In his mind, he toyed with illusions of Eighteenth or Nineteenth Century expeditions or even playing out the imagery of "Raiders of the Lost Ark".

As they came up on a small country bridge and a wooded creek, Waha pulled over to the side of the road, announcing it was time for a break. Juri's weight on the back of the bike and the contesting deliberate detour had taken a toll on Waha. He squatted Asian style next to the bike under a swatch of shade for an inordinate amount of time in what would have been an excruciating posture for Juri. Waha's comfort was evident as he surprisingly lit up a cigarette. It didn't fit his slight and gentile manner. Juri pulled out a liter of drinking water from his pack and poured a cup for him.

Although he couldn't see the temple from the road, he knew they were close because of all the telltale makeshift structures and vendors next to the dirt path. Just past the refreshment stands, on the tree-lined road, was a small bridge with two sculpted Nagas in the form of arching cobras guarding the causeway to Beng Mealea. Two rows of headless sentinel lions,

275

spanning both sides of the track, were the first signs of inflicted damage by the Khmer Rouge or possibly the vandalism of earlier poachers. The collaboration of trees and stone guardians produced a tall regal hallway effect sided by a now empty dried-up moat. Because Beng Mealea was so distant from Siem Reap and the many sites in and around Angkor Wat, the usual steady stream of tourists dwindled to only a handful willing to make the long trek. The frontal approach to the main structure was mostly rubble of cascaded stone blocks as a result of Khmer Rouge artillery practice. Signs of the jungle encroaching were everywhere. The one or two Cambodian soldiers on site were a little late in protecting the heritage of the Khmer kings. The front walls of the temple for now were left in repose. A newly hewn hardwood ramp and stairs led over the piles of stone blocks and into the rest of the temple complex that fortunately was left standing. From the top of an interior wall, the site was remarkable. Vines draped from hundreds of ancient trees with their huge buttress roots engorged in the remaining structures. The jungle owned this Twelfth Century construction. You could see why this was a prime film location for Hollywood.

Juri stopped for a long look before descending into a deep-dive of antiquity. The impulse to climb everywhere was undeniable. The disorder of all the branches and the ornamental stonework of the partially intact temple structures begged to be scaled. Boulder hopping turned his mind to narratives of the ancient Khmer kingdoms and what it was really like when this place was in its prime. Would the ritual and ceremony have made sense to him? Would the routine of the everyday have been familiar? He chose to take it all in on an elevated and shaded walkway atop the library. The treetop ramp ran along the roofline of the remaining structures. At that level the archaic stone elements of the temple "jig-sawed" perfectly with the newly cut wood of the aerial walkway that took all sorts of peculiar geometric angles around the heaps of ruin. He found a maze of sanctuaries and colonnades that wound up and around the back wall of the enclosure. A 12-year-old boy appeared out of nowhere and with the silent motion of a finger, gestured Juri to follow him. What did he have in store for the tall foreigner? The boy guided him through a serpentine of dark narrow openings and into an inner sanctum with a low-ceilinged passage that looked like a horizontal chimney. The opening required stooping and even crawling to proceed. It led to several secret chambers, qualifying him as an unindicted Tomb Raider. The view as they scrambled out into the sunlight offered up a remarkable vantage of the entire temple grounds in a mysterious dappled light.

Lunch for the young boy and Waha was on Juri at one of the resident stalls back where they parked the motorbike. Waha recommended the Tom Ya soup with chicken. After the meal they saddled up the bike, paid their respects to the boy and charted an alternate course to avoid backtracking to Siem Reap. After passing through a succession of villages, they again attended to their thirst at a local roadside attraction. A flirtatious young female proprietor produced a machete beheading the top of a chilled coconut again and served it with a flex straw. Instead of the usual plastic table and chair, this time they made their way over to a slatted bamboo platform under some shade. It had a comfortable trampoline effect. Juri reclined a bit and the cooling breeze against the dampness of his t-shirt played well to his body temperature. Curious residents hustled over to get a word with the kicked-back outsiders. Juri was in the dark. He didn't understand a word Waha was telling them. Back on the motorbike, passing huts transformed into storefronts, suggested they were back in Siem Reap. All in all it was a rewarding day off the beaten track. At the guesthouse, Waha waited for Juri to take a shower, grab his bag and then book it back to the airport to catch the return flight to Phnom Penh.

The last day was a day of goodbyes. Just when you got to know friends and co-workers, it was time to return. The richness of any journey was colored by the relationships that were struck up with the local inhabitants. The land around Angkor and all the Cambodians he had the opportunity to get to know were what made this trip unique and a contrast from a typical tourist vacation. There were people like Mardi, Phea and Waha. The different NGO staffers, the same lively tuk-drivers and the considerate hotel staff were all part of making the stay something to be remembered. And then there were the children. They gave unconditional love and play and the most difficult to leave behind, especially his little friend Phiseth. CDCC was the first group in the morning and always easy to visit. In the Afternoon he visited Little Sprouts, the Maryknoll NGO that had charge of HIV positive orphans. Because of funded HIV drugs, children's health made a remarkable improvement since the introduction of taking the "cocktails". Their exuberance and playful activity made them appear, at least outwardly, typical of kids that age. A billboard of photos of the children at the seashore with visitors was telling, since none of the kids pictured were present on the playground. The head of the orphanage said that since the Clinton Foundation supplied Little Sprouts with donated drug regimens over the last year, the mortality rate had improved dramatically. One last time at HOA, he took the tuk past the Russian Market and climbed the steep stairs to the second floor and the large open-air balcony where he engaged his favorite and closest group of children. It was impossible to do anything without feeling like family. He approached Phiseth to explain he had to leave. He carried him into the first room and asked the house matron to translate. Juri struggled with the emotion in Phiseth's eyes. The office afforded some privacy from the other children. Juri opened his familiar yellow daypack and pulled out another folded-up purple backpack. It was his parting gift to his newfound friend. The excitement on his face relieved Juri's dread. He explained that he wouldn't see Phiseth again until next year. Juri didn't have a complete grasp on how Cambodians dealt with the concept of time. At the moment, he wanted to be in denial about going. Back at the Goldiana, a revitalizing shower and a cup of herbal tea helped a little.

Volunteerism, if he was honest and assessed his experiences, always brought on feelings of worth, enrichment and graced him with a pleasure unattainable through self-indulgence.

The flight home found him sitting in the exit aisle again with elbowroom on both legs of the return, one of those small conveniences that made a difference for transoceanic crossings. Eva Air was ungodly cold. The cabin temperature had everyone bundled up in multiple blankets. His dreams were of the tropics.

Tui Tai
CHAPTER 30

The Tui Tai wasn't the sleekest of modern-day, ocean-going vessels but she had plenty of character and you could tell she had logged her share of nautical miles. Just shy of 140 feet, the boat was a classic motor-sailing ketch. It had two things going for it that set it apart from the other vacation boats they might have settled for. It was headed for some of the remotest parts of Fiji rarely sailed by conventional charters. And secondly, they were asking passengers to pitch in and contribute a share of simple medical supplies for some of the villagers on those distant islands as part of their passage. Things like antiseptics, bandages and aspirin, all supplies that were difficult to procure in those far-away places. The packet of medical relief would go a long way in meeting the needs of the islanders. Juri thought this kind of forward thinking was rare coming from a boat charter company.

Ava and Juri boarded Air Fiji for the transpacific flight to Nadi, followed by a shaky crossing on a Pacific Sun propeller-driven island hopper to Savusavu. The De Havilland Twin Otter, at least on that leg, was not one of the more comfortable connecting flights they had experienced. Vanua Levu, the second-largest island of the Fijian chain, had an impressive rugged spine of lush mountains in the interior that generated a lot of thermals affecting the short flight. Mt Batini, the highest peak, broke the clouds at 3,645 feet above sea level. They were met at the airport by two pickups from the Tui Tai and set out on the southern coastal road for about 30 miles to go aboard. As the trucks crested the dirt road on top of the headlands overlooking Natewa Bay, they got their first glance of the boat anchored below in an absolutely deserted cove. They parked on a patch of flat grass near the shore where a Zodiac tender was already waiting for them. Shoes off, they tiptoed into the rubber dinghy. They stowed their gear and enthusiastically enjoyed their approach into the wind. When they were close enough, they could see the individual crew members—all hands-on deck—clothed in matching light blue island print shirts and blouses playing what Polynesia, Micronesia and Melanesia all had to offer on traditional ukuleles. Fiji was uniquely the only place in the Pacific where all three cultures shared an island. Joining them on the flight, in the truck and now on board, was a couple about their age. Yves and Renee had to work much harder for this journey than Juri and Ava. To get there, they had to fly across two oceans all the way from France to Fiji, a significant undertaking, underscoring their commitment to travel. They both had a biting sense of humor that played well to inciting conversation and lightening the mood. Time and time again, good fortune was with them on this trip. For a ship that usually had an overflow capacity of 24 passengers on previous sailings, for multiple inexplicable reasons Renee and Yves and Ava and Juri were the only confirmed travelers on this particular voyage. Both couples booked modest cabins but were upgraded to the two elite captain's suites when they boarded. They had the run of the ship all to themselves and the service staff far outnumbered the four of them. There was always someone there to pamper them. They were treated like the affluent. They felt privileged. Meals were served on the top deck at an open-air 40-ft table under a canvas sheet strung to the rigging. Fruits and vegetables from the most recent island were sliced up and the entree reeled in from the stern of the boat. Fresh was the operative word. You might add savory and a little seasoning. On board every morning a loose itinerary was *white-boarded* up. But going against the grain, the four would usually point out a pristine white sand beach on a passing motu or a little surf break off a reef and they would drop anchor and fire up the motor on the zodiac and tender everyone wherever they wanted.

As the Tui Tai set sail, it brought back 'Neverland' from the deep recesses of where we file our youngest dreams. The South Pacific had a way of bringing out the wonderment of the child in him. Fertile green isles in blue tropical seas were off the starboard side. The Polynesian Island of

Kioa was the first port after leaving Vanua Levu. They tied up to a long pier without any railing that seemed to lead to nowhere. There weren't any signs of humanity, just hillsides of thick jungle. Only a single dirt track shadowing the shoreline gave purpose to the wharf. A pickup truck came out of the overgrowth from a village they couldn't see. It drove out on the dock to unload and upload supplies with our ketch, a fair exchange of island goods. Juri watched the makings of island economy from the vantage of the sun deck just outside his cabin.

In this particular stretch of ocean, islands were never out of sight. The next island on the itinerary was right there on the horizon for everyone to see. Taveuni was dramatically large compared to most on their sailing course. The Tui Tai cruised into a shaded tree-lined cove with three unoccupied private residences. The crew took 20 minutes to anchor and seriously secure the ship to a couple of major banyan trees staking out their plot of beach for the afternoon. Ava was watching the seamanship from the top deck rail and lost grip on her mask and snorkel. Hearing her audible concerns, one of the younger crewmen in his shorts dove into at least 40 feet of clear water to save the day. A table was spread out with a tropical banquet and later on, the passengers and the crew divided up to play volleyball at a net just off the beach.

The tender took the four of them to a stretch of the coast near a waterfall and a huge crooked tree full of birds of varying faiths. The avian choirs sang their hearts out for the approaching visitors. On the sand, next to the chute of white water coming off the outcrop, were two white-draped massage tables for Yves and Renee. Juri and Ava chose two out of a string of kayaks and paddled around the point to unseen beaches. A couple of miles down an empty strand, they came ashore just to put a few footprints in the sand of a pristine beach. In the afternoon, a couple of crewmembers took them all to Bouma National Heritage Park where they walked a wooded path that followed the ridgeline along the coves and bays of the shoreline. The next morning Maafu and Juri took the Zodiac for a surf check. It was a distance from where the Tui Tai was anchored. At full throttle, the salt spray peppered Juri in the face as he hung on to the rope leader on the gunnel of the inflatable. His jungle hat was cinched tightly under his chin and the brim was filling with air like a sail. Off to the left he could see the backs of swells approaching the shore in a crescent shaped bay. The waves weren't huge but certainly manageable. It was deep-water surfing off a narrow reef. He spent over an hour playfully testing the waters while Maafu was content dropping a fishing line just outside the line of breakers. That's all Juri needed was for him to hook a bloody fish and attract the sharks while he was in mid-ocean half a mile from shore.

They were now out in the passage between Vanua Levu and Rabi Island. They were slated for some community outreach at a local school. The entire student body performed Fijian cultural dances in traditional tapa and feathered headdress. The familiar South Pacific sway fit seamlessly with the vocalization of the songs. It was a true foreign exchange as the dancers gestured their visitors to join in on the ceremony. The ensuing laughter and smiles revealed the delight of the children as the guests struggled with the performance. The remote, farthermost reach of the sailing and most interesting interaction with villagers occurred in the Ringgold Islands on Yanuca. They were welcomed into an authentic Fijian community by a group of islanders in traditional sarongs and led to a longhouse that was basically a hundred-foot palapa with woven grass mats for flooring. They partook in a Kava ceremony in the evening with the full moon on the water's horizon. In appreciation for medical and art supplies that the visitors brought, there was a lavish cookout with a skewered pig over a fire and fish and chicken with breadfruit wrapped in banana leaves cooked in the ground over heated rocks. It was the dancing that was out of the ordinary. The women were exceptionally exotic and graceful but it was the men's dance that was completely engaging and unexpected. Eight shirtless Fijians in short sulus wrapped around their waists had broad green leafed garlands around their heads and wrists and were all absolutely cut like statues of NFL linebackers. Sitting in cross-legged fashion on the mats, they were going through a series of almost violent martial arts choreography with their torsos, arms and hands. They struck out with the intense physical force of jabs that might unhinge their joints in a series of fierce movements timed with the guttural chants of an exquisite furious ballet. They were seated so close to each other that if any one of them had moved out of sync they would have cold-cocked the guy next to them into the neighboring lagoon. When they pounded the floor with their hands, the garlands on their wrists snapped with savagery that literally shook the ground. All the sounds that were the repercussions of those abrupt staccato movements were part of the music. In all his travels through the Pacific he had never seen anything that matched that kind of performance.

On the loop back to Natewa Bay, this time they sailed down the leeward side of Taveuni. They kayaked uninhabited small island beaches and up mangrove waterways. The four hiked forested slopes to a 150-foot waterfall swollen with raging rainwater. The most tourist thing they did was stand with one foot in the present and one in the past on each side of the International Date Line. The last day, anchored in a bay off Taveuni, a whale calf mistook the boat's hull for her mother and kept swimming around and under them for about 20 minutes until she realized her miscalculation. Farewells and Goodbyes always felt a bit awkward but expressed needed acknowledgment of appreciation. They paid respects to the crew of the Tui Tai and to Yves and Renee then dusted the road back to Savusavu.

Five kilometers shy of town on the Hibiscus Highway they pulled into a grassy lane with an arching arbor of flowering shrubs that tunneled towards the ocean. The driveway opened up onto a very large gardened lawn with a tropical beach house that faced the water. Located on an absolutely ideal lagoon, it was paddling distance to two small motu islands just off shore. The property was about five or six acres of prime Fijian shoreline and they had it all to themselves. The Pearl Shack was the home of a third generation of one of the original settler families in Fiji. They owned and ran the major pearl operation on Vanua Levu and decided to purchase an additional place closer to town where their oyster hatcheries were located in Savusavu Bay. They occasionally rented out the beach house and Ava and Juri were delighted to have it for a full 10 days. They reserved the house as an extension of the boat excursion and it turned out to be one of the serious highlights of the trip. The cottage was located on one of the nicest stretches of beach on the whole island. The house was set back a little from the water with open-air construction and a wrap-around deck allowing the trade winds to blow through the full-screened windows, keeping it cool day and night. It had the beach toys; kayaks, surfboards and a small playful reef break about 200 yards directly in front of the house. Their hosts' grandparents lived in a house at the east end of the property and Bear, their dog, would visit anytime they were on the beach. Juri threw fallen coconuts toward the water and the mixed pit bull-boxer would rampage after them violently, shaking his head from side to side, ripping at the husk. The dog turned out to be a good-natured terrorist.

From the edge of the water the calligraphy of a palm tree leaning horizontally with a suspended rope swing arced over the shallow surface of the lagoon. A large banyan tree offered ample shade on the sand and doubled as a lean-to for the kayak, surfboards and rented motorbike in the heat of the day. Other than the short runs on the yellow Vespa into town to stock up on supplies at the outdoor market from local farmers and fishermen, they never wanted to leave their enclave on the secluded beach.

The Virgins
CHAPTER 31

Travel for them, was notably searching for options. Did they want to remain permanently in California or relocate to the perfect tropical hideaway? That was the burning question. On Moorea, Ava and Juri found what they thought was the answer. There was a piece of property on an idyllic Tahitian beach they might commit to, adjacent to their friend Kevin's place. It was tucked away near the water facing three small motus in the lagoon. They pursued emigrating and started paperwork that came to a grinding halt when they were confronted with a choice they couldn't make. They would need to quarantine their cats for one month in Australia. They had *This* and *That* since they were kittens and they struggled even entertaining shipping them off in cages that far away and for that length of time. It was time for plan B.

A deep dive into regulations for persons relocating with animals revealed that the US Virgin Islands required only a current letter from a veterinarian that cited vaccinations were up to date for US residents. They purchased tickets to scout out the Virgin Islands as a new possibility for resettlement. Jurij spent two years living on St Kitts and grew to love his time in the Caribbean with West Indian people. They were especially interested in St John's and St Croix. St Thomas was the administrative center of the islands and was far less laid back than its two sister islands. St Johns was an esthetic jewel and primarily a dedicated national park. They reserved lodging on the south side of Cruz Bay, walking distance from the town center. The island definitely had its share of beaches that made the pages of most of the travel magazines. Trunk Bay was world-class especially with its million-dollar view from the lookout on the elevated north shore road. Cinnamon Bay was also one of those rare beaches that attracted its share of visitors. St Johns and St Thomas were closely connected by a ferry ride. The passage took only about 20 minutes. All that was happening was easy to spot from each of the two islands. From the south side of St John's you could only see the lights of St Croix on the distant horizon if it was a clear night. The ferry Ride to Christiansted took a considerable 4 hours and 25 minutes. St Croix was much further removed from her two sister islands that absorbed most of the tourist traffic.

Ava and Juri flew into Henry E. Rohlsen Airport, named after one of the famed Tuskegee Airmen of World War II. They staked a quiet plot of sand near the Cottages by the Sea on West End Bay, south of Frederiksted. St Croix was an island that was laid out east to west. The more affluent expat community was mostly concentrated on the east end and local families tended to occupy the middle and west side of the island. There was a clear division between the two major enclaves on the island. Christiansted was at the center of soft rolling hills of east facing tracts of land while Frederiksted lay at the foot of the more mountainous topography of the northwest and the flat coastal plain of the southwest. A pleasant two-mile hike in the sand from the Cottages and the quiet beaches of Sandy Point offered seclusion. The area was designated a national wildlife refuge for a variety of sea turtles that included the largest of all sea turtles, the Leatherback, and during different nesting seasons, the Hawksbill and Green turtles.

Going in the opposite direction towards the northwest corner of the island just past Mahogany Road, Rainbow Beach attracted visitors with its restaurant bar on the sand and a watersports shop that afforded kayaks, jet skis and other water toys. There was also an outfitter that trucked in horses for rides along the beach and up into the rainforest. On occasion, Juri opted for Rainbow Beach because it was one of two beaches on the island where competitive volleyball was played. North of there the population density quickly thinned out. Following the shoreline, there was a scattering of homes along Hams Bluff Road until there was nothing but bare cliffs at road's end.

The feel of the north coast was distinctly different, rugged and more removed from most the east end beaches and the ones around Frederiksted that most travelers frequented. Much like the north shore of Hawaii, the terrain catered to the adventurous. Ava and Juri stayed at a place called Waves at Cane Bay. It was a modest two-story structure overlooking the sweeping panorama of the mountainous coastline. Their room sat above the open patio of the bar and restaurant that was built directly on the rocks where an imposing natural pool was constantly replenished by the breakers. A charging right breaking wave sped past the pool and into the bay. It was the kind of urgent wave you had to pay close attention to because of the rocks. There was another surf spot just walking distance from the inn where a concrete boat launch and deeper channel cut through the surging waves. A narrow beach fronted by a restaurant and a dive shop attracted divers to a location called "The Wall". The reef had a precipitous drop into the abyss and ran well beyond most of the north shore of St Croix. It was one of the few elite dive spots accessible from shore not requiring a boat. On any given day, divers in black wetsuits could be seen migrating the two hundred yards of shallow bay to the edge of the underwater shelf. Word was that a few years back a shipwreck carrying an antique carved carousel came to rest on a sandy ledge in 35-40 feet of water. It was said that divers could grab ahold of tarnished brass poles and sit on sculpted wooden stallions. Cane Bay turned out to be one of the finer snorkeling areas on the entire island. They gravitated to the north shore because of the laid-back ambiance and its natural undeveloped temperament.

Christiansted was the capital and largest city making most of the rest of the St Croix feel rural. Everything seemed to radiate out from the near center of the island. Where you lived on the island made a statement. The upscale homes of Shoys and Teagues Bay contrasted notably with the residences in communities like Prosperity and Le Grange. Frederiksted was an old colonial Danish town. It had the remnants of a bygone era and its esthetic charm attracted artists having a discerning and forgiving eye. On the strand just south of Fort Fredrik and the pier in a promenade of arched colonnaded buildings stood The Caribbean Museum Center for the Arts.

Taking a Sunday morning walk along the deserted strand, too early for people to be up and about, they noticed the doors to the Art Center were swung wide open. Curious they stepped in to peek to see what was happening. They were invited in by a Crucian woman to see the museum. Daphne the director of CMCA, along with an assistant, were hanging an exhibition slated to open the following week. Conversation led to her enquiry into Juri's history as an artist and professor. Because of that chance meeting, Daphne suggested that he contact Tralice, a board director and a docent who oversaw the Artist in Residency Program at the museum. After subsequent meetings and board consideration, Juri was awarded the residency for the upcoming summer. July would mark his return to St Croix where he would be lodged at the museum center compound for the full month. He exhibited his work in the gallery and gave workshops for the youth of the island. In the evenings he was the only one on the property after the day staff went home. It had the feeling of living in a luxurious private villa. Next-door was the compound where they threw lavish parties and the address of the elected representative from St Croix, who held a non-voting seat in the Capitol building in Washington D.C. Juri would sit on his second story balcony and watch the goings on. The Art Museum housed in a historical Eighteenth-Century colonial had a classical landscaped courtyard used for events and social gatherings. The building and grounds were leased to the museum by a major art collector who lived mid-island at Shoys. Warren was an eminent American economist of some renown and a likeable, well-placed contributor in the community.

The artist fraternity on St Croix was substantial. Juri was surprised and impressed by the quality of artists on island that included painters, sculptors and musicians. The culture had a history, both long-term and contemporary. The museum center was the hub of the art community on the island and fostered social and cultural events. At one of those events, he met Lars who was a student in the art department at Cal State Long Beach when Juri was a graduate student. After school, Lars settled down as a painter and worked as a graphic designer at an ad agency in LA. Time and time again, it was a small world. Although they had never met before,

Lars knew many of the same people in Juri's circle of friends. Lars had also done a residency at the museum in previous years and chose to make St Croix home for the immediate future. His daughter also lived on the island and worked at Rhythms, the restaurant bar at Rainbow Beach. He and Lars hung out together the month Juri was there. They shared war stories, talked art, reminisced college days and pretty much spent time on the beach.

Juri's art opening was on the Fourth of July. The holiday was a big deal on the island. The reception was calculated to coincide with a fete in the park on the strand with multiple Reggae bands, food vendors and fireworks off the end of the pier. He felt that the crowds at the museum gallery were more a function of spillover from the carnival atmosphere in the streets rather than the nature of his work. Whatever it was, there were throngs of revelers dancing to the music, enjoying the cuisine and taking in art. It was a rewarding evening. A woman whose brother used to own the candy store in Laguna Beach bought one of Juri's original oils from his *Monument Series*. Sandy was an artist herself, an accomplished jeweler who lived out near Butler Bay on Hams Bluff Road. Her boyfriend Marc owned a large spread with plenty of acreage out further at North Side that had some meaningful ruins from plantation days on the property.

With Tralice's help they kick-started the children's workshop, which concentrated on drawing during the first week. They played games to loosen up the lessons and their mark-making skills. Juri had them take common objects and draw them with the off hand, left-handed if they were naturally right handed and vice versa. He then taped their hands together at the wrists and asked them do two handed drawings. Another drawing game was to tape a large marker to the end of a slender bamboo stick and do "sword fight" drawings on a large piece of paper taped to the wall. The subject matter was always some everyday simple object they were familiar with and had on their possession such as a set of keys or a pair of eyeglasses or an old shoe. The idea was to take away a little bit of their control with their drawing tool, which they mostly relied on to use in a specifically technical way. Without that particular type of control, they were forced to use their skills in a more accepting fashion that resulted in surprising outcomes. The drawings were awkwardly beautiful, truthful and even graceful. And what was unexpected was when the restraints were lifted their drawings became more masterful. Not just technically meritorious but linearly poetic and fluid. The experience addressed confidence and added to their competency and an understanding of what drawing was about.

In the second week of the workshop the students addressed color and painting. More advanced for some, but they did some basic color exercises to learn how to use color perspective to understand where things fit in a painting. What subjects came to the foreground and what objects receded to the background taught them to look into a color composition in a functional way no matter how realistic, stylistic or abstract their style was. There was a six-year-old boy in the class who barely came up to Juri's waist in height who was an absolute prodigy. He did paintings that were comparable to some of his college students in California. He had no right to understand color the way he did. He was an intuitive. He made Juri proud and he made the rest of the class look good. They were more confident because of this young artist. During the end of his tenure at the museum center, they exhibited the student work in the satellite gallery adjacent to Juri's work. A second reception attended by proud parents and the artistic community of St Croix showed up to rave reviews of the children's artwork. It was the most pleasant surprise of the summer.

Ava and Juri returned to St Croix the following summer for a full month with the intention of possibly making the island a permanent home. This time they rented a small unit on Marc's property at North Side. It was across the road from the beach at Monk's Bath the oldest swimming pool in the Caribbean. Legend has it the Knights of Malta carved the small saltwater pond out of the rocks in the Seventeenth Century.

The small-world syndrome delivered him another unexpected set of circumstances once again. On the last year's visit to St Croix, he met Colin and Phyllis who coincidently turned out to be college friends of Dan, someone Juri knew well from volleyball tournaments in Aspen Colorado. To make the story even more random and intriguing, Colin, a world ranked professional tennis player originally from down under had competed a couple of years prior against Juri's brother Frank in a national tennis tournament in Phoenix. The world continued to become smaller and smaller. He loved that these moments of happenstance and chance seemed to haunt him wherever he traveled. To him they underscored that the universe had a resplendent sense of humor. In quantum physics Bell's Theorem postulated particles that contacted by chance through travel no matter how briefly or insignificantly would always from that day forward resonate with each other. Maybe it explained the unforeseen coincidental connections with strangers along the way. Ava always said he attracted these kinds of chance meetings. On one particular occasion shortly after they met, they were in the middle of nowhere in the California desert when they stopped at a remote road stop miles off the beaten path for refreshments. Walking in they heard an audible... "Juri...what the hell are you doing here" from a voice out of his past.

Ava and Juri were invited to Colin and Phyllis's for lunch. Also included, as guests were Warren and his wife, the same Warren that was presently the landlord of the Caribbean Museum Center for the Arts. It was indeed a small island in middle of the ocean. The artist community on St Croix definitely had a grip on him. He spent the bulk of his time on that specific incarnation of Caribbean travel working on a mural project. Hill Street, in Frederiksted, was a location chosen for local artists to ply their skills to the bare walls of older structures in town. Heading the project, Elizabeth, a self-described aging renaissance lady, was one of the matriarchs of the Crucian art scene. An accomplished painter who was known for her underwater sculpture park in 20 feet of water off of her beachfront home. Snorkeling and taking in art worked just fine for her. Juri, Ava, Elizabeth and Larry worked on the twenty-foot mural over the course of his last stay on the island. The mural paid tribute to a 1927 exposition at the Louvre on African Art. A month after Ava and Juri returned to California Maria, one of the deadliest category-5 hurricanes to ever hit St Croix, devastated the region. It took an unexpectedly long period of time for the island to rebuild and in no small measure put into doubt some of their future plans. For the two of them it turned out to be a sad reality they wished wasn't part of the equation. While it really came down to the availability of health care in this part of the world, the cyclical reality of ever increasing tropical storm patterns required a rebooting of relocation plans.

Far East

CHAPTER 32

China

They chose a full dose of Asia for two months and they would be on the run for the entire time. Raymond, the preeminent ticket broker they used for long hauls, arranged for affordable first-class cabins LAX to Vancouver then business class sleepers all the way to Beijing. All in all, they would have 14 scheduled legs in the 63-day journey on an assortment of planes, in addition to a number of boats, ferries and trains. They were all on time without any glitches. It turned out to be an absolute miracle. That was a lot of itinerary without any hiccups. The travel gods were definitely kind to them. Juri hadn't been to China for over 45 years since before major changes immediately after Chairman Mao's death. During his previous visit, people were still wearing Mao suits with an emblazoned red star on their small military style hats. China was coming out of its Cultural Revolution then and he was curious to see how different the country was now. So much of Chinese life had shifted because of a prosperous world economy and the communist government allowing for entrepreneurship. Most of the population especially the young wore modern western clothing. Instead of bicycles and horse drawn carts the main mode of transportation were automobiles and motorbikes. While China had its share of problems it seems they went from its dynastic period directly into the twenty-first century and seemed to skip some of the trial-and-error period that most western countries struggled through after the industrial revolution.

Current day Beijing was a bustling mix of old and new. Prototypical architecture had more than its share of historic landmarks that somehow meshed compatibly with innovative enterprising glass structures of the modern Chinese business world. The acclaimed architectural wonder of the most recent Beijing Olympics, the "Birds Nest" Stadium was only one of many contemporary jaw-dropping structures scattered throughout the capital. The new Beijing was a leading proponent of the world's most daring architecture, yet it had more than its share of the most recognizable historical sites on the planet. It had both the best of the new and the most revered of the old.

Juri had developed a habitual ritual whenever he arrived at a new destination to get the lay of the land. Getting a fix on where one was grounded, always secured the psyche. Maybe it was genetic memory passed on by his ancestors as a defense mechanism. Whatever it was, it seemed to be spontaneous and automatic. He learned not to go against his intuition. Like those many years before, he landed in Beijing under the cover of darkness. The lateness of the arrival cloaked his visual take on his surroundings. Much like during his first visit, he would have to wait until morning to see where he was.

Instant gratification put him in a world distinctly different from anywhere else. The upward curve of roofline corners immediately suggested he was enjoying breakfast in the most foreign of places. The soft low-lying mist washed over the palace grounds like it did in Chinese dynastic brush paintings. He was in an exotic eastern landscape and was both an observer and a participant.

They took lodging in the Prime Hotel, one kilometer from the Forbidden City and Tiananmen Square because it was central to their future explorations. They were within walking distance of many venerated sites and their outlying interests could easily be reached by the well-functioning subway system that accessed the entire city all the way out to the distant airport.

Out in front of the hotel, the street pulled them in both directions. The massive structure of the National Art Museum was on the right and an emblematic little temple on top of a small hillock was off to the left. For some inexplicable reason, they chose to walk west towards the less obvious as they absorbed their first taste of street life. The diminutive shrine wasn't on the city's list of top 10 sites but it had a certain beckoning call. In the few miles they walked, the city blocks transitioned from the past to the future then again back to the past. Ironically out of place, a gothic western stone cathedral stood defiantly back from the sidewalk and a few hundred meters further up the avenue, a Starbucks on the bottom floor of a contemporary glass high-rise stared them in the face. Both seemed to be strangely out of context. Rich magenta-colored flowerbeds embedded in the walkway alongside lavender blooming trees lined the streets. Gaming character heroes occupied a sculpture garden. It was all there to be seen. They took a turn down a wide alleyway into throngs of people jamming a street fair. On the right, a vendor was selling scorpions on a stick and another was blocking the flow of foot traffic, pulling a thick sticky wide rope of taffy across the sidewalk. The serpentine patterns of sweet tugged candy in midair mesmerized pedestrians. It was a carnival sideshow not unlike the snake oil salesmen of the Old West. Unfamiliar foods, fruits and broths were sold on the side. Octopus tentacles dipped in sesame seeds and gunnysacks full of protein-rich cockroaches were available for the brave. There were stalls with small glass aquariums at the foot of seated customers where diminutive fish nibbled between submerged toes serving as an adequate form of pedicure. That particular stretch of street, awash with a sea of humanity, fulfilled one's shopping needs and also aroused an ample amount of curiosity. China itself seemed much of an enigma.

Word of mouth couldn't prepare one for the cultural and architectural onslaught of the Forbidden City, the world's largest palace complex, ushered in on the senses. Long a mix of history and lore, the legend preceded itself. For Juri it hadn't changed much since his last visit. It was akin to a reunion with an old friend. The historic site was a complex of 720,000 square meters encircled by a six-meter-deep moat and a ten-meter-high wall. It was a fortified garden maze of buildings that housed the royal dynasty and its entourages. The commoners presently viewing the grounds would not have been allowed during the Forbidden City's golden age. The sheer numbers and volume of edifices on palace grounds were mind-bending. Just standing in the presence of the labyrinth of structures was unsettling. The massive red ornamented gates must have taken an army to open and close. The primary courtyard lay open beyond the gates and seemed to showcase a long myriad row of buildings laid out in an orderly fashion. Above the rooftops the complex seemed to spill out all the way to the horizon. It put the observers in awe of what it was in the human spirit that inspired the grand structures of shared history.

Immediately across from the Forbidden City was where past and current Chinese history seemed to spring into being. Tiananmen Square was adjoined by scores of government buildings where the principal decisions that affected the people of the country were made and where hundreds to thousands of protesters were killed by the military. Burned into the collective conscious of the world was the enigmatic image of a lone individual standing up to the peril of an army tank. Those events probably were a factor in future worldwide democratic movements to follow, including the Arab Spring. Juri couldn't help but think the events that occurred in Tiananmen Square, between his two journeys there, shaped the world's view on present-day China. Yet, willing crowds of Chinese still passed through identification lines just to view the changing of the guard on the square and to catch a glimpse of the Forbidden City.

The Great Wall of China, the Summer Palace, the Temple of Heaven and the Palace Museum were only some of the abundances of major historic constructions built in the past that merited attention. With these sites, China put her enigmatic affluence out there for the world to see. It underscored a history that went back to the dawn of recorded cultures. China undisputedly counts itself as one of the significant early civilizations.

China also has its share of contemporary idiosyncrasies. In Harbin, near the Mongolian border, the world's largest ice festival displayed unparalleled architectural ingenuity every winter. When they disembarked the train in the station it was bitter cold. At the festival grounds, it was hard to grasp what was there directly in front of them. Entire replicas of notable structures from around the world were reconstructed life size out of blocks of ice with large boom cranes and the same technology used to erect modern cities. The river provided the building material and architects, the creativity. Constructed in a period of a little over two months, each year the theme changed. What Ava and Juri witnessed were places of worship from around the world, true to scale, erected out of ice. There was a life-sized reconstruction of St Peter's Square. Right in front of them was a chilly version of the Vatican next to the unmistakable iconic spires of Angkor. The Taj Mahal and the Temples of Pagan were neighbors carved out of ice. It was a whirlwind world tour built out of frozen water, which simply vanished, replenishing the river after the spring thaw. The structures were visually enhanced at night by the colored lights that were embedded in the block ice. Daytime Harbin was distinguishingly different from the nightly version. He made a note to himself that the annual festival was a candidate for every esthetic's bucket list.

After a two-hour-and-fifteen-minute flight from Beijing, the medieval walled city of Xi'an, with its massive ramparts, encompassed approximately five-and-a-half square miles of the old city. Their hotel was just outside the southern gate, protected by sculptured dragons adorning a series of pillars.

From their room high on the seventh floor, they had an inspired view of all that was happening behind the city fortifications. In the morning they rented bicycles and pedaled the wide elevated cobblestone road atop the wall encircling the entirety of the ancient city.

Most travelers to Xi'an probably come for the most acknowledged archeological site discovered in the last century. Local farmers, while digging a well in 1974, uncovered the Terracotta figures of the armies of Qin Shi Huang, the first emperor of China. During Juri's first visit to China, the site had yet to be unearthed. In all, the buried terracotta army of more than 8,000 life-size sculpted soldiers, along with chariots and horses, were excavated in three separate pits. The dig is archeologically unique and a one of a kind find. Each individual figure is a distinct portrait and no two are alike. A roofed stadium-size structure protects the clay figures from the elements. They are aligned in formation in the exposed trenches where they were originally buried. The display is breathtaking, not only for its artistic merit but also for its colossal scale. It is a site unparalleled anywhere in the world.

The last stop in China was a picturesque boat ride down the Li River to Yangshuo, the wonderland pinnacled region just southeast of Guilin, seemingly right out of an illustrated children's book. Limestone karst formations jutted up out of flat valley floors like green fingers reaching across the landscape. This vista of spires went on for miles, overlapping each other by varied shades of color perspective. The landscape was nature's way of marking its place in the foreground, middle ground and background. It was truly a labyrinth of flourishing natural towers, a vista of depth perception that delighted the child in us all. The fairytale setting for this precious jewel of a river town with its cascading tributaries flowing into surrounding waters made for a water dance that washed clean the many miles they had traveled. There wasn't a straight road to be seen because of all the twists and turns in this natural setting. On the river back to Guilin, they passed a fisherman in a long prow vessel with a trained cormorant on a leash that would dive in the water and return with the catch of the day. The highlight was a ten-mile bamboo raft trip past the limestone karsts drifting through pristine river landscapes. At their last hotel in China, they booked an evening show on the lake that was a production on the water of theatrical acclaim. In a small outdoor amphitheater on a lake setting, costumed performers amazed an international crowd to the nightly display of lights, costumes, dancers and props. The ensemble purportedly was influenced and choreographed by the celebrated opening ceremonies of the previous XXIX Olympiad. It was an avant-garde spectacle that featured red-clad figures coming out of the dark, walking on submerged planks seemingly floating just above the surface of the water, with the distant peaks of Guilin lit by far off floodlights in an array of colors. It was a surrealistic visual assault on the senses and hard to grasp what was staring you directly in the face. Your eyes kept playing tricks on you until you realized it was actually your mind.

Thailand

It was raining before they boarded their flight. They watched their aircraft being prepped, through expansive glass panels in the lounge. The blast of the jet engines blew streams of water rivulets across the tarmac. An arriving airliner created an eerie shroud of mist and spray as it touched down. Bangkok was the next stop on a trail of destinations that were beginning to pile up. It was definitely still Asia, much as a font spelled out in the same alphabet, but in a distinctively different typeface. The message was still exotic but the character was completely different. Thai culture was not as orderly as the previous one in China. It wasn't as regimented, only more frenetic. The hustle made one wary. The street was on full alert. You had to stay on your toes. It helped if your antennae were well tuned and in good working order. They hired a tuk driver at the airport who said he knew where their hotel was. It was just after dark and he dropped them next to a canal and walkway leading into a maze of alleyways that kinked into a congested unknown neighborhood. They looked at him with that "you gotta be kidding" expression so he went the extra mile to escort them to their guesthouse, crossing a footbridge into a charming little villa within the walls of a beautifully landscaped courtyard. It was a relief to be staying in a welcoming place, when for a moment it looked every bit as if it was going to be on the sketchy side. The room was on the second floor with a view of the spires of the Royal Palace from the balcony. It was a prime location, within walking distance of the riverfront and all the major temples and recognized sites. They had a bird's eye view of what transpired in the narrow winding walkways and alleys of this particular quarter of the city. They broke out a couple of cold Singhas to put a chill on the heat of the day. From their perch, they watched two neighbors in the narrow alley below, sitting across from each other in white plastic chairs in front of their respective front doors so close they could almost touch. They were trying to carry on a conversation in the absence of a front porch. A puzzled thread of zigzagging paved trails, never straight, wound through the entanglement of poorly constructed hootches and huts. From his second story vantage point, Juri noticed a motorcycle pinball along the ridiculously narrow pathways, just a few blocks away. It found its way with barely enough room, darting through the confusion directly in between the two neighbors' dialogue. Undaunted, they took the motorized interruption in stride without missing a beat.

A short walk from their little villa was the imposing Royal Palace and its impeccably manicured grounds. Because the spires and rooflines of the king's buildings stood well above the palace walls, they were visible from most anywhere in the river walk area. The Chao Phraya was a still, slow moving, massive body of water and was the main transportation corridor through the heart of Bangkok. Unusual watercraft labored up and down the river's channel. It divided the city in half. Well-meaning Europeans affectionately labeled the western portion the "Venice of Asia". A network of canals made water traffic a predominant form of commerce. There were wooden dugouts tied up together to make patchwork of floating markets where local farmers sold their goods. One had to have sturdy sea legs to negotiate stepping from one canoe to another. The floating market, a particularly popular photo op on the tourist junket, was obligingly colorful and unique to the western eye. He remembered his first trek to this part of the world over 30 years prior. A brief water-taxi ride to the main temples in the central part of Bangkok took them to the Golden Buddha, known as the Wat Trimit Withayaram Worawihan to the Thai people. The five-ton solid gold statue, a national treasure, was once encased in concrete to conceal its true value and as the story goes placed out in plain sight.

At Wat Pho, the giant 46-meter long Reclining Buddha has its own structure housing the massive prone figure of gold and inlaid mother of pearl. The effigy is so big, that in the confined space, it was difficult to back up and get a discerning perspective of the sculptured form. Wat Phra Kaew was said to enshrine two bone fragments of the Buddha under the Golden Stupa's spired dome and was one of the unmistakable landmarks of the ancient city. There was the steep precarious climb up weathered stairs of the Temple of the Dawn on the west bank of the river. As a counter to a full day of temple itinerary, they walked some of the shops of the city that ironically consisted mostly of antique stores and craft stalls.

Juri remembered when Marty, his roommate and former volleyball partner, first went to Thailand over two decades ago. His first trip was for two weeks, then every subsequent trip after that he stayed longer. Eventually he relocated to Patong Beach on Phuket Island and officially became an expat.

Ava and Juri planned a few weeks' stay with Marty on this leg of their Asia trip. They hadn't seen each other in a couple of years because in Marty's words he said he had no reason to go back to the States. It was just before the pandemic and the beach at Patong was hopping with tourists seeking its ideal tropical waters and spirited nightlife. They spent 10 days in Patong, taking in the beaches there and to the south at Karon and Kata. Ava and Juri went on to Kho Phi Phi for a week, the island made famous for its spectacular secluded vistas in the Leonardo DiCaprio film *The Beach*. Experiencing Maya Bay, it was easy to understand why they went all that way to make a beach movie where nature was the star attraction. It was without question an incomparable one-of-a-kind location. It was one of those places when merely looking at photographs, let alone being there in person, that left one speechless. They stayed at an isolated bungalow on the hillside above an absolutely ideal beach with other islands on the horizon. That week- and-a-half was breathtaking and ideal. It was tough taking the ferry back to Phuket and Patong. The plan was for the three of them, Ava, Juri and Marty to fly to Siem Reap to visit Angkor, the capital of the Khmer Empire from the Ninth to the Fifteenth Centuries. Leaving Phuket behind, little did they know then the changes Thailand would have to endure. After Covid-19, the place turned into a ghost town. Previously semi-secluded beaches became relics of the past.

Cambodia

An early-morning minibus ride to the Phuket airport put them on a plane to Siem Reap and the "mother of all temples" among the resplendent ruins of Angkor. The three of them subscribed to something more about the *temples* than the status quo of current contemporary archeology. Their conclusions from readings begged the question that the *temples* might be much older than consensus had it. Was it possible that the Khmer were not responsible for the construction of Angkor but simply its inheritors? The purpose or function of all of Angkor would be in question by that answer. Juri had now visited the structures spread out over 150 square miles on four different occasions and each time he felt stronger towards more controversial answers to the origins of the ancient constructions. The engineering required to pull off the architectural fabrication of the many sites in the Angkor area is at the very least staggering to comprehend. The idea of hewing the massive blocks to such precise tolerances and then transporting them from distant quarries leaves more questions than answers, especially with the technology available during the Tenth Century. Might the accepted answer of worship as a purpose be re-examined for such a monumental undertaking? Could it be that commerce and mining might be possibilities in terms of probable answers? Water is a vital factor in the mining of gold. Almost every structure built in the Angkor complex has an extensive moat or aqueduct. From an aerial perspective, much of the topography looks like conical deposits or mining tailings. Most of the ancient structures have horizontal, longitudinal empty chambers or hallways that no one yet had a satisfactory clarification for. And then there are the peculiar literally "off the wall" pictographs of Stegosaurus and Triceratops that are hard to explain away, particularly for Khmer from over a thousand years ago. Angkor is an enigma, an especially beautiful and haunting one. During the summer solstice the sun rises directly over the main tower. That demands astronomical logic. It begs to be experienced in real time. Regardless of when it was built, it is a definite must see. Angkor Wat, the main and best known of the entire Angkor complex, is the world's largest "religious" site. It is so important to the history and culture of Cambodia that it appears on the national flag. The main towers of Angkor Wat seem to vibrate. There is a type of electricity in the air that can be felt much like around a power plant. It is a highly charged place. Looking down at the footprint of the "temple" from atop one of the towers, the whole layout looks much like a circuit board. And that is true of most of the structures in the contiguous complex.

Bayon, the next immediate structure on the temple-hoppers itinerary, made an impact on Juri. The massive heads embedded into the walls of the building were all individually different, yet posed the same features and were placed randomly about the edifice. Giant ancient faces glared down at you from almost every conceivable point of view. It was as if someone was always staring at you over your shoulder. Between all the sites where the tuk-tuks parked waiting for touring clients, were tarp covered stalls of vendors offering trinkets, nourishment and quenched thirsts. After three days of chasing temples, only a small portion of the major sites was checked off the list. He rode on lengthier excursions out to Banteay Srei where some of the most delicate, elegant and elaborate architectural carvings existed in the world. And then Beng Mealea, a site used for target practice, left in rubble by the Khmer Rouge and a near *"Indiana Jones"* experience, took another two days.

If we were to literally believe some of those mythic murals along the colonnades as some notation of the past, it was asking a lot from history. Not that the archeologists got it a hundred percent right. The effigies were in an array of skin colors ranging from green, to red, to blue. The alien creatures looked as if they stepped right off the mother ship. What Juri welcomed was that every entryway brought total surprise. It was expectation of the unexpected. The architects came from another planet and the design from another universe. Were they built as temples as historians say or were they constructed eons before for other purposes and bequeathed to the people that occupied that part of the Khmer Empire at Angkor?

Siem Reap was a pleasant enough town that welcomed the throngs of antiquity buffs. Tourism brought with it a sense of a secure economy. The marketplace thrived in the streets and shops. There was a friendly pace in the hustle and bustle of the town center. The walk along the river front park was calming and the sidewalk cafes offered food and drink to satiate any appetite. It dawned on Juri, for a country that not too long ago endured a horrific genocide, the people seemed genuinely happy. There was no overt pall hanging over the population. It seemed a true anachronism to see the gracious smiles shared so freely. Despite its history, the Khmer were a kind people.

In a wet market in Siem Reap, they bought some man kaeo or what Mexicans call jicama. It was a turnip-like root plant that remarkably quenched one's thirst in the absence of water. Those markets were always a place to exhibit your risk-taking skills, since most of the fruits and vegetables were novel and unrecognizable to most westerners.

Not much for goodbyes, it was still a departure. Marty was headed back to his home base in Patong and Ava and Juri headed south along the Mekong to Cambodia's capital of Phnom Penh. Quietly, Juri was aware this might be the last time he would see Marty in some time. It was good to have had his company, but now it was back to their comfort zone of traveling in tandem.

Juri took Ava to all the sites he had experienced in the two years of working with Art and Social Action in Phnom Penh. The Killing Fields and the memorial monument to the Khmer Rouge atrocities, the Russian Market, the renowned flea market in the bowels of the city that manifested a number of the city's blocks of stalls and vendors of anything the heart desired. The Royal Palace was the residence of King Norodom Sihamoni with its preeminent Khmer architecture on exhibit for all to see. They also visited with old friends and colleagues of Juri's from Pannasastra University he worked with on his two previous visits to Phnom Penh. It was a small personal reunion he was happy to share with Ava.

Vietnam

It would be his third visit to Vietnam, a country significant in shaping his young life. The third time was a charm with a brief stopover in former Saigon and then his first return to Nha Trang where he was stationed as a Psyops warrior during the Tet Offensive. Except for the runway at the airport, there were no apparent signs of the war buried in those many years from the past. Vietnamese lived in a socialist country but were every bit as entrepreneurial as Americans. Street vendors ran when word of approaching police inspecting business licenses got out. Walking by an ocean front restaurant, they were struck by the oddity of a saltwater crocodile roasting on a skewer of a rotisserie. Nha Trang was still a seaside resort with its tropical waters and café society. People got out at night to remedy the heat of the day. The oceanfront promenade was crowded with pedestrians and, for a moment, Juri recalled milling on an evening beach way back when. The vestiges of his recollections were faint. Memories were blurry and quaint. Too much time had passed and therefore change was inevitable. There were flashes of well-acquainted places and distant memories. Being on the ocean, it was easy to adjust to the now. He was in the moment and fully present, which was probably better than being stuck in the unpleasantries of the past. Nha Trang was a vibrant coastal town. Jumping in the surf again left warm feelings all around and the salt water had a calming effect. He wasn't sure if his memories lacked clarity or that the world had just changed with time. But what he definitely never understood was why some former soldiers he knew, came home with their demons and why some carrying similar experiences didn't.

The first part of the train trip to Hue, the old imperial capital of the Nguyen Dynasty, hugged the coastline and the South China Sea. Intermittent small islands and harbors dotted the shoreline. Most of Vietnam was still a jungle. It was a wonderful introduction to how simple people along the coastal enclaves lived. The train turned out to be a looking glass into how the way of life for typical Indo Chinese hadn't changed much. Hue was a traditional walled city with an impenetrable fortress surrounded by an imposing moat. The palace grounds were an invitation to witness the inner sanctum of bygone Southeast Asian court life. A small section inside the walls was earmarked and left as a reminder of the destruction from the Vietnam War. The remains of a collapsed building, intentionally left exactly as it was immediately after an American bombing raid, was a stark reminder of that unceasing war. Near the site on a concrete pad, the skeleton of a Huey Helicopter, the most iconic symbol of the war, stood like a lone sentinel. Dragon boats, Asian versions of Viking ferocity, sailed along the low-lying mist of the Perfume River cutting the city in half. The river walk was Hue's version of Nha Trang's shoreline promenade. It was the hub of social activity after the sun went down.

A short flight to Hanoi, which was the heart of enemy territory during the war and now the undisputed capital of Vietnam, took a little over an hour. The bus ride to the Lake District in the city center from the outlying airport consumed more time than did the plane ride from Hue. Their hotel was in the old quarter a block or two from the restaurants and shops on the lakeshore. At the southeastern end of Hoan Kiem on a small island was a starkly wonderful little pagoda that was lit up and reflected color off the surface of the water. Across from the other shore, back a few avenues, was the Ho Chi Minh Mausoleum. A French colonial Opera House built in 1911 was a formidable landmark between the lake and the river. Walking the shoreline of the lake for lunch and ice-cold green coconuts, with an inserted straw, became a ritual. Spooning the jelly-like pulp was his favorite part. Crowds were especially large during nightly street concerts and acrobatic performances in the park skirting the lake. Hanoi was a sprawling metropolis, large by any measurable standard, with an area well over 1,200 square miles and a population of over five million people.

Ninh Binh Province, 100 kilometers south of Hanoi, was an easy two hours away by bus and well worth the effort. The region of limestone karsts and winding tributaries snaking through dramatic pinnacles and open caves made for an adventurous riverscape. The boat guide they hired was a slight woman in her late forties with an unusual technique for propelling the hand-hewn craft. Instead of typically facing the stern and sculling the oars with her hands, she sat in the stern and faced forward towards the bow and powered the wooden boat with her feet. She was remarkably adept at keeping the bottom of her feet on the oars without ever slipping off. She didn't use straps of any sort. This took pressure off her back and allowed her larger leg muscles to absorb the load. Another advantage this ingenious method of rowing gave her was a clear forward view of anything in her path instead of having to crane her neck and repeatedly look over her shoulder to calculate her way. It was totally engaging to watch her nuances as she adjusted her course. The valley floor was absolutely flat and the limestone formations jutted straight up towards the sun. The lush river landscape was a deep jungle-green hallway and the channel was so narrow there was a procession of boats shadowing each other in the sunlight, mostly single file. It looked as if the boat guides were all peddling bicycles instead of rowing oars. It was an eminent Zen moment and a remarkably tranquil setting. Human silence was always best when listening to nature. The eyes and optic nerves digested the experience and with the simple repetitious water lapping, the soundtrack delivered the musical score through the action of the oars.

Back at the hotel in the old quarter, they mapped out a trip to Cat Ba at the travel desk. In the morning they would catch a bus to Haiphong, which served as the port to Hanoi. In the north, everything that came in by boat went through Haiphong. From there it was a rapid-fire hydrofoil water transfer to Cat Ba Island, the southern extension of better known and established Ha Long Bay but without the many tourists. Like Ninh Binh Province there were the enigmatic karst formations, however in this region, they came directly out of the water instead of a valley floor. Through the entire bay there were endless hoodoo needles piercing out of the submerged arms and coves in between the islands. They stood like inert fountains decorating every estuary and channel. It was one of those select places where nature demanded respect. Drifting on the surface of the water, it was a slalom course inside a cathedral of inlets. It was a revelation of spires that left everyone dumbstruck. Most intruders were stunned silent. A diesel powered inboard with an ample shade awning constructed of 2 x 4's transported them to any beach or rock pinnacle they wanted to explore. It was a vast area to cover. Lunch was offered up on a barge that served as a floating restaurant. At the top of the bill of fare was a profuse course of natural beauty. It was a privilege, he felt, to be there in the middle of it all and he was paying his respects.

Back at their lodging on the Cat Ba waterfront, from their seventh-story balcony they had an overreaching view of the harbor with its rebellion of flagged boats, barques and junks. The bay front road hugged the hillsides and coves where both ends of the concrete almost came full circle at the entrance to the crescent harbor. Around the eastern landfall was an outcropping that led to a series of beaches that were interconnected by an iron catwalk on the sheer vertical rock face of an exposed cliff. Down in front of the resort along the beach was a small group of men sledding, more than pushing, a huge palm tree on a makeshift trailer rig in the sand of a landscaped area. From high above they looked like seven dwarfs whistling while they were going off to work.

Ava and Juri rented motorbikes for the day and used two wheels to survey the area along the coastline and some of the interior valleys. Cat Ba, as an island, collected its visitors in one small concentrated location around the harbor. Most the hotels were strung out along a stretch of harbor front overlooking the bay that ran for a little more than a mile. But the lion's share of the archipelago was open and wild except for a few villages and settlements where the locals put down their belongings. It was made up mostly of natural hill land or rural farming enclaves. At one point, they came across a massive cave system that was used as a military hospital sheltered from the bombing of the war. The cave had a series of caverns that went deep into the mountain. There were some exhibits with rudimentary mannequins of doctors, nurses and patients and even some hospital beds and intravenous apparatus. The valleys inland from the sea were undeveloped and pastoral. The motorbikes were a welcome change to the public transportation they had used most of the time on their Asian journey. They were able to get off the predetermined track and go where intuition took them. It gave them a sense of freedom of what exploration was, after all, really about.

Travel continues its magnetic pull. He was always drawn to islands, to the tropics and to mother-ocean all his life. He could not fathom why his visits tended to be temporary. It was an enigma. The search to find his place still pursues to this point. All he could think of was that it is the journey and not the destination. There was no conclusion, no beginning, no middle and as of yet no end.

Ingram Content Group UK Ltd.
Milton Keynes UK
UKHW022028200323
418891UK00020B/180